D0296311

REGENERATION
The story of the Dome

Also by Adam Nicolson

Restoration, the rebuilding of Windsor Castle
Perch Hill, a new life

REGENERATION
The story of the Dome

ADAM NICOLSON

HarperCollins*Publishers*

HarperCollins*Publishers*
77–85 Fulham Palace Road,
Hammersmith, London W6 8JB

www.**fire**and**water**.com

Published by HarperCollins*Publishers* 1999
1 3 5 7 9 8 6 4 2

Copyright © Adam Nicolson 1999
NMEC logo © NMEC 1998
and NMEC licensed materials and illustrations © various agencies

Adam Nicolson asserts his moral right to
be identified as the author of this work

A catalogue record for this book
is available from the British Library

ISBN 0 00 257 130 7

Set in Times and Gill Sans

Printed in Great Britain by
HarperCollinsManufacturing Glasgow

For my children
Tom, Will, Ben, Rosie and Molly.

Contents

The normal state of nature is not one of balance and repose; the normal state is recovering from the previous disaster.

Stephen Budiansky,
Nature's Keepers, The New Science of Nature Management, 1995

Still the Queen kept crying 'Faster!' but Alice felt she *could not* go any faster. The most curious part was that things around them never changed their places at all: however fast they went they never seemed to pass anything. 'I wonder if all the things move along with us?' thought poor puzzled Alice.

Lewis Carroll,
Through the Looking-Glass and What Alice Found There, 1872

Acknowledgements

'Has it been more muddled than most things in which you have been involved?' I asked Michael Heseltine in the spring of 1999.

'Yes,' he said. 'The time pressures on this, the scale of it, the unexplored nature of it, the political complexities of it, the interplay of media, sponsorship, waiting for other people to initiate – this was a hugely ambitious project.'

'And muddle is inseparable from things of this kind?'

'Yes. No criticism in that. It is remarkable that they have found a way through.'

This book describes an organisation finding its way through. It is the biography of an embryo, from the moment of conception to the moment of emergence. But that analogy is not really adequate. There was no certain genetic formula by which the Dome could come into being. Its genome had to be invented at the same time as the foetus had to develop. What to do and how to do it? What to be and how to be it? For month after month and year after year those questions hung tangled together over the Dome. To write the book was my idea and I suggested it to the New Millennium Experience Company (NMEC), the quango which built the Dome, and to HarperCollins. Terms were agreed with Jennie Page, the chief executive of NMEC: it was to be an objective account, neither pro- nor anti-Dome. I should be able to read their background papers (but not necessarily to quote from them) and have access to their staff and consultants, as long as they would see me. NMEC would have a right to read the text before it was printed; and to correct errors of fact. They were to have no veto over anything simply because it was awkward or uncomfortable.

I have undergone some heavy encounters with Jennie Page in the course of writing this book – the definition of a 'fact' is not always as easy as one might imagine – but I remain immensely grateful to her for having the courage and integrity to allow me to do it. Few other chief executives of such a complicated, troubled, multifarious, politically sensitive and enormous enterprise would have dared. Its scale is difficult to grasp. As a small measure, a little under £10,000 has been spent on the project for every word in this book.

I would also like to thank Simon Jenkins, not only for playing a central part in originally persuading Jennie Page, but for championing my cause with the Millennium Commission, of which he was a member. He succeeded with NMEC, but he failed with the other commissioners. They decided not to assist me in any way. Apart from Jenkins himself and Michael Heseltine, no current commissioner spoke to me, and I was not allowed to see any commission papers that were not already in the public domain. In a book whose time constraints were already extremely difficult – work began in February 1999 and the manuscript was delivered in October – this fearful, uncooperative and outdated attitude did not make life easier.

By contrast, the politicians, their advisers, civil servants, employees of NMEC, their design companies and the sponsors whom I have interviewed were all generous with their time and insights. I would particularly like to thank Ian Brack, head of policy at the Millennium Commission, for his acerbic intelligence, consistent helpfulness and wry perspective on the whole phenomenon.

My agent Caroline Dawnay and her assistant Annabel Hardman have given me, as ever, invaluable advice and encouragement. At HarperCollins, Susan Watt has stood by this book through thick and thin and has been the model of a supportive publisher. Sophie Nelson has done a superb job of copy-editing in unprecedentedly difficult circumstances. My thanks to Juliet Davis for dealing with the pictures, Amanda Starkey for all her help, and to Liz Wilhide for letting me see in draft her book on the construction of the Dome itself. Finally, my love and apologies to Sarah and the children for the way this vast octopus of a task clambered into our lives and took up permanent residence there. No family has better reason to celebrate the coming of the millennium.

ADAM NICOLSON

List of Illustrations

Section 2

Line drawing of the exterior of the Dome. Photograph ©
    NMEC/Richard Rogers Partnership.
Jennie Page, Ian Liddell and Mike Davies. NMEC/QA Photos Ltd.
One of the masts is lowered into place. Photograph ©
    Reuters/Popperfoto.
Robert Ayling. Photograph © NMEC/Network Photographers.
Jennie Page. Photograph © NMEC/Network Photographers.
Liam Kane. Photograph © NMEC/Network Photographers.
David Trench. Photograph © NMEC/Network Photographers.
Ken Robinson. Photograph © NMEC/Network Photographers.
Jeff Hawkins. Photograph © NMEC/Network Photographers.
Claire Sampson. Photograph © NMEC/Network Photographers.
Sam Chisholm. Photograph © NMEC/Network Photographers.
Michael Grade. Photograph © NMEC/Network Photographers.
Millennium Dome launch at the People's Palace, February 1998.
    Photograph © PA News.
Body Image. Photograph © NMEC/Hayes Davidson.
Spirit Level. Photograph © NMEC/Hayes Davidson.
Living Island. Photograph © NMEC/Hayes Davidson.
Serious Play. Photograph © NMEC/Hayes Davidson.
Aerial view of Millennium Dome, March 1998. Photograph © London
    Aerial Photo Library.
View of the Dome from the north side of the Thames, May 1998.
    Photograph © Mark Power/Network Photographers.
The cable-net complete, April 1998. Photograph © NMEC/QA Photos
    Ltd.
The first of the Teflon-coated panels are installed, April 1998.
    Photograph © Brian Harris/The Independent Picture Syndication.
View from the Docklands Light Railway. Photograph © Mark
    Power/Network Photographers.

Section 3

'Mr Mandelson has assured us it will be all right on the night'.
    Photograph © Solo Syndication.
'Just you wait till they find a sponsor for my bottom half'. Photograph
    © Solo Syndication

Michael Heseltine and Peter Mandelson, June 1998. Photograph ©
Gideon Mendel/Network.
Tony Blair and workers at the 'Topping Out' Ceremony, June 1998.
Photograph © PA News.
The Dome, December 1998. Photograph © Chorley Handford.
The Dome at night, December 1998. Photograph © NMEC/QA Photos
Ltd.
The amphitheatre under construction, March 1999. Photograph ©
NMEC/QA Photos Ltd.
The Millennium Show, stilts training class. Photograph ©
NMEC/Gideon Mendel/Network Photographers.
Litmus Group. Photograph © Jillian Edelstein/Network
Photographers.
Politicians. Photograph © Jillian Edelstein/Network Photographers.
Eva Jiricna. Photograph Gaston Bergeret.
Tim Pyne. Photograph Kate Phillips.
Zaha Hadid. Photograph Steve Double.
The central amphitheatre, June 1999. Photograph © NMEC/QA Photos
Ltd.
The Millennium Pier. Photograph © NMEC/QA Photos Ltd.
Skyscape. Photograph © NMEC/QA Photos Ltd.

Section 4
Computer-generated illustration of 3D Floorplan. Photograph ©
NMEC/Hayes Davidson.
Computer-generated illustration of Learning. Photograph ©
NMEC/SHAM.
Computer-generated illustration of Work. Photograph ©
NMEC/SHAM.
Computer-generated illustration of Rest. Photograph © NMEC.
Computer-generated illustration of Mind. Photograph © NMEC/Hayes
Davidson.
Ron Mueck and his sculpture for Mind, September 1999. Photographed
by Gautier Deblone, courtesy of the Anthony d'Offay
Gallery/NMEC.
Computer-generated illustration of Faith. Photograph © NMEC/Hayes
Davidson.

Computer-generated illustration of Self Portrait. Photograph ©
NMEC/Hayes Davidson.

Computer-generated illustration of Home Planet. Photograph ©
NMEC/Hayes Davidson.

Work in progress on Home Planet in August 1999. Photograph ©
NMEC/Network Photographers.

Computer-generated illustration of Living Island. Photograph ©
NMEC.

Computer-generated illustration of Journey. Photograph ©
NMEC/Hayes Davidson.

Computer-generated illustration of Shared Ground. Photograph ©
NMEC.

Computer-generated illustration of Body. Photograph © NMEC/Hayes
Davidson.

The Dome, June 1999. Photograph © NMEC/QA Photos Ltd.

CHAPTER ONE

Marking the Millennium

Although the Dome weighs less than the air it contains, and although it seems to perch on its riverside site, scarcely touching the land on which it sits, it has, nevertheless, a vast and overwhelming presence. It is both light and enormous. Visitors gasp when they see it for the first time. They smile at its size. It elides the scale of a natural object with the precision and intricacy of a man-made thing. It is a Teflon Ayers Rock and a giant toy. It is visibly taut but visually relaxed. When the wind blows over its surfaces, the huge white body moves, breathing slightly, as if it were a tent, which it isn't. It has grandeur of scale but the colours of a building on holiday. It's the Pantheon on the beach, a sunshade for an entire seaside resort, an envelope for something, or for nothing in particular, a container for that most literally insubstantial of things – a moment when the dates change.

This building, whose genius is in many ways its simplicity, enshrines a set of ideals and ideas that are of unparalleled complexity. Its roots are tangled. It certainly wouldn't exist without the Millennium Commission – or at least without one or two of its more enthusiastic and evangelical commissioners. The Millennium Commission wouldn't exist without the National Lottery, which funds it; there would be no National Lottery without the government of John Major; no John Major in Downing Street without the discontent that began to leak out in late-eighties and early-nineties Britain over the divisive legacy of the Thatcher revolution; and of course none of the discontent without the revolution which preceded and engendered it.

This is all part of the Dome's ancestry. Twined together in its identity are many contradictory strands. In July 1996, for example, Michael Heseltine, Deputy Prime Minister, Millennium Commissioner, chairman of the government committee overseeing the Millennium Festival, and a shaping figure in the Dome's story, described his aspirations for it:

> I want millions of visitors to visit this country, share in the festival and go away deeply impressed, much excited by British achievements. The excellence of UK companies, the pre-eminence of the City of London as a financial centre, the technological prowess, the innovative genius will leave an indelible impression.
>
> We can do that only in partnership with our leading companies. It is not a bureaucratic concept of central government, or a whim of the Millennium Commission. It is about selling ourselves and our country.

In other ways, the Dome has come to embody something very different: post-Thatcherite notions of consensus, inclusiveness, togetherness and the ideal of 'a country at ease with itself'. That was the very phrase which, in November 1990, John Major had scribbled in the car on his way back from Buckingham Palace to Downing Street, the morning he became Prime Minister.

Six and a half years later, as the ministers of the new Labour government and their special advisers pondered and debated the future of the Dome, they had before them the business plan of the company which had been set up to build it. What was the Dome for? the politicians were asking. Why should they continue with it? Was it something worth doing? Was it worth the huge sums it was going to cost? What was going to be in it? The plan put it like this:

> The overall purpose of all Millennium activity is to re-energise the Nation. The ultimate aim of the Company, therefore, is to change perceptions, more specifically:
> • to raise the self-esteem of the individual
> • to engender a sense of pride in the wider community
> • to enhance the World's view of the Nation.

Whatever was done, it went on, would have to be 'popular without being populist, quality without being elitist and challenging without being inaccessible'. There is a scale of ambition here – even emotion – which, baldly stated, is surprising in a government or quasi-government document. There is the assumption behind these words not that Britain was great, or that its brilliance needed trumpeting, but that, as a group of individuals, as a society and as a global presence, it was in need of repair. Britain is described as a damaged culture, with low self-esteem, shrinking pride and a diminishing position in the world. The Dome was there to do something about it.

These aims did not exist in a vacuum. They had been shaped by the audience to which they were addressed. At a board meeting of the Dome company during the run-up to the election the directors had agreed that 'the strategy would be to provide a new government with something that was theirs. An incoming government would be our most important audience. They would need to be sold the feel and value of the exhibition and emotionally buy into it before detailing how it would be delivered.'

If the language was intended to tell ministers what they wanted to hear, and if the company was painting the Dome as a New Labour scheme before New Labour realised it, this wasn't a purely cynical exercise. The Dome is founded on a whole set of motivations – commercial, communal, triumphant, therapeutic, opportunist, millennial. The coexistence of those tensions defines it. It is both a lid over multiplicity and a network of cables under immense strain. The history of the Dome cannot be understood, neither its travails nor its triumphs, without grasping that. It is not and was never intended to be, as it was so often portrayed, some big top show at the godforsaken end of an abandoned piece of south-east London; a manipulation of the market; or a presentational piece of fluff – although it involves aspects of all those things – but something more than that, a tool and a lever with which to shift the country into a new view of itself and a new approach to the future. The idea behind it was not only to celebrate the millennium but to regenerate a nation, to make it new, to mark the millennium with newness.

It begins with the National Lottery. Since the early nineteenth century the country, or at least its governing elite, had been suspicious of lotteries. As early as 1569 a state lottery was being run for improvements to harbours. Over the next 250 years more than 100 lottery bills were introduced to Parliament, almost all of them designed to finance public works. A 1739 scheme was set up to raise funds for Westminster Bridge; another in 1753 was devoted to an early project for the British Museum.

The 1823 Lotteries Act brought all that to an end. One last draw was to be held in 1826 and from then on lotteries were banned. For over a century they virtually disappeared from the British Isles. The only exceptions, to which nineteenth-century Home Secretaries turned a blind eye, were the Roman Catholic lotteries that were organised to raise funds for new Catholic churches needed after the 1829 Catholic Emancipation Act, and the raffles which Anglican congregations ran in imitation of them. Even as late as 1919 the Bishop of Manchester persuaded the House of Lords to vote down a bill to establish a Premium Bonds scheme for war wounded – a lottery by another name, with permanent tickets in a repeated draw – on the grounds that gambling was immoral. In the United States, throughout most of the nineteenth century, lotteries were run for educational purposes and the relief of poverty, but not in Britain. George Orwell's 1948 account of the lottery in *1984*, where the masses are tricked into believing that one or two lucky individuals receive vast, life-changing prizes which don't actually exist, can be taken as the average mid-century attitude to lotteries in Britain: sops for the credulous, a symptom of corruption and essentially deceitful. 'It could be you' meant, in fact, that it almost certainly wouldn't be.

In the deep geology of the Dome, these are some of the formative layers: a puritan suspicion of gambling (lotteries have always thrived better in Catholic than in Protestant countries; a 1924 Irish lottery – itself a gesture of freedom from the British state – had included as one of its prizes a bust of Leo XIII, presented by the Pope himself) was tempered by the idea that if the proceeds of a lottery were put either to important governmental purposes – a bridge, a harbour – or to buildings which could be identified as morally good – churches, chapels, museums – then they could, at the margins anyway, be tolerated. Fun in a good cause, the irresponsibility of the one restrained by the straitjacket of the other: this formula lies deeply buried in the personality of the Dome.

After the Second World War the idea of a national lottery surfaced again. In the early 1950s the Treasury was able to kill it, convincing the government as a whole that it was a bad idea to raise large sums of money outside the conventional tax system and then spend it on ends that were

4

not dictated by the Treasury itself. At several critical moments, particularly in 1996 and 1997, the natural treasury dislike of lottery projects – Kenneth Clarke and Gordon Brown were equally antipathetic – was a factor in the life and survival of the Dome.

A window for very small, very local lotteries had been opened by the 1934 Betting and Lotteries Act, and in 1976 a Lotteries and Amusements Act had allowed local authorities to set up lotteries with prizes up to an earth-shattering maximum of £12,000. Meanwhile, the rest of the world was beginning to play on a far larger scale. The Sydney Opera House was financed from lottery revenues, as were the Barcelona Olympics. By the early 1990s every other European country except Albania had a lottery and there were national lotteries in 116 countries worldwide.

Britain was becoming a lottery anomaly. The 1978 Royal Commission on Gambling, chaired by Lord Rothschild, had concluded that lotteries were 'at the soft end of the gambling spectrum and would not be socially harmful if introduced to Britain'. The Rothschild Commission, true to its sceptical and moralist inheritance, had recommended that a national lottery should be established to raise money for the 'arts, sport and other deserving causes'.

Nothing happened. The Rothschild recommendations foundered on the rock of Margaret Thatcher. The tone of crusading moral vigour which she brought to government; the new emphasis on the virtues of self-reliance and hard work; the moral disgust at any idea of something for nothing; and the distaste which, on the basis of her essentially nineteenth-century Methodist beliefs, she had for the dangerous and socially erosive forces of gambling: all these factors made the idea of a national lottery impossible and unacceptable to a Thatcher government. If the 1980s in Britain involved an enormous growth in the acceptability of self-gratification and material acquisition, and if it witnessed an enormous expansion in the amount people were prepared to borrow, that was nevertheless founded on the idea, however paradoxically, that the spending should be deserved, a natural reward for those who had earned it. Multimillion-pound prizes for a £1 stake, the double rollover and the midweek draw, all handed out on the basis of balls popping out of a bingo tube, could form no part of that vision.

'Mrs Thatcher thought sound money and control of expenditure was what government was about,' Norman Lamont would later reflect acidly.

'Mr Major thought it was about something else, like making people happy.' If that remark exaggerates the differences between the Thatcher and Major administrations, it nevertheless points to one of the reasons why the National Lottery came into being under one and not the other. John Major himself has reflected on why, in 1992, he was so keen to set up the lottery. It was part of his vision of completeness, of healing the disruptions which the Thatcherite period had done so much to create.

'I believed, and still believe, that the arts, sport and the built heritage enhance the quality of life for everyone. They are part of a rounded life, yet the opportunity for everyone to enjoy them was clearly not there. Some people were more capable than others of viewing or taking part in sports and the arts. I was concerned to ensure that a child who lived in a tower block had the same opportunity in arts and sport as the child who was the heir to rolling acres. It was part, if I may return to an old phrase, of what I thought of as a classless society.'

Why those causes? 'It was largely,' Major said, 'because they were under-resourced and would always be under-resourced by any government. For any government – Conservative, Labour or mishmash – the competing demands of health, education, pensions and defence will always come first, because that is where the pressure and the need have always traditionally been. The purpose of the lottery was to raise funds without taxation for those essential components of our national life.' The figures were stark enough. In 1991 social security had absorbed £74 billion, almost exactly a third of the total government budget, health £31 billion, education almost £30 billion, defence a still enormous £27.3 billion, yet to see any great peace dividend from the end of the Cold War. 'Recreational and cultural affairs', as the Central Statistical Office describes them, were allocated no more than £3.9 billion. The lottery would more than double that.

There were other less high-minded reasons. Expensive market research conducted by the Conservative Party in the course of 1991 on what people wanted from their government concluded that 'the party's strategy should be based on offering people "hope" and "peace of mind"'. These soggy terms – which were ridiculed by people inside Number Ten at the time and yet had a curious way of floating back up to the surface at intervals during the history of the Dome, confirming the suspicion that the bigger the question, the vaguer the answer – were nevertheless evidence of a griping discontent in the country in the early 1990s. Precisely the same terms would be thrown up by research conducted in the mid nineties by agencies as diverse as the Labour Party, BA and BT. They seem to indicate the existence of a real need.

By 1992 the recession, a pendulum swing against the Lawson boom of the late eighties, had worsened. House prices had collapsed, national income and industrial production were both dropping precipitously. Unemployment had climbed from 1.6 million in mid 1990 to 2.6 million by the early months of 1992. The Tory middle classes were badly affected by this recession, in a way they hadn't been by the downturns in the 1980s. Every evening the news bulletins carried announcements of business failures, approaching 1,000 businesses a week by the end of 1991. More people than ever before were failing to keep up with their mortgage payments. Negative equity – until then an arcane economist's term, meaning the debt on a property exceeding its market value – became familiar both as phrase and reality.

Government finances were hit from both sides. Tax receipts dropped and social security payments rose. In 1992–3 government spending rose by 5.8 per cent in real terms, £8.6 billion at current prices. Half of that increase was involuntary, funding the huge, demand-led social programmes to which all governments are committed. Half the increase was due to increased funding for, among other things, the health service (£1.65 billion, a pre-election commitment by Major himself, overruling Treasury ministers) and defence (£800 million, largely as a result of the costs of the Gulf War).

It is scarcely surprising, in these circumstances, that Major should have turned to a national lottery. As an idea, it didn't have to be invented. It was already there, waiting on the shelf. A lottery could turn over, it was thought at the time, perhaps £1.5 billion a year, raising perhaps £300 million a year for the five good causes (figures that rose to over £5 billion and £1.7 billion respectively, as the pent-up demand for a lottery surged into ticket-buying when it was launched in November 1994); the funds could be spent on national and local luxuries, the pleasures of life rather than its grim necessities; and it could be a vehicle for the social cohesion with which, above all, the Prime Minister identified his own job and purpose.

The National Lottery was announced in a White Paper in March 1992. There had been a suggestion that Norman Lamont might refer to it in his pre-election budget, but he did not want to distract attention from his new 20p base rate for income tax and, besides, there was the traditional Treasury antipathy to the idea of a lottery.

The White Paper, 'A National Lottery Raising Money for Good Causes', was launched by Kenneth Baker, the Home Secretary. It is a cautious and in some ways apologetic document. It quoted the Rothschild finding that 'gambling should not be positively encouraged because, if taken to excess, it can cause misery for the individual and his family, and have damaging consequences for society as a whole'. As a counterbalance to that iniquity, it was made clear that the money would be going to four good causes: the arts, sport, heritage and charities. There is no mention of the millennium. This was deliberate. The existence of a Millennium Fund, as one of the ways in which lottery money was to be distributed, was revealed only in the Conservative Party manifesto for the approaching general election.

The idea of a Millennium Fund had not been around for very long. Ken Baker, as Home Secretary, had informed his private secretaries' office of the possibility of a National Lottery only eight weeks earlier. The officials there had tried to dissuade him from going ahead with it, guessing, on no more than gut instinct, that a national lottery would be a commercial failure in Britain. But it was scarcely in Baker's say-so. There was some evidence that Britons might already be starting to play foreign lotteries. And anyway, it was a pet project of the Prime Minister's. Baker was keen for English cathedrals to be one of the specified recipients of the money. Cathedrals, at the suggestion of his officials, were extended to the national heritage more generally, but an echo of Baker's enthusiasm survives in the White Paper, where cathedrals are mentioned, for the last time, as a possible destination of the millennium money.

In the manifesto, with John Major's smiling face gleaming on its cover, the Millennium Fund appeared as the last-minute ragbag of ideas it surely was. There is more of an emphasis on the past than on the future and an air of slightly haphazard suggestion hangs over the whole project.

The fund 'could be used, for example,' the manifesto said airily, 'to restore the fabric of our nation: our great inheritance of buildings which symbolise and enrich our national life.' Local restoration schemes for canals and rivers; new sporting facilities for cities in general and Manchester in particular, if it were to host the 2000 Olympics; bursaries for young and recently retired people to 'change the face of the United Kingdom by the year 2000' – these were the methods by which 'we can use our increased leisure time, energy and money to improve life for ourselves and our families'. In the middle of this slew of good intention and lack of definition, where most of the so-called millennial ideas were already catered for under the other lottery distributing bodies, there is this paragraph:

> To help another major city [i.e. not Manchester] – chosen by competition – to hold an international trade fair designed to be a showcase of British innovation for the twenty-first century.

There, almost unrecognisable, is the fertilised egg of the Dome, a cell or two, scarcely formed, at the very beginning of its long and troubled gestation. Each one of the elements of that paragraph – another major city, chosen by competition, international, trade fair, showcase, British, innovation, twenty-first century – was to provide the raw material for years of debate. Not explicit, but implied by this hurried, last-minute insertion into an election manifesto, is another element, the taste of which continued to flavour the Dome for the rest of its life: the hint of political opportunism.

As Britain entered the last decade of the millennium, its inhabitants tended to be more conscious of what was wrong than of what was right. Cultural conservatives, of which there were many, could see only the break-up of old norms and old forms. As was widely publicised and discussed in press and Parliament, more and more people, for example, were living alone. By 1992 a quarter of all households consisted of one person, twice the proportion 30 years earlier. The figure represented, it was said, the disintegration of community, the death of the family, the atomisation of modern life, the end of sociability.

The pattern of a radical, modern, disruptive trend imposing itself on an old but still largely dominant inheritance is repeated again and again in the picture of early-nineties Britain. The number of divorces, as was persistently bewailed, had doubled since 1971. Less often was it remembered that the British were among the most uxorious people in the world. The rate of marriage in Britain was higher than anywhere else in Europe except Portugal. Although there was a real growth in the number of lone parents, from 8 per cent to 16 per cent over the previous 20 years, that again was not the overriding picture. Marriage, families and parents living with their children continued to be the usual way in which Britons lived. It was the form not the fact of marriage that had changed. The shotgun wedding was the only casualty.

More children under five were at school than ever before. A fifth of them had been at school in 1971; by 1991 that had risen to more than half. Class sizes had shrunk. A class with more than 30 pupils was now almost unheard of (less than 4 per cent) in secondary schools. At all levels, in all social classes and in every part of the country girls were now outperforming boys. The electronic revolution had yet to hit. There was only one 'microcomputer', as they were still called, for every eighteen pupils in British schools.

Britons did not feel as rich as they were. Over the previous 20 years their real disposable income (the amount of money they could actually spend after inflation had been taken into account) had risen by 70 per cent. That was the long view but everyone ignored it. Dominant in the country's mind was the real fall in income, by a matter of 1.6 per cent, between 1990 and 1991, the first time it had dropped in ten years. It hit the poor even more severely. They had not benefited from the years of growth, and the gap between rich and poor had grown. A man in the poorest fifth of the population earned the equivalent of £96 in 1979 and £100 in 1990. Over the same period the earnings of the richest fifth grew on average from £289 a week to £402 a week.

Britain had become a consumerist nation. Spending on food, which had absorbed nearly 20 per cent of all household expenditure in 1976, had now dropped to 12 per cent. The rest of the money was going on goods which had flooded into British homes. Only a minority had computers, CD players, dishwashers or tumble driers but far more households had deep-freezes than did not, and the same applied to washing-machines, microwaves, telephones, televisions and VCRs. Foreign holidays had quadrupled since the mid sixties, and in 1991 630 million day trips from home were made, costing Britons £5.2 billion.

Despite that clear growth in material well-being, Britain continued to be coloured by a culture of discontent and sense of mutual dissatisfaction. It was about a society in which so much seemed to be so available but so little was enjoyed. There were now almost 32,000 doctors in practice (up by a third on 1961), issuing an average of eight prescriptions per person per year (nearly double the number 30 years before). People in Britain felt no better. Only the Dutch spent more time off work during the year due to illness, or the suspicion of it. Britons going abroad had the uncom-fortable and justifiable feeling that others were doing better. In Europe, only in Greece and Portugal could the British holidaymaker feel that his money was going further than it did at home. (Even ten years earlier Britons would have felt richer on holiday in Belgium, Ireland, Italy, Holland and Spain as well as Greece and Portugal.)

It was generally said that the public domain was shrinking away, that people were retreating into the privacy of their increasingly lonely and defended houses. The American idea of 'defensible space' as a route to contentment had taken hold. It was widely claimed that membership of clubs, societies and community bodies was falling, that participation was something the British no longer enjoyed or even required. The truth was more complex.

Certainly trade union membership, from a historic peak of over 13 million in the late seventies, had sunk, and quite sharply, but 10 million Britons still belonged to a trade union in 1991. If that was old-form corporatist participation, the astonishing rise in charitable giving during the 1980s in many ways embodied its successor. The amounts covenanted to British charities more than trebled in the ten years to 1992. Membership of the mainstream Christian churches was falling slowly (nearly 7 million in 1990 from over 8 million in 1975) but membership both of other churches, such as the Mormons and Jehovah's Witnesses, and of other religions, particularly the Muslims and Sikhs, was rising. There was no evidence that either spirituality or a sense of community was deserting the shores of this island. Almost a quarter of the population participated in some kind of voluntary work, even though men were much less likely to do so in every social class. Some of the more old-fashioned organisations, such as the Mother's Union and the WI, suffered a serious loss of membership, but others, particularly those targeted at children, were growing fast. The Cub Scouts added nearly 100,000 members in 20 years to 1991; the participants in the Duke of Edinburgh's Award scheme grew from 122,000 in 1971 to 200,000 in 1991. Politically, despite the general verdict that the population was fed up with politics and politicians, the participation in general elections remained constant at about 75 per cent between 1979 and 1992. The British turnout for Euro elections, though, remained at about a third of all those eligible, by far the lowest in Europe.

Almost everyone, 99 per cent of the population, watched TV. The lower social classes watched more – almost 32 hours a week – but even that was less than it had been five years earlier. Very nearly the same number, 96 per cent, either visited or entertained friends and relations. There was no evidence to show that the TV age had diminished people's sociability. Three-quarters listened to music, more than ever before, 60 per cent (a rising proportion) went to the cinema at least once a year and more than 60 per cent read books, a figure that was increasing slowly but consistently throughout the 1980s. Just under half either gardened or DIYed, or both, and slightly fewer enjoyed going for a walk. An astonishing quarter of the population claimed that they made dresses, sewed or knitted at some time in the four weeks before the Home Office conducted its survey into needlework in the middle of 1990.

As for outings, 6.5 million went to Blackpool Pleasure Beach and an amazing 5.1 million visited the British Museum, double the figure ten years earlier. The Tate Gallery had also doubled its number of visitors in the same period, although both the Science and Natural History Museums in South Kensington had suffered a near-catastrophic collapse in their attendance when admission charges were introduced there in the late eighties.

This was Britain in the early nineties: cultured, wary and largely conservative, in the more old-fashioned sense of that word. People knew what they liked – they spent 118 million days on general sightseeing tours in Britain in 1989 and the National Trust was by far their most popular charity; they were insular, fearful of Europe but travelling there more than ever before. Britain was not particularly modern; it was a country in which the public domain was in parts shrinking away, in parts thriving, slightly directionless in the aftermath of the Thatcher revolution, unsure which elements to take up of that complex and self-contradictory movement, part libertarian, part authoritarian, part nationalist, part globalist; part drumming up the old virtues, part advocating the rejection of old habits in favour of the clean sheet of the free market.

If an organism draws part of its character from its own genetic background and part from the environment in which it emerges and grows, then it should not be surprising that this picture of a multiple Britain in the 1990s should in many ways affect both the process by which the Dome came into being and what the Dome turned out to be. Britain was multicultural in a wider sense than the coexistence of several ethnic traditions within its shores. Modernising trends could be identified, but only against the background of older and still vitally persistent ways of life. Class difference remained a powerful reality but the old habit of a cultivated establishment deciding what would be best for the masses, conceiving of its role as 'a mission to inform' – that was no longer acceptable. The deeply ranked vision of society that lay behind it had been blown away by the populism of the Thatcher years. The BBC itself, under pressure in a globalising market, was moving away from the earlier understanding of its role as an organ of the elite, broadcasting high culture to the masses, to a more populist vision in which those who paid the licence fee received what they wanted for it – in other words a market service, not a form of televised museum. The licence fee was no longer to be a tax on the poor to fund the expensive diversions of the rich. In time, that principle was to provoke many outraged accusations that the BBC was dumbing down.

Exactly where the Dome was to place itself on this national cross-grid of high and low culture, high-mindedness and commercialism, national tradition and global reach, the past and the future, heritage and modernity, was to remain a source of energy and tension throughout its life. It was never quite resolved. These strains within a dynamic society form a set of conundrums which cannot be unravelled. The tension between them is what the society is. If the Dome was to strike a chord in the nation as a whole, and if it was not to be seen as the plaything or cosh of a particular group, it had to remain open to the multiplicity that surrounded it. Those who worked on the project took comfort from time to time in the contradictoriness of the accusations that were thrown at them: too worthy, too Disney, too commercial, too governmental, too populist, too inaccessible, too much, too little, godless, holier-than-thou, red-top, broadsheet. As long as this polygon of discontent remained nearly circular, they felt, they were probably doing all right. The Dome would have been a failure if it hadn't been profoundly self-contradictory.

To everyone's surprise, not least their own, the Conservatives won the 1992 election. They had survived a 2.1 per cent swing to Labour. If the swing had been greater by a couple of percentage points, if Neil Kinnock had become Prime Minister in April 1992, it is conceivable that there would have been no lottery, no Millennium Commission and no Dome. The vast majority of the Labour party, in early 1997, would advise Blair not to back the project. It had squeaked through the first of its many narrow gateways.

Government by its nature is immensely slow. This is due partly to the viscosity of its culture, its habit of moving slowly; partly to its sheer size and the need to accommodate the demands and influences of the various elements within it; partly to caution; and partly to its preoccupation with everything else. As a result, the millennium project got off to what outsiders considered a slow start. Although the idea of a lottery and of a millennium strand to it was a manifesto commitment in the spring of 1992, endorsed at the general election, and although national lotteries were commonplace throughout the world and did not have to be reinvented in Britain, not until eighteen months later, in October 1993, did the National Lottery etc. Act receive the Royal Assent and become law.

The intervening period had been taken up first with designing the structure of the new department which was to run it, secondly with the arrangements for distributing the lottery funds and thirdly with an argument over whether the Treasury would have a role in the control of lottery proceeds.

According to Sarah Hogg, head of John Major's Policy Unit at Number Ten, the new department was something of an anomaly: 'The Prime Minister decided to bring arts, libraries, sport, the media and tourism together, and to give this amalgam a seat in the Cabinet. But what on earth could such a ministry be called? The Ministry of Recreation? Awfully fifties. The Department of Leisure? Terribly seventies. The party chairman [Chris Patten] suggested "The Ministry for Things I Want to Do on My Weekends".' A rapidly produced thesaurus came up with the Department of National Heritage (DNH), a dead term which neither encompassed what the department did nor carried much conviction, let alone excitement. The press, identifying the core of the Prime Minister's interest in the project and stripping it of any attempt at gravitas, called it the Ministry of Fun. The new Labour government in 1997 would call it the Department for Culture, Media and Sport, on the Italian model.

David Mellor, as its first Secretary of State, soon became embroiled in a tussle with the Treasury over the control of lottery money. Ken Clarke, the Chancellor, wanted it but Major himself was adamant 'first, that resources should be additional to existing public expenditure; and, secondly, that other areas of expenditure – very important, but legitimate taxpayer-borne expenditure – should be specifically excluded'. Lottery expenditure was to be additional to the spending that stemmed from general taxation and came through the Treasury's control.

This central notion of 'additionality', as it came to be called – a pendant to those other wonderful neologisms of the early nineties, 'subsidiarity' and 'contractorisation' – was intended, of course, to make lottery money invulnerable to the raids which the Treasury, in alliance with the big spending departments, would be chronically tempted to make on it. Additionality was designed as an institutional fence to safeguard what might be called the 'delightful' aspects of the lottery. Without it, the lottery would be sure, in time, to be absorbed into the massive, joyless expenditure on the national necessities, which no one would notice and would do little to further Major's aim of making people feel better. It is one of the great ironies of the Dome story that this safeguarding of lottery money, this allocation of public money to national enjoyment of life, has been the source of the greatest popular discontent. 'Why not spend it on schools and hospitals?' every taxi-driver, barman and newspaper pundit continued to ask year after year throughout the nineties. It was the one attitude to the Dome which spread across all classes and all regions of the country. Various answers were given: because that's not what it says in the Act (civil servants); because we wanted to do something more (Conservative politicians); quite a good idea, let's look at it (Labour politicians). When Labour came to power in 1997, they would indeed divert lottery money into an educational stream, via the New Opportunities Fund and the National Endowment for Science, Technology and the Arts (NESTA). For the Tories in 1993, that option was not on the agenda. Major wanted the lottery to be independent of the rest of government finance, and that prime ministerial support won the argument for his friend, David Mellor. Besides, without the lottery the new DNH would effectively have been eviscerated.

Hayden (later Sir Hayden) Phillips, an official at the Treasury since 1988, was given the task, as its first Permanent Secretary, of setting up the new department, drawing up the National Lottery Act and devising the bodies and systems by which the lottery revenues would be distributed to the various good causes. A keen fly-fisherman, culture buff, India-phile, he is described by other officials in the department as 'ace, funny, a fixer, always able to find his way around a problem if he wanted to. The approach was always: "Let's find a way to talk about it" rather than: "Oh, well, that isn't what the documents say."'

The design both of the Act and of the Millennium Commission bear the mark of Sir Hayden Phillips's ingenious mind and his intricate structures have been essential components of the Dome's history. 'There shall be a fund,' the Act says unequivocally, 'maintained under the control and management of the Secretary of State and known as the National Lottery Distribution Fund.' The Treasury was to have no part in it. Each of the five good causes was to get a fifth of the fund. For the Millennium Commission '20 per cent shall be allocated for expenditure on projects to mark the year 2000 and the beginning of the third millennium.' That careful form of words was chosen to short-circuit the pedants. Technically, the third millennium begins on 1 January 2001, after the full 2,000 years of the first two millennia have elapsed. But that isn't what the world thinks or feels. The general understanding is that the new millennium begins on 1 January 2000, the moment when the 999 rolls over into 000. The act's terminology straddles those horses.

The relationship of the Millennium Commission both to the government and to the rest of the country was subtle and complicated, the subject of long deliberation within the department. The Act said quite clearly that 'the Millennium Commission shall not be regarded as the servant or agent of the Crown'. It could make grants towards projects it considered appropriate, and spend money in deciding which projects were appropriate (clauses which were to be a lifebelt for the Dome in

1996). Nevertheless, the commission was far from independent of government control. The Secretary of State had to approve both numbers and pay of the commission's staff (and in that he had to get the agreement of the Treasury). The commission had to comply with directions given to it by the Secretary of State on the policy of what was appropriate, what was millennial, and also on how to put that policy into practice. The commission had to tell the Secretary of State anything he wanted to know at any time and get his permission to do anything he felt like instructing them to ask permission for. Without recourse to legislation, simply 'by order', he could also alter the amount of money going to any one of the five good causes. In other words, the commission was independent in little but name. It 'shall comply with any directions given to it by the Secretary of State as to the matters to be taken into account in determining the persons to whom, the purposes for which and the conditions subject to which [it] distributes any money' and it 'shall comply with any directions that the Secretary of State considers it appropriate to give … for securing the proper management and control of money'. It was a government body, created by the government, funded by public money (which happened to be outside the stream that flowed through the Treasury), and it was to do what the government, in the form of the DNH, told it. Both policy and the systems of financial control were set from above. Apart from that, the commission was free.

Not quite. In addition to that institutional straitjacket – and one can perhaps see in it the residue of suspicion that has always hung over lotteries and the money they produce – Hayden Phillips installed two further layers of political control: no powers of initiation; and ministers as commissioners. According to a direction given by the Secretary of State under the powers of the act, the commission would not be allowed 'to solicit particular applications'. It could not suggest or invent any of its own projects. It had to ask people what they would like to do, evaluate the suggestions and then give grants to those it liked. If it wanted to do something, such as set up a great national exhibition (and no one wanted to do that), the Millennium Commission was not allowed to do anything itself.

This provision, which was to hobble and hamstring the commission in its attempts to put together a great national exhibition through 1995 and 1996, is now seen by many as a major flaw in the legislation. Sir Hayden considers that 'hindsight working overtime'. The lack of initiating powers was a product of two things: a reluctance on the part of the Treasury to allow a quango to have a completely free hand in spending its money; and some characteristically 1990s intentions about the responsiveness of spending bodies to popular wishes. The government, it was said, didn't want to create a set of quangos which were then going to tell people what to do. They wanted people to come forward with their projects, on the basis that those who had bought the lottery tickets had after all provided the funds.

'What those with hindsight who now say this was not the right thing to have done are telling us,' Sir Hayden says in the fully rounded, Jamesian manner of the Whitehall mandarin, 'is that we at that stage should have had in our minds what it was that the Millennium Commission some two years later would decide it wanted to do. We should then have said, and I can see this argument, that there are two sorts of millennium project: one is grant-giving – people come forward with their projects; the other is doing something directly. We ought therefore to have given the Millennium Commission powers to run an exhibition of its own. But to have done that would have required some remarkable foresight, able to predict that those might have been the requirements of the body which we were at that stage in the process of setting up, alongside and in many ways parallel to the other bodies, none of which was to be, we were quite adamant, an intrusive bureaucracy.'

They didn't have that foresight and, partly as a result, the idea of a great millennium exhibition very nearly foundered on several occasions in 1996. The inability to initiate slowed the process, and the slowness with which the Dome came into being made the public and press impatient with it. In that way its bad image and over-careful institutional structure were intimately related. The Festival of Britain had been arranged more simply in 1951, when a temporary government department was established. No arm's-length relationship to government; no quasi-independence; shorter and less complicated routes for decisions to be made; a greater speed of execution; but very statist, very fifties, and even less likely to be politically acceptable in the nineties than it had been in the fifties.

Sir Hayden now turned his attention to the composition of the commission itself. Here was the final layer in the subtly tissued relationship between government, commission and country. There were to be nine commissioners, appointed by the Queen (in other words chosen by the government). None was to be paid, and their travel costs and other expenses had to be approved by the Treasury. Two of them were to be government ministers and one nominated by the opposition. This was a neat arrangement. The spending of what turned out, because of the success of the lottery, to be £2 billion of public money would clearly involve the government, at least with the bigger projects. With ministers on the commission (the Secretary of State at the DNH was the commission's chairman from the start) that involvement could be intimate and uninterrupted. But because the programmes for the bigger schemes were bound to stretch across at least one general election, it was important that the opposition had its nominee too, reducing the danger that important projects initiated under one government might be tainted in the eyes of its successor. Such a large and overt political presence on the commission pleased the Treasury, giving some additional political control over lottery expenditure. It was also a realistic acknowledgement that the Millennium Commission's setting up, activities and purpose were all from the beginning profoundly political. This was the state marking the millennium.

This set of interlocking arrangements, as elaborate as an orrery, whose very workings gave pleasure to the officials who could watch it in action, was a compromise that was characteristic of Britain in the nineties. It was not anti-statist or anti-governmental, as anything either a decade earlier in Britain or in the United States would surely have been. This was not privatisation. It recognised both the part government could play and the benefits government could take in becoming involved in marking the millennium. Nor was it uncompromisingly centralist and governmental, as anything two decades earlier in Britain or at any time in France would have been. It was consensual, third-wayist before its time.

The bill to set up the National Lottery was moving towards the statute book in the autumn of 1993. The Department of National Heritage began to consider who the six non-political Millennium Commissioners might be. Heather Wilkinson (later Hancock), the brilliant and voluble young private secretary of Hayden Phillips, 29 at the time, was allocated the task. Having previously worked for Kenneth Baker in the Home Office, she had walked into Phillips's office immediately after the election – she had never met him – and told him that she thought he needed her as his private secretary if he was going to set up a new government department, and he had taken her on. Hooked by the excitement and scale of the idea, Heather Wilkinson was, from the time she left Phillips's office, the principal person in the United Kingdom working on the millennium until Christmas 1993. In time she was to become the first acting director of the Millennium Commission.

They decided not to make the commission formally representative of all the usual bodies. It would look too much like the establishment once again setting itself up to give money to its pet projects. So they moved on to something not very different: the usual list of the great and the good. Officials in the department were keen for the commissioners to be paid but Peter Brooke, who had become Secretary of State in September after David Mellor was forced to resign over a string of sex scandals, was against it. The great and the good did things for the public benefit without pay. That was not a principle he wanted to erode.

Wilkinson was not keen, however, to trundle through the same list of names that are always thrown up on these occasions and so she wrote to hundreds of people asking for suggestions. Most of the replies suggested the Dalai Lama and Prince Charles. Others, who looked better at first, turned out, on investigation, to be poor at delivering: 'all mouth, no trousers', as Wilkinson puts it; or, worse, looked good on paper and then failed to attend meetings, or if they did turn up never said anything.

The process of collecting names and sifting them was taking weeks. Turf wars developed between departments. The Secretaries of State for Scotland, Wales and Northern Ireland all wanted to nominate their own commissioners. They weren't allowed to. One or two of them then said that if they weren't allowed to nominate their own commissioners, they wanted their own lottery. That demand was also turned down. All they got was the chance to comment on the shortlist and submit their own names to the DNH – every other member of the Cabinet was given the same chance.

By Christmas the final list was delivered to Number Ten. After the holiday it came back: 25 per cent of the names were different. The main casualty was Mary Ann Sieghart, the young leader writer on *The Times*.

The list of commissioners was published in the New Year. The two government ministers were Peter Brooke, as Secretary of State at the DNH, and Michael Heseltine, whom John Major had personally invited to take on the role. Heseltine jumped at it, quite openly thrilled at the idea of a new budget to spend. 'This was obviously a very exciting opportunity to invest an unheard of sum of money in a range of projects that were in many fields where I had a personal interest stretching way back. There would be a huge number of opportunities that would be in the environmental, heritage, scientific and cultural worlds. One could see this huge cash flow, unprecedented in history.' It was unmissable.

The Labour nomination, the personal recommendation of John Smith delivered months previously and to the surprise of many, was a businessman, Michael Montague, who had made a fortune in Calor Gas and other enterprises and had been chairman of the English Tourist Board. He left the Commission and was made a life peer by the incoming Labour government.

The non-political commissioners were selected to fill up as many slots as possible in the diverse cultural grid of modern Britain. It was important, above all, that the commission was not sniped at on the basis of the people it contained. And it hasn't been. The final selection was as follows: Brooke; Heseltine; Montague; Heather Couper, the astronomer and television presenter; the Earl of Dalkeith, heir to the Duke of Buccleuch, Scottish environmentalist and landowner, admired by commission staff for his courtesy and strong sense of social justice; Robin Dixon (later Lord Glentoran), the Northern Ireland industrialist and athlete; Sir John Hall, the Newcastle entrepreneur and football proprietor; Simon Jenkins, ex-editor of *The Times*, ex-deputy chairman of English Heritage and now a columnist on both *The Times* and the London *Evening Standard*; and Miss Patricia Scotland, the black QC, later to become a Labour peer and minister as Baroness Scotland following her resignation from the Commission.

They met for the first time on 23 February at Spencer House, just off Piccadilly in central London. A delicious dinner was provided (good food and comfortable hotels would continue throughout the life of the commission). The atmosphere was not immediately easy and the meetings of the commission would never become convivial. This was a set of people chosen largely for the differences between them. They scarcely knew each other. It would be difficult, officials thought, to imagine them ever going out to dinner together. Their natural lack of cohesion also made life awkward for commission staff. 'It was like trying to herd cats,' one of them said.

That first meeting was a little dull. Commissioners had to deal with papers on staffing, choice of chief executive, the handling of money, the delivery of accounts, the relationship to the DNH and the rest of it. Peter Brooke chaired it skilfully. Michael Heseltine, President of the Board of Trade, said little but, when he spoke, was listened to carefully. Of all those around the table, he was the one with the greatest natural authority. His presence loomed over the others, 'his dominant silence adding to his grandeur', as one of those present put it. Some of the commissioners said almost nothing, perhaps overawed by the circumstances.

The commission got off to a leisurely start. The millennium was still just under six years away. The lottery itself had not been launched. The other distributing bodies were even further behind. Peter Brooke went around the table asking what, if any, were the priorities in people's minds for the spending of the money. Nothing had been specified either in the Act or in his own directions as Secretary of State. Some quirky ideas were ventured. One male commissioner suggested that they should put everything they had into covering over all the pavements across the whole country 'so that ladies don't get their hair wet when they go shopping'. Another thought that the entire sum might be devoted to burying the wires of the nation's electricity grid and telephone network, an idea which the officials duly investigated and found to be too expensive. It would cost at least £10 billion. A Millennium Commission satellite, football stadiums in every town, new hospitals: none of the suggestions was up to much.

Despite the dinner, there was quite an austere underlay to the tone of the gathering. The millennium was not, commissioners were adamant, a question of drinks and fireworks. Committees were needed to administer different parts of their brief, including personnel (which Michael Montague would chair) and finance, taken by Sir John Hall. Then Simon Jenkins spoke: 'We'd better have an exhibition committee, a festival committee, a great event to mark the millennium.' In 1976 Jenkins, interviewing many of the survivors, had made a television documentary on the 1951 Festival of Britain. It was one of his enthusiasms. But his suggestion now met with total silence. The table of commissioners looked glum. To Jenkins it seemed perfectly clear that not one of them had given a moment's thought to a great event to mark the millennium. Peter Brooke, who was keen on the idea himself, then said, 'Well, Simon, you'd better be chairman of the Festival Committee.' Michael Heseltine said he wanted to be on it. Sir John Hall and Michael Montague were to become its other members. Around the rest of the table there was a studied lack of enthusiasm. Jenkins went home that night aware that he might well have a struggle on his hands.

CHAPTER TWO

Roots of the Idea

The earliest public suggestion for a millennium celebration was put forward by Bevis Hillier, the journalist, art historian and biographer of John Betjeman. On 28 March 1989 his letter was published in *The Times*:

> Sir, May I suggest that it is not too early to start planning a British exhibition or festival to celebrate the year 2000? Like the Great Exhibition of 1851, it should have a cosmopolitan aspect rather than the insular character of the 1951 Festival of Britain. It should be a celebration of the western world's accomplishments, not just a crowing manifesto of our own.

Hillier, who had curated a celebrated show on the 1951 festival at the V & A in 1976, was angling for the job of Millennium Festival director himself. He had just returned from five years as a columnist on the Los Angeles Times, was looking for something to do and had the relevant experience. Sir Gerald Barry, the mastermind of the 1951 festival, had given the whole process its impetus in September 1945 in much the same way, with an open letter to the Chancellor, Sir Stafford Cripps. The letter was printed in the News Chronicle, of which Barry was editor at the time. Like his predecessor, Hillier was getting in early. It was to be a disappointment that he was never to be invited to become a Millennium Commissioner or to join any part of the project.

His letter to *The Times* had suggested, among other things, a Domesday Book of modern Britain, 'a great survey of our land', involving artists, writers, photographers and the local communities. In several ways – in the website sponsored by Tesco's, Schoolnet 2000, where children are encouraged to describe and chronicle their country now; and in the Dome zone, Self-Portrait, where there is a photographic collage called the 'Andscape', a wall of faces brought together by the artist David Mach, and a depiction of national neuroses and failings by Gerald Scarfe – Hillier's suggestion (even if the use of that word 'land' has something of a 1951 air about it) did indeed eventually emerge as part of the Dome itself. It was the piece of Dome content with the longest history.

Hillier had sent a copy of his letter to Mrs Thatcher. She passed it on to her Arts Minister Richard Luce, who eventually replied to Hillier, saying that it was 'rather too early to start thinking about these things'. She also spoke to Peter Palumbo, at that time chairman of the Arts Council, asking him to put forward suggestions for celebrating the millennium. This he did in the council's annual report, incorporating the Domesday Book idea among others.

Unaware of these developments, the borough of Greenwich was also considering the millennium as an engine for the regeneration of its own disintegrating industrial landscape. A rumour was in the air that an American broadcasting network was making early enquiries into the possibility of using Greenwich, the home of time, as the headquarters for its own millennium coverage. The Americans were said to be interested in acquiring the world-exclusive use of Greenwich as a name and a location for the whole of the year 2000. British *amour propre* in government circles, and in Greenwich itself, felt that such a literal sell-out would reflect badly on the state of the nation. Had we come to the point where a TV station could buy up our millennium for its own commercial ends?

None of this caused many ripples. It was all too far away. Britain in the nineties was not, except at the lunatic margins, millenarian. Or at least not in the obvious sense of that word. There was no expectation that the coming of the year 2000 would herald an Armageddon, a cataclysmic fight between good and evil, after which the 1,000-year reign of Christ on earth would begin. If some of the Cold War rhetoric of the Reagan and Thatcher years had drawn energy and fire from its Christian and millenarian inheritance – Reagan's famous characterisation of the fight against the Soviet Union as 'a struggle with the most evil empire the world has ever known' was clearly millenarian, at least in its coloration – that bi-polar vocabulary and frame of mind had now fallen away. The collapse of the Soviet Union and the events of 1989 in Europe had brought it to an end. Managerial, post-ideological politics, of which the Major regime was a symptom, were now to be the dominant form. The state was no longer a scourge of the wicked but an enabler. Both the creation of a big, employing, asset-owning state in the old socialist way; and its running down, according to the rhetoric of the New Right, were to seem equally out of date. Government's legitimate role, to use a phrase first employed in Britain by John Major, later adopted with enthusiasm by Tony Blair, was now 'to give a hand up, not a hand out'. The new emphasis was on a therapeutic politics, in which normality, social coherence and national community seemed like the natural priorities. These were to provide some of the central ideological strands in the making of the Dome.

Nevertheless, there remained, as a powerful instinct in 1990s Britain, infused into the substratum of national consciousness, the remnants of what might be called 'soft millenarianism'. The set of ideas which looks for turning points in history; which emphasises change more than continuity; which conceives of crises as moments beyond which all shall be different; which values newness for its own sake: these are the echoes of a millenarian frame of mind. When the Dome company, with the help of wordsmiths at M. & C. Saatchi, the advertising agency, came up with the slogan 'It's Time to Make a Difference' in the spring of 1997 – Peter Mandelson would later insist on dropping the 'It's' in an attempt to make its leaden rhythms more snappy – they were doing no more than distilling the residual millenarianism of the age. The focus on the possibilities of the future; the implication that things before 'the time' were bad; and the possibility of personal involvement in widescale change: all of these would be recognised, in admittedly far more ferocious terms, by the members of those fundamentalist and apocalyptic sects which occasionally seared their way into the world headlines via the activities of the Survivalist militias in the United States or the catastrophes in Jonestown or Waco.

This can be overstated, but it would be equally mistaken to ignore it as a shaping force in the Dome. Modern, secularised, soft millenarianism takes many forms: environmentalist (the world is heading for eco-disaster; only through joining us, and through changing both your heart and your lives, can the world and the future be safe); technological and electronic (new machinery, the electronic virtual community, can provide a new democratic happiness accessible to all – or to all with a modem anyway); globalist-libertarian (the concerned corporation, attending to the well-being of its market and free of the shackles of an over-regulating government, is the route to a universal future happiness); educationalist, spiritualist or deconstructionist (free yourself from the stiff and constricting categorisations of all the old ways of using your mind to emerge into a brilliant future filled with new possibilities); and physicalist (look after your body and abandon your indulgences if you want to be happy) – every single one of these mentalities found its place, however transmuted, in the Dome.

Many of those who were closely involved, such as Sir Hayden Phillips, the Permanent Secretary at the DNH – and this is an answer that was widely shared – put their justification for doing something in the negative: 'There was and is a public expectation that something would happen to mark this great date change. If provision had not been made, the government of the day would have been heavily criticised for being either Philistine or incompetent or both.' That is questionable and in the course of the Dome project many would question it, usually on the basis that this millenarian gesture was a diversion of resources away from the proper, normal needs of people and society.

The left-wing Labour MP Jeremy Corbyn voiced this point of view in November 1996. Virginia Bottomley, then Secretary of State for National Heritage, had made a fairly bland statement of the position. 'I and the Millennium Commission,' she said, 'regard the marking of the millennium as a moment of great importance, when we should be able to make a statement about our achievements, abilities and potential as we move into the next century.'

Corbyn was angrier: 'Does she think it would be better if, as a nation heading into the twenty-first century, we set the real objective of ensuring that every homeless person had a roof over his head and that there was no longer a housing shortage? People who are desperate for a roof over their head, or somewhere decent to bring up their children, are not excited by the idea of 2,000-feet-high office blocks, a ferris wheel or exhibition centres. Does she think that we should be considering this country's social needs as a priority and an indication of how we want to live in the next century?'

Until the turning of the millennium itself, that would also be the tenor of popular sentiment. In an NOP poll conducted in February 1999, for example, 60 per cent of those polled said the money spent on the Dome should go to the NHS. Another 29 per cent wanted it spent on education. Fewer than half said the Dome was an 'appropriate' way to mark the millennium. Only one in three considered a monument of any kind a good idea. Seventy per cent 'strongly believed' too much cash was going to the Dome. Two respondents out of five were 'not at all likely' to visit it. Despite that extraordinarily heavy emphasis on 'real needs', two successive governments were to decide that 'making a statement' was a necessary priority. It was what lottery money was for.

The British are habitually reluctant to make their governing ideas explicit. Jennie Page, who, as chief executive of the Millennium Commission and then of the Dome company itself, has in many ways devoted more of her life and energies to this project than anyone else, says simply that 'when doing something like this, you cannot tell what the deep and underlying reasons are. Perhaps, in retrospect, we will be able to see. For the present, it is impossible to say. You cannot analyse the movement of every muscle you make as you play a tennis shot or if you hit a snooker ball. If you did, if you attempted to, you wouldn't be able to make the shot. You would be paralysed by self-consciousness. You have to do it, then look back on it, and only later understand exactly what it was you were doing.'

For the Millennium Commissioners, there was a pair of more down-to-earth models: the Great Exhibition of 1851 and the Festival of Britain a century later. Although those two exhibitions were part of a much larger and longer international tradition, spreading in particular to France and the United States, the precedents that mattered in the mid 1990s were British. In March 1994 Simon Jenkins, as chairman of the Festival Committee, wrote a paper for the commission on the precedents they might consider. It made one essential point: they did it then, we've got all this money, we should do it now.

The 1851 exhibition, 1951 festival and 2000 experience clearly form part of a single tradition. The parallels between them are striking. On 21 March 1850 Prince Albert gave a speech in the Mansion House. Albert, dressed as an Elder Brother of Trinity House, delivered a text he had learned by heart to the chief officers of state, ambassadors and the representatives of some 200 towns across Britain. Change the rhetoric slightly, and it is a speech that might have been made in the 1990s. Albert talked about the future and globalisation: 'The distances which separated the different nations and parts of the globe are rapidly vanishing before the achievements of modern invention, and we can traverse them with incredible ease.' About education: 'The languages of all nations are known, and their acquirement placed within the reach of everybody.' Technology: 'Thought is communicated with the rapidity and even by the power of lightning.' The virtues of modernity and competition: 'Gentlemen – the exhibition of 1851 is to give us a true test and a living picture of the point of development at which the whole of mankind has arrived in this great task, and a new starting point from which all nations will be able to direct their further exertions.'

If the ambition was similar, so in some ways were the doubts. Mathematicians calculated that the Crystal Palace would blow down in the first strong gale. Engineers said the galleries would fall in and crush the visitors. Political economists prophesied a scarcity of food in London owing to so vast a concourse of people. Doctors feared that owing to so many races coming into contact with each other the Black Death would return as it had after the Crusades. Moralists predicted that England would be infected by all the scourges of the civilised and uncivilised world; theologians that this second Tower of Babel, a shrine to material hubris, would draw upon it the vengeance of an offended God.

Even as the opening day on 1 May approached, and even while the Crystal Palace was springing a thousand leaks, as the drains backed up and the water poured on to the exhibits from the holes in the cast-iron columns designed to receive the handrails for the galleries, and even though, according to the Queen's diary, 'My poor Albert [became] terribly fagged,' his response remained phlegmatic: 'I can give no guarantee against these perils.' They did not materialise.

Some of the cultural elite despised it. Cultural conservatism, in which only the authentic and the hand-made were a touchstone of worth, was alive in the 1850s. Ruskin could see only 'the carved bedsteads of Vienna, the glued toys of Switzerland, and gay jewellery of

France … the petty arts of our fashionable luxury'. As for the Crystal Palace itself:

> The earth hath bubbles, as the water hath:
> And this is one of them.

Pugin told Sir Joseph Paxton, the one-time gardener at Chatsworth and designer of the Crystal Palace, that he had 'better keep to building green-houses'.

All the fears which would fill the Dome-makers' minds had troubled the Crystal Palace too. There was the problem of crowd management and visitor flows. At one time 93,000 people pushed into the glass cathedral in Hyde Park, but it didn't matter. It was 'never so crowded as a lady's successful *soirée*'. Modernity was there in 1851 – gas cookers, combine harvesters, Staffordshire glazed waterclosets – but even then visitors were alive to the ambiguous moral consequences of mechanisation and the effect it would have on traditional work practices. Exhibits were a failure: the Koh-i-Noor diamond initially looking rather dowdy compared with the Hope diamond from South Africa, at least until it was redisplayed against black velvet and lit by gas. Many exhibits arrived long after the exhibition had opened and so the catalogues, printed in English, French and German, were useless.

The whole organisation was as deeply embroiled with the commercial world as the Dome was to be. Schweppes provided the refreshment, paying £5,500 for the contract, which it then subcontracted to two other firms. A million bath buns, 32,000 quarts of cream and 33 tons of ham were consumed. The question of legacy, what would happen to Paxton's invention, was also alive throughout the summer months the exhibition was open. In June Henry Cole, the impresario behind the whole scheme, anonymously produced a pamphlet arguing for the retention on its Hyde Park site of the revolutionary and by now widely loved building. 'Shall we keep the crystal palace,' he asked, 'and have riding and walking in all weathers among flowers, fountains and sculpture?' It was not to be. The exhibition closed on 15 October, after 6 million visitors had been through it; the building was empty by mid November and it was sold for £70,000 the following spring, a sum added to the door receipts of £356,278 and the £67,514 that had been taken for season tickets. It was re-erected in Sydenham in south-east London.

There is no doubt that in the making of the Dome, the fact that, 150 years before, another remarkably similar enterprise had been embarked on, weathered its difficulties and survived to succeed was a source of deep reassurance. This had been done before. And if the courage and persistence of their Victorian antecedents provided a model for those nurturing the Dome in its darker days, the gap between the criticism it suffered in preparation and the praise it received – generally – on delivery also gave them a buffer against the brutal press attacks to which the Dome was consistently subject.

Architecturally, commercially, culturally, socially and politically, the Great Exhibition provided a template on which the Dome could – at least roughly – be modelled. Despite the widespread scepticism that had accompanied its beginnings, the exhibition made a profit of £170,000, which was invested in the land in South Kensington where the great Victorian museums now stand and in a foundation which continues to provides grants for scholars to this day.

Even Prince Albert's dreams of universal harmony had their effect. Having been to see the exhibition, a London preacher, the Reverend George Clayton, had told his congregation in Walworth that 'this scene of sublunary glory affords a faint representation, a humble type of the heavenly world, with all its incomparable brightness and inconceivable splendour. Let us soar on wings sublime, far above the reach of those inferior things, and take a glance "within the veil". I invite you to behold the palace of the skies.' The atmosphere, needless to say, did not last long. By 1854 Britain was at war in the Crimea. Its devastating winter of death and incompetence, of vast, useless suffering and unprecedented waste meant that most of the millenarian dreams which the exhibition had summoned up soon vanished.

All the great exhibitions, *expositions universelles* and world's fairs, which over the next 150 years followed in the wake of the Crystal Palace, declared soft millenarian intentions. All proclaimed in their opening ceremonies that they were to be about brotherly love and universal acceptance. All were going to change the world. None of them did. Their underlying justification was more hard-headed. As Paul Greenhalgh, historian of the fairs and head of research at the V & A, has found in unpublished papers held in the Public Record Office, Sir Edward Grey, the

Liberal Foreign Secretary in the build-up to the First World War, wrote to his opposite numbers asking why they concerned themselves with these hugely expensive exhibitions. 'All the replies,' Greenhalgh says, 'focused exclusively on economics and politics, on the promotion of national industries and imperial ambitions. None of them mentions culture, even though the public rhetoric was consistently cultural. These were behind the scenes, non-published discussions, the conversation of the elites, the place where the reality could be revealed. And the reality was that people took part in exhibitions to sell their goods and promote their national profile.'

In the twentieth century, when people became bored with looking at machines, the pill had to be sugared. In Britain, France and even more in America, the high moral tone and seriousness of the early exhibitions were increasingly accompanied by funfairs and other amusements. It was not only giant corporations that built their own vast pavilions; smaller-scale enterprises began to colonise the exhibition sites. Successful American fairs before the Second World War often included pavilions housing naked women in artistic poses. At San Diego in 1935 nude girls played with a robot by a pond. At New York in 1939, alongside an electric eel that was wired up to some magnesium flares, one stripper, Yvette Dare, had trained a macaw called Einstein to remove her bra to the sound of tom-toms from the neighbouring Seminole village.

If there are some aspects of this tradition which the Dome does not reproduce, in many other ways it clearly draws on elements of what went before. It is focused on a single giant building, in which engineering is taken to the point where it becomes indistinguishable from architecture – the Crystal Palace had made gigantism the *sine qua non* of these shows; even the primary colours, the red and gold tarmac, the yellow masts, the blue fencing, the white roof fabric, reproduce Owen Jones's Crystal Palace colour scheme. The Dome is packed with high technology; aims to reach a mass audience, with wholesome messages emphasising brotherhood or community. It is utopian in its attempt to create optimism and an increased self-esteem; promising a future filled with technological abundance, swayed by the requirements of business and government. A theatre in fact for the articulation of those forces, it is determined to be neutral in the face of the conflicting demands put upon it. It is an amalgam of the triumphant and the slightly disturbing, the inrush of modernity which all the fairs represented; a quintessentially

Victorian idea in its physicality, in its promotion of a grand site where people would learn about aspects of the world they didn't previously know; attacked before it was opened, adulated once it was. The Dome could scarcely be more obviously a child of its tradition.

But in key areas it is not like previous exhibitions. The earlier tradition was to trumpet the contents before the exhibition opened, so that the public would have a clear idea of what it might be coming to see. The great age of these exhibitions occurred before mass electric and electronic media had been invented. They were in many ways the precursors of those media. The Dome has been reluctant to advertise its contents, less certain perhaps in an age of widespread spectacular entertainment that what it had on show would be very different from what people had access to anyway.

Most of the great exhibitions and *expositions universelles* both embraced enormous art exhibitions and sponsored large, serious and pioneering intellectual gatherings. The Paris exhibition of 1900, for example, was accompanied by the largest medical conference of all time, attended by thousands of researchers from all over the world. The Dome, Paul Greenhalgh suggests, 'might have been the ideal opportunity for an epoch-breaking conference on the meaning and reality of globalisation. It has not done that.'

In the mid nineties, particularly in the mind of Simon Jenkins, the one exhibition which loomed largest was the Festival of Britain. It had been intended as 'a Tonic for the Nation', a brightening of the grey skies in austerity Britain. Gerald Barry had been adamant that the absurdities of the previous generation were not to be repeated. 'There would be no Hall of Woollens,' he had announced, 'or Pavilion of Sweetmeats or Garden of Horticulture; there would be no mammoth mounds of apples or effigies of Royalty in edible fats.' (There had been a Prince of Wales in butter at the 1924 British Empire Exhibition at Wembley.) This was to be modern.

The festival had originally been conceived in 1943 by the Royal Society of Arts as an international exhibition with a strong emphasis on trade. It would demonstrate to the world the British recovery from the war. Other nations would be invited to exhibit. It was in that way to be more 1851 than 1924. It soon became apparent, though, that the extensive war damage made it impossible for that to go ahead and so the plan was pared down. It was to be a show about Britishness, its land and people, with an exhibition of the arts alongside. The result was an event that slid towards insularity, more inward-looking (a decision was even taken to ban foreign foodstuffs from the South Bank restaurants and cafés), more old-fashioned and more trivial than its great predecessor a century before, but perhaps more fun. Justifying this lightness of tone, Barry knew, he said, 'that the British had been too busy making history for the last ten years to be in need of a gigantic, ponderous history lesson'.

Once the idea of an international trade fair had been dropped, the Chancellor, Stafford Cripps, had decided that he did not want the Board of Trade involved. The budget was cut to one sixth of what had originally been proposed, and Cripps passed responsibility for it to Herbert Morrison, Lord President of the Council, who presented it to the House of Commons on 7 December 1947. Other ministers were not particularly keen to take it up and Morrison was the only senior minister without departmental responsibilities. In a remarkable parallel to the situation of his grandson Peter Mandelson in 1997, Morrison wanted to take on the festival because it was one of the very few projects for which he had direct responsibility. Everything else in which he was interested could only be done by persuading other departments to do what he asked.

Morrison set up a non-political Festival Council to be responsible for major decisions and appointments. Its members were Kenneth Clark, John Gielgud, Malcolm Sargent, A. P. Herbert, R. A. Butler and another leading Tory, Colonel Walter Elliot. They chose the South Bank site, rather than Osterley or Battersea Park, which had also been discussed. Barry was appointed and he then engaged both Hugh Casson and Ralph Tubbs as architects. Both had done work for him at the *News Chronicle*.

It was a deeply establishment exercise. According to the writer Michael Frayn, it had 'a herbivore character: upper-drawer, amateur, a posh, BBC-approved enterprise'. It was largely conceived on the lawns of Barry's house at Petworth in Sussex, where the designers 'paced the lawn in pairs, like the Walrus and the Carpenter, trying to grasp the immensity of our task and marshal the shapes and ships and sealing wax into some kind of order'.

Frayn's herbivores were the

'radical middle classes, the do-gooders, the readers of the *News Chronicle*, the *Guardian* and the *Observer*; the signers of petitions;

the backbone of the BBC. In short the gentle ruminants, who look out from lush green pastures which are their natural station in life with eyes full of sorrow for less fortunate creatures, guiltily conscious of their advantages, though not usually ceasing to eat the grass.'

In a foreshadowing of the nineties, the carnivores hated it – a waste of money when foreign currency was short and there were still Britons without a house. How could a Dome of Discovery be justified when there was still a famine of wood, steel and skilled labour? It was also foreign in influence when Europe was rife with communism. For the right-wingers, such as Evelyn Waugh, the Beaverbrook press and Sir Thomas Beecham, it was a 'monumental piece of imbecility'. For puritan left-wingers, it was a middle-class indulgence with no opening or appeal for the working-class people in whose name it was being created. All of them poured an unending river of abuse on the scheme.

In October 1950 the festival budget was cut by £1 million but Morrison argued fiercely that to abandon it would be like going into mourning. 'Is that the way to buck ourselves up when we are in difficulties? I do not think it is. It is profoundly important that we should keep the self-respect and morale of the British people on a high level. I want everyone in Britain to see it, to take part in it, to enjoy it. I want to see the people happy. I want to hear the people sing.'

The preparation was a nightmare. Work started on the cramped and rubble-strewn site on 26 July 1949, with less than two years to go. Progress was pitiable. By 31 December 1949 only 831 out of the 6,000 required drawings had reached the contractors. The switchboard girl at the festival office used to answer with the words: 'Festering Britain here, how can I help you?' Jacob Epstein, from whom the Arts Council had commissioned an important piece of sculpture for the festival, was turned away from Hugh Casson's office by the doorman because he looked like a drunk. Professor A. R. Richardson, a traffic expert, predicted that London would come to a halt. The Dome of Discovery was alive with rats until a matter of hours before the royal opening. Morrison 'listened swivel-eyed and whistling under his breath' to Casson's anxieties, always encouraging and always optimistic. Eventually it was done.

Those who liked it loved it. Eight and half million visitors came to the

South Bank between May and September, the five months for which the festival was open. Despite the wet, the British casualties in the war in Korea, the defection to Russia in May of Burgess and Maclean, there was a sudden feeling that the future – or at least the future with a U certificate – had arrived. Dylan Thomas was ecstatic:

> 'What everyone I know likes most in it is the gay absurd irrelevant delighting imagination that flies and booms and spurts and trickles out of the whole bright boiling; the linked terra-cotta man and woman fly-defying gravity and elegantly hurrying up a w.c. wall.'

Visitors to the festival were sometimes found forming queues to nothing. Over 100,000 came on one beautiful summer's day. There was dancing in the evening to Geraldo's Embassy Orchestra. Tractors rose and fell on hydraulic plinths in the Countryside Pavilion. There were husky dogs for the polar display (sitting on salt to simulate snow), and battery hens and Jersey cows (which had to be milked) in the Pavilion of Agriculture. It was the world of Daks, Kia-Ora and BOAC, the sort of place, according to one visitor, 'Dan Dare strove to defend in 1999 from the appalling Treens of the Red Moon'.

This was the landscape, as William Feaver has said, of 'Braced legs, indoor plants, colour-rinse concrete, lily-of-the-valley splays of light bulbs, canework, aluminium lattices, Cotswold-type walling with picture windows, flying staircases, blond wood ... All these became the Festival style.' The festival, in other words, was responsible for more visual pollution than any other single event or influence in mid twentieth-century Britain.

Labour lost the subsequent general election, even though they won more votes than the Conservatives. Attlee had delayed the date to take account of what he imagined would be the positive effect of the festival, but there is no evidence that it changed the outcome either way. A departmental committee at the Board of Trade chaired by Lord Ramsden had insisted, when the idea was resurrected by Gerald Barry, that if there were to be an exhibition, progress had to be made in the real world as well:

> 'To justify the heavy expenditure of money and the large allocation of labour necessary to make an exhibition a success, it is essential

that in the meantime there must have been adequate progress made in the provision of dwelling houses, schools and other public institutions already promised, and in addition sufficient industrial buildings of all classes provided to enable industry to function efficiently.'

The real world would always matter more, however universal and well-intentioned the aims of an exhibition. All the world was not a stage.

After the election the new Minister of Works, David Eccles, immediately ordered the South Bank's demolition to make way for a garden that would be used the following year to help celebrate the Coronation; only the Festival Hall and the National Film Theatre were spared. There was nothing of the festival left, except in people's memories. It had been hell in preparation, diverting in effect, essentially unimportant in its legacy, but had added something to the gaiety of life. It had not been too expensive. It had been worth doing.

With this long, wide background to the history of national exhibitions, with any number of options available as a precedent for what might be done, it is not surprising that the Millennium Commission was approaching the question with caution in early 1994. Even a passing knowledge of large-scale exhibitions would reveal that they were dangerous propositions. The commercial advantages that might accrue from them were nearly always invisible and could only be guessed at (a possible £3 added to the national economy for every visit to the 1924 Empire Exhibition was one estimate), while several shows had lost clear and large amounts of money: Paris in 1900 had ended up 40 million francs to the worse; the Montreal Expo in 1967 had bankrupted the city.

Perhaps as a result of this history, perhaps out of native caution, half the commissioners were against an exhibition in principle; more than half felt that it was going to be impossible to deliver in time, either economically or physically. In this gut judgement, they were running up against the feelings of three powerful political figures: their own chairman, Peter Brooke; the President of the Board of Trade, Michael Heseltine; and the Prime Minister. It was clear that at some time during that spring of 1994, Brooke would have to make a policy statement on their spending priorities. Would they include an exhibition?

A tussle developed between the commission and Number Ten. Major's office, under the guidance of Sarah Hogg, wanted the Millennium Commission to agree to fund projects which might also be eligible for funding from other lottery-distributing bodies. In particular, Number Ten wanted the commission to give money to the Royal Opera House, which was also receiving money from the Arts Council. No one at the time imagined that the lottery would be so successful that the revenue stream going to the Arts Council anyway, as part of the 20 per cent designated for the arts, would be sufficient to fund the Opera House on its own. The commission stood its ground. Its money was for its own projects. It ruled out (except in Scotland, Wales and Northern Ireland) funding anything that was naturally in the remit of any other lottery distributor. Commissioners, essentially reflecting the strong regional allegiances for which they had been chosen, made it clear that they weren't going to pick up other people's difficult projects for them. As for the exhibition, they stalled. It was not clear to them whether an exhibition was going to be popular in the country. No one could say if it was something Britain wanted. Most of them, thinking of what might be done around the United Kingdom, did not consider a great central statement a priority.

The speech Peter Brooke delivered on the evening of 22 June 1994, largely drafted by commission staff but eventually with a text agreed by Number Ten, bears the scars of this history. 'We expect to be the sole source of the lottery funds for the majority of the millennium projects we support,' it said, papering over the battle that lay behind those words. The projects he described were to be of four possible kinds: large capital projects of national significance, probably twelve of them, probably receiving about £50 million of grant each; capital projects with a more local impact; bursaries; 'and, perhaps, a millennium festival'.

There is a confusion in the text, a symptom of what was going on in the commission at the time. Brooke described the kind of large-scale national projects they were envisaging: environmental, scientific, educational, engineering-based, which together would take up 50 per cent of the money they had to distribute. He continued: 'We would like to use the other 50 per cent or so to support capital projects of local significance and a millennium bursary scheme.' Fifty per cent on the national landmarks and 50 per cent on these other ideas would leave nothing for an exhibition. At this stage the likeliest outcome looked like no exhibition at all.

The commission began its consultations around the country. Belfast, Birmingham, Bristol, Cambridge, Cardiff, Edinburgh, Inverness, Leeds, London, Manchester, Newcastle, Nottingham, Oxford, Plymouth and Southampton were the scenes of a series of lunches. No one could ever claim that the Millennium Commission had failed to get out of the metropolitan shadow. Between 30 and 40 people came to each lunch, chosen by commission staff, a total by now of ten civil servants packed into the top floor of Vincent House in central London, 'our rat-infested garret, not very nice at all,' as one of them described it. At the lunches there was always a token one or two local councillors but mostly those who had been involved in local community projects and voluntary initiatives. Youth, the old, science, environment, community, urban renewal, health, education and society – the anticipated priorities emerged. The local anxieties matched them: the commission had no regional structure; time was short; the kind of rules and stipulations that would accompany any grant would strangulate initiatives.

It is not surprising that local people talking to commissioners largely chosen on the basis of their own local significance should be more keen on funding local projects than any great national fanfare for the millennium. The idea of an exhibition received what is called 'a lukewarm response'. Throughout 1994 it was still a long way down the commission's agenda. The focus was on the local projects, large and small, and the fate of the exhibition was little considered. For Simon Jenkins, 1994 was a year in which the only question relevant to the exhibition was not what, who, how or where, but whether.

The September meeting of the commission took place in the Basil Hotel in Basil Street behind Harrods. Another lunch, hot because Michael Heseltine insists on a hot lunch. By now it was predicted that the lottery, to begin in November, would raise £1.6 billion for millennium projects. Under Heseltine's prompting, the commission had decided to fund no more than 50 per cent of any project. 'I argued strongly for that, based on my experience of regeneration, where we had been gearing one to four, in some cases more, in the London Docklands. I knew we would be better off in management terms with partners who had an incentive to deliver and we would serve the cause, the broad cause, much more dramatically if we could double the cash. So that simple decision turned £1.6 into £3.2.'

The Millennium Commission's choice of 50 per cent funding was mid-range in the spectrum of other lottery distributors. The Sports Council funded 90 per cent of several projects; the Arts Council occasionally went as low as 25 per cent. The average for all lottery distributors was just below 50 per cent. If the Millennium Commission had decided that it could vary the amount by which it funded different projects, and if, for example, it thought it had been able to fund an exhibition to the tune of 90 per cent or more, many of the problems which were to beset the idea would have evaporated. The decision not to do this was partly because of Heseltine's insistence on 50 per cent. But it was also because the commission itself felt that 'spreading the risk also spread the responsibility'. That was true both in management and financial terms and so would always be better for a project.

The staff recommended to the commissioners that, in order to clarify the process, they should deal first with the twelve big projects, then move on to smaller projects and bursaries. That, convenient as it might have been, was not accepted by the new chairman of the commission and Secretary of State at the Department of National Heritage (DNH), Stephen Dorrell. Everybody had to be invited to apply at the same time, big and small, otherwise the whole enterprise would look like an establishment affair and the majority of people would feel excluded. The commissioners agreed and it was decided that everything should happen at once: the commission was to get new offices in Little Smith Street, acceptably within the division bell for the politicians, but which also needed refurbishing; headhunters had to be found who would be able to produce candidates for a permanent chief executive; a logo was to be devised; management consultants taken on to advise on the guidelines for major capital projects. The exhibition was still a long way over the horizon.

In the meantime, they had managed to choose a new chief executive. The persuasive and urbane Nicholas Hinton came with a good reputation for having turned around the fortunes of Save the Children. But he had his drawbacks. He knew nothing about major capital projects, had no real experience of life in the public sector and was unaware of the strict proprieties which governed it. Even before he took up his post, he attempted to lay down guidelines for the division of responsibilities between himself and the commissioners. As they saw it, he wanted too much and gave them too little. He attempted to appoint a close friend and right-hand man as his deputy. Suddenly the relationship between Hinton and the commissioners began to go downhill. He ordered some leather chairs for his office which cost £1,000 each. Commissioners, fearing that Hinton was both wayward and headstrong, in danger of bypassing them on major decisions, tried to persuade him that his own responsibilities should be subject to the greater control of the commissioners themselves. The two parties could come to no accommodation and at an emergency meeting at a hotel in St James's the commissioners decided to sack him. They felt badly served by the headhunters and by those from whom they had sought references. Hinton left the job the day he arrived in it. He would die of a heart attack early in 1997.

Still without a chief executive, but with Heather Wilkinson still acting in that capacity, the commission made progress on everything except the question of the exhibition. Application guidelines for all other projects were launched; staff rose to 24; a panel of 60 expert advisers across the country was drafted in; a labour-saving computer system was set up, intelligent enough to assess whether proposals were eligible for a grant.

The commissioners remained largely sceptical about an exhibition, with the exception of Simon Jenkins and Michael Heseltine. Even they couldn't agree on what form it might take. Jenkins's emphasis was largely on the fun, large-scale, high-profile, huge range of components, spectacular feel and social energy of something like the Festival of Britain; Heseltine's, as President of the Board of Trade, on the possibility of a trade fair for the next millennium, the new Great Exhibition. Progress was made more difficult by Heseltine's preoc-cupation with other matters in government. In him, the exhibition idea had a powerful backer but it was a power which was not easy to use. A year had passed since the commission had been established.

In the early winter of 1994 another open competition was run to find a chief executive. Hayden Phillips advised Heather Wilkinson not to put herself forward for the post. At the same time the commissioners were urging her to apply, even though Phillips had warned her that if the commissioners gave her the job, the government would have to step in on the grounds that she was too young to do it. That is almost exactly what happened. Wilkinson was told that she was going to be offered the job by some of the non-political commissioners but it was clear that Stephen Dorrell and the government were against it. Wilkinson was indeed very young, now 30, and it was clear that there would be tough and testing times ahead for the chief executive of the commission.

In December 1994 there was a flurry of activity, which concluded with Dorrell calling commissioners to a special meeting in Little Smith Street. Here they were introduced to Jennie Page, the immensely successful and widely respected chief executive of English Heritage. Dorrell recommended to the commissioners that she should become their own new chief executive. They agreed.

The feelings among the commissioners were mixed. In one way they had been bounced into a decision. Their choice of chief executive had been overruled and their independence had been compromised. They had folded under pressure. But they had got Jennie Page. In early 1995 she was 50. She had long and wide experience of life as a civil servant at the Departments of Environment and Transport, in nationalised industry at the British National Oil Corporation, on the margins of state and private enterprise in the Docklands Corporation, in a quango at English Heritage, and in the private sector as vice-president of an investment company. She was also on the boards of Railtrack and Equitable Life.

She was acknowledged as a tough and immensely competent operator, able to command detail over a huge range of subjects, to persuade and to browbeat, to excel both at the big angry meetings at which large numbers of consultants have to be brought to heel, and at all the necessary word-in-your-ear, why-don't-you-come-in-for-a-drink oiling of the system. She gathers her lieutenants around her, inspires great loyalty in them and is loyal to them in return. Her tendency to establish a core team of the like-minded around her can make others feel excluded, a sense on the project which was at times exacerbated by its sheer difficulty. The strain and anxiety which were features of the Dome at intervals throughout its life had the effect of bonding together those who had been through it. The links between them were forged by hard times. Anyone who arrived later could never hope to share in that emotional intimacy and intensity.

Jennie Page is a virtuoso at playing the complexities of Whitehall politics – 'corridor-experience', as it is called – subtle, obstinate and doggedly hardworking. She took one holiday in the eight years up to 2000. She is literate – an English graduate from London University – cultured and numerate. She can be fierce. She is adept, to use the civil servant slang, at 'getting all her ducks in a row', at mobilising allies, squaring opposition, covering her bases, not moving until ready to move. She can be funny and angry. Her prejudice is against revelation and in favour of a certain blank, non-reactiveness to difficulty, a technique which buys time and keeps powder dry. 'She is practical and pragmatic,' according to Bob Harris, deputy leader of Greenwich Council, 'hard to read and difficult to sell to.' Her own conception of her managerial style is that she absorbs the blows, placing herself between those who have to do the job and those who are attacking it from the outside, allowing the doers to do, protected from the critics. Others see a more dynamic approach. One senior civil servant says, 'She creates a fire-zone around her. It's like the Marines going into the jungle around Hue. Destroy everything around you and you can see what's coming. Then you can shoot it.'

She worries. She wakes up at night, reading in the small hours. She's passionate, swears when roused, is impatient and inspiring. One man involved in the Dome called her 'this fizzing Mrs Tiggywinkle. I took to her as soon as I met her.' Stephen Bayley would brutally describe her in his diary as a 'noisy mouse; no slave to fashion or fitness. Has learnt shouting and effing and blinding from her time under Jocelyn Stevens [at English Heritage], but probably lacks his vision and precision.' One Labour minister calls her 'a cross between a porcupine and an armadillo'; another 'vigorous in negotiation'.

As Page herself points out, it was noticeable that many of those phrases used the old, instinctive male technique when approaching powerful women of 'diminishing them and demonising them by animalising them'. This was all part of the interesting and complex gender-theatre in the Dome. One of Page's most celebrated *obiter dicta* at the Millennium Commission was: 'I have seen the future and it's female.' Certainly she gathered other highly impressive women in many significant positions around her. At the same time, there were, inevitably on a construction project, the usual vast male egos swimming in the pool.

Perhaps those remarks were a symptom, above all, of the Dome being the first project of national significance on which the women mattered as much as the men.

Virginia Bottomley considers Jennie Page 'a soulmate' and thinks her 'magnificent. She is tenacious, energetic, focused, won't take no for an answer and has great integrity. It may be she should delegate more but it may be if she had we wouldn't be where we are today.' Michael Heseltine has nothing but praise for her: 'You can't overstate the significance of the quality of chief executive. And in presenting the decisions and mobilising the information, you can't get better than Jennie Page. The papers are always there, they are extremely comprehensive, questions are answered, and she has that extremely important quality of a public servant, of a permanent secretary really, of being able to lead the discussion without pretending that she is taking the decision. A formidable performer, a very excellent public servant.' It can safely be said that no one has been more important in making the Dome than Jennie Page.

Sir Jocelyn Stevens, chairman of English Heritage, had been deeply reluctant to let her go. Stormy meetings between Stevens and Hayden Phillips, Permanent Secretary at the DNH, took place in Phillips's office in Cockspur Street. Dorrell and Phillips were torn, recognising how difficult it was to have someone like Page ripped out of an organisation without knowing who her successor might be but acutely aware that the Millennium Commission needed someone of Page's standing. Some horsetrading took place and the scheduled cut in English Heritage's budget that year failed to materialise. 'If Sir Jocelyn later did better in budgetary terms than had been expected,' a senior civil servant in the department now says, 'I wouldn't dream of speculating why that might be. I imagine he had arguments of merit, I imagine we thought that English Heritage was a priority.'

It was Whitehall's version of a transfer deal. As part of it, Page had to work out her full three months' notice at English Heritage. In Simon Jenkins's house in north London, Heather Wilkinson wept over her disappointment, feeling that the commission had folded before government, and that the commissioners had revealed themselves as weak-willed. That was not how they saw it. The Millennium Commission now had a chief executive with drive, coherence, vision and the quality which in an earlier age was called 'bottom'. She was also someone who believed in an exhibition. Jennie Page was an old friend of Simon Jenkins. Throughout the years of the project he would at intervals give her lunch or dinner to persuade her, amidst all the difficulties, that, if only she knew it, these were the greatest years of her life. He had convinced her that the exhibition was something the commission must do. The government had been dragging its heels. Draft documents sent to Dorrell's office were taking weeks to be returned. The commissioners were appearing timid over the idea of an exhibition, reluctant to commit to anything. Michael Montague in particular was hostile. And time was running on. With Page's arrival in the job in March 1995 that would change and the idea that would eventually become the Dome quickened into new life.

CHAPTER THREE

Getting Something Started

'This whole thing has operated by the bumble bee rule,' Jennie Page said early in 1999. 'Science has been against it. Take it to pieces, analyse it and it can't fly. How we got here is amazingly odd.' There would be many fuzzy passages between Page's arrival at the commission and the day of the millennium itself, but her own beginning as chief executive of the commission was characteristically forthright. 'The Millennium Commission plans to support a festival in the year 2000,' the first public document produced under her aegis says. That had never been stated in such definitive terms before.

The commission had not suffered any great change of heart. Like the country at large, most of the commissioners continued to be only quite interested in an exhibition. This document is more a symptom of Jennie Page's unmatched ability to play it long. For months the commissioners found themselves unable to make a decision on the exhibition. There was always more that could be found out. There was always another next step. Taking it would not commit anyone to anything but not taking it might prevent them from doing something later. In this way, with a dangling of options and a subtle steering of a natural inertial drift, progress towards the Dome was made.

The document issued in March 1995 was not an edict but a request, a consultation, a suggestion of directions in which people's minds might like to go, an invitation for ideas. Although there was no discernible enthusiasm for an exhibition in the country, there was a clear desire for one among the politicians. It was, as a member of staff at the commission put it, 'the kind of thing politicians like – big, showy, dramatic, flattering, a kind of focus for state largesse. Of course the politicians wanted one.' The question had moved over from 'whether' to 'how'. But the commission could not itself initiate one. The 1993 Lottery Act prevented it from doing that. There was already a real demand across the country for big capital projects which would be in line for large grants. They came in particular from those parts of Britain which over the years had become used to receiving central government aid for local schemes. But there was no market for grand national festivals on an immense scale to celebrate the millennium.

The commission therefore had to create a demand which it could then satisfy – at least to the tune of the ceiling it had set itself: 50 per cent of the projected costs. It is in many ways a curious process. The state invents an idea; tells the country about it; requires a body other than itself to express a demand for it; offers to part-fund that body; then insists that the body, although independent of government, should not be entirely free to do what it likes with an idea which it never had but which it must nevertheless claim as its own.

This strange wrinkle in late-twentieth-century British government was a matter in which the entire Dome project found itself embroiled for the best part of the next two years. It was not only a question of procedure. Giving shape to the wrinkle was an ideological point about the relationship between government and business, part of the continuing love-affair in late-twentieth-century Britain with the businessman as the man of vision. 'Our millennium projects are probably going to be those that would not otherwise happen,' Peter Brooke had said a year before. 'If there were no Millennium Commission, they would not get off the ground. We do not wish to see "business as usual" ideas dressed up with a thin veneer of celebration.' On the other hand, he had gone on, it was not to be a purely statist affair. 'A millennium festival would need support from business, industry and the cultural sector.' What was meant by 'support' was not obvious but the project was expected to be commercial, driven and guided by commercial principles. It was to be business but not 'business as usual'. It was to be commercial but not entirely commercial. It was something no business would naturally undertake but business was being asked to undertake it anyway.

There was a way of squaring this circle. In Jennie Page's words, 'We recognised that it was never going to work if there wasn't some kind of legacy interest in here, something which allowed a commercial organisation to take a profit afterwards. What we were really saying was this: "There is a development opportunity here. You will get the benefit of it if you are prepared to take the risk of doing something for the public good in the first year."' It was a straight quid pro quo: risk now, profit later.

In other words, the Millennium Commission grant, to an amount as yet unspecified (although the figure of £100 million was in the air), would bridge the funding gap between what the government wanted – a *grand projet*, a landmark, an unprecedented experience – and what the public would be prepared to pay for. The carrot for the operator was the prospect of being left with a hugely enhanced site after, perhaps, breaking even on the exhibition. The commission itself would carry none of the risk.

Those were the elements of a complex proposition which was workable only if the conditions were precisely right: the costs and projected revenue of the scheme proposed; the amount the commission was prepared to put in as grant; the cost of getting the site in order; the actual value of the site at the end of it; and the risk of putting on a show which by definition was to be unlike anything ever experienced before. If any one of those figures were out of kilter, the whole scheme would capsize. The viability of such a method – compared to a straight government-sponsored *grand projet* route: one client, one aim, one process – was, even at this early stage, anything but robust.

The consultation paper mentions both festival and exhibition but the exhibition is its focus. As a document, it is a miracle of prescience, comprehensiveness and conciseness. Anyone who looks at the long and confused history of the Dome and sees in it not the inherent difficulties of bringing off such a thing at the ambivalent margins of the modern British state but the failings of the people who have been attempting to do it, should look at this consultation paper and ask himself if he could have done it any better.

It moves briskly through the relevant questions and factors to consider: first the precedents of 1851 and 1951; then the setting up of two competitions, one for the site and one for those who wanted to design and operate the exhibition. (The coherent rationality papered over the slight Alice-in-Wonderland air that hung over this exercise: neither sites nor operators, of course, had any idea that they might yet exist.) The site was to be accessible by road and rail (no hint yet of an anti-car policy); there was to be some thought given to urban regeneration (not yet the critical factor it would become), and to whether the buildings should be permanent or temporary. The document makes it quite clear that the Millennium Commission would be intimately involved throughout, that the commercial possibilities for sponsorship, licensing and straight-forward gate receipts were substantial and that operators should not assume that the commission was a bottomless pit of funds.

These few brief paragraphs outlined the agenda for the next two years. Only one section looked weak and uncertain: 'SHAPE OF EXHIBITION' the cross-head declares in bold capitals:

We want the Exhibition to be the most exciting and enjoyable experience available at the Millennium anywhere in the world. The Exhibition should be accessible to the widest possible audience and should use the latest ideas in interactive technology and exploit the opportunities for shared experiences of entertainment and education.

The hyperbole contrasted starkly with the balanced coherence of the rest of the paper and, as usual, overstatement masked something of a vacuum. The problem of content, which was to trouble the project well into 1998 and beyond, was already alive and well. What was it to be about? And how was it to be about it? Those queasy questions on subject-matter and manner would not go away. The commissioners found it difficult to commit to the exhibition largely because these questions were so difficult to answer. No one could agree on whether it should be forward-looking or backward-looking or a bit of both. Or about science or culture or national community. More lunches were held for cultural gurus and panjandrums but nothing much came out of them. An opinion poll was commissioned from Bob Worcester at MORI to ask the public what the exhibition should be about, how far they would go to see it and whether it was worth doing. People came back with a series of quites: they were quite interested; they would travel quite far; they thought it was quite worth doing. They didn't know what they wanted but they knew at least that, if they were going to be entertained, whatever was offered had to be

Above: Queen Victoria opens the Great Exhibition in Sir Joseph Paxton's Crystal Palace. The building was the Dome's grandfather: gigantic, populist, technological, modern, a mass medium in physical form.

Below: Muddle and last-minute panic in 1851. Enter Albert. 'Oh! Mum – Please, Mum – here's a to do! – here's all the company come, and the street's full of carriages and brooms – and there's such a row! – and the candles isn't lighted, nor the supper ready, nor the man dressed who's to wait, nor the music, nor nothing.' from *Punch* April 1851.

Fun and formica in austerity London, 1951. 'Clad in the proud livery of Festival beauty,' the *London Illustrated News* captioned this photograph of the Festival of Britain site, 'and, in spite of all prophecies to the contrary, ready in time, it presents a scene of remarkable architectural beauty in the modern manner.' Visitors would remember above all the Skylon 'pointing upward with modern aspiration' and the Dome of Discovery. It was on precisely the site where in 1999 British Airways' giant wheel would be erected.

Right: Right wing scepticism interrogates Utopian exhibition idealism in 1951. Enoch Powell subjects Herbert Morrison, the Labour minister in charge of the Festival, to his famous inquisitorial stare. 'What do you mean – symbolic?' Morrison's grandson Peter Mandelson would be asked over and over again the same sort of question about the Dome in 1997–8, more often than not by Tory politicians.

NO VISIBLE MEANS OF SUPPORT

"What do you mean—symbolic?"

(The Vertical Feature for the South Bank Exhibition is now under construction.)

Below: The Millennium Commission in 1994. Front row, from left to right: Patricia Scotland QC; The Rt Hon Peter Brooke CH MP; The Rt Hon Michael Heseltine MP; Professor Heather Couper FRAS. Back row from left to right: Sir John Hall; Robin Dixon; Michael Montague CBE; Earl of Dalkeith; Simon Jenkins.

Left: A model of Imagination's 'Millennium Central'. The Birmingham scheme featured an avenue of ten time 'zones' with the 'Big Time' arena at one end and the spectacular Tower of Time ride at the other. The sheme envisaged that much of the content, excitement and involvement in the exhibition would be generated by a four year programme of activities throughout the nation.

The evolution of the Greenwich Peninsula

Below: In the late 18th century, the low flat extent of Greenwich Marsh is surrounded by the Thames beyond the towers of the Royal Naval College at Greenwich. The site of the Dome, on the northern tip, was in use as a rhubarb farm.

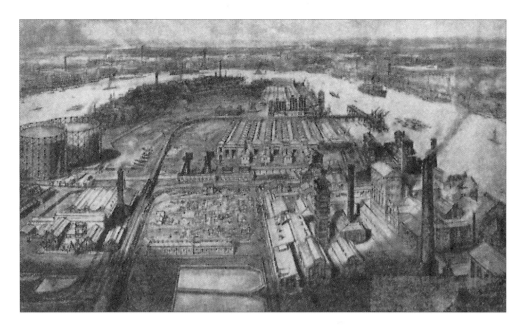

Above: A view of the peninsula in the 1920s. The South Metropolitan Gasworks occupy the middle distance with their two gasholders on the left. The smelliest part of the works, the purifying plant, was placed on the tip of the peninsula, the site of the Dome.

Below: The Greenwich peninsula in August 1996. A single gasholder and the coaling pier remain. Otherwise the site is clear except for the prominent white ventilation shaft of the Blackwall Tunnel. In the background, Canary Wharf, the NatWest Tower in the City and the many bridges across the Thames can be made out. On site, British Gas had just begun its statutory clean-up.

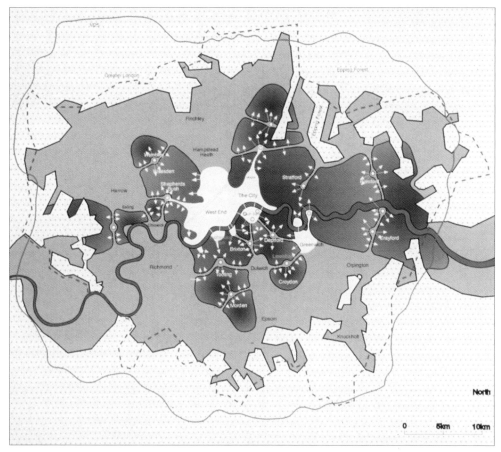

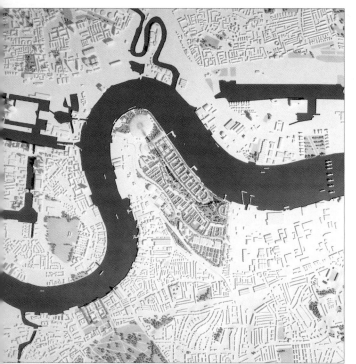

Left: A model of part of the East End of London shows the Greenwich Peninsula sticking up like a thumb, with the Dome at its tip. Canary Wharf is due west of it, the Royal Docks to the east and historic Greenwich at the bottom of the meander to the south. The area covered by the British Gas site, as developed by the Richard Rogers Partnership masterplan, is shown darker than the rest.

Right: June 19 1997: The new government says Yes. Bernard Ainsworth of McAlpine Laing, the construction management company, takes Tony Blair, John Prescott, Chris Smith and Peter Mandelson around the site. Peter Mandelson rubs his hands. Jennie Page and Claire Sampson were trying to get down there to meet them but were stuck in traffic.

Left: A poverty map of London produced by the Richard Rogers Partnership. A central core of the West End and the City is rich (coloured white). A tongue of money stretches north from there through Hampstead and Finchley to the wealthy outer suburbs. Apart from that, a ring of poverty (shown black) encircles Central London. Both Greenwich and Stratford were clear targets for strategic regeneration which could begin to fragment the poverty belt.

Right: July 22 1996 the day on which British Gas began cleaning up the site. Deputy Prime Minister Michael Heseltine arrives at Greenwich for a photo-opportunity to promote the exhibition to be held there. Sir Peter Levene follows closely behind.

The sight that greeted Heseltine and Levene: the
battered meridian sign, dereliction and decay.
Canary Wharf looms from across the river.

phenomenal. But if the commission didn't know what it was going to give them, how could they possibly meet that expectation? And if there was no great public hunger for this kind of thing, would the absence of an exhibition be such a catastrophe? These questions would continue to be asked by commission staff throughout the rest of the decade. Some senior people there never even visited the site of the Dome.

Into the teeth of that scepticism Simon Jenkins continued to fire his volleys of enthusiasm. The country would be open to public ridicule, he reiterated, if it did nothing. He was agnostic on whether it should be singular or plural, a single great gesture or the dispersed festival on which most of the other commissioners appeared to be keen. Some thought that an electronic cyber-exhibition on the Internet, or a version of it, might be exciting. But, Jenkins felt, hanging over the whole issue was the Great Exhibition question: 'If they could do it then, if they could get 6 million to come to Hyde Park 150 years ago, why can't we do it now?' For him, the idea of a global electronic village and virtual congregation was a fallacy. The more the world became dependent on electronic media, the more desperate it was to congregate. 'Pilgrimage,' he said, 'is never more alive than now. As the sense of locality and community gradually ebbs from everyday life; as it becomes ever more difficult to extend your web of acquaintance; and as the sense of authenticity in objects and experiences diminishes in an endlessly reproduced world, so people hunger for the real thing at which thousands of others are there to share it with them. The huge gathering, whether it is a rock concert, a great show at a museum or the Olympics, is a necessary counterbalance, and is something people actually want to do, in the modern world.'

That said, the response rate to the March consultation paper was appalling: 2,200 sent out, 62 replies and those almost content-free. That was to be expected. People do not respond to things whose implications they don't understand and which they have not thought of themselves. Meanwhile, the response to the other aspects of the Millennium Commission's work, their large- and small-scale projects and bursaries, was very positive. In the end they would receive over £13.3 billion of grant applications for a huge diversity of projects: a national cycle network, a vast forest in Scotland, bridges, village halls, exhibitions on life, the earth, the environment, stadiums and so on.

The exhibition had to be pushed and driven to the point where the country would come to realise that it wanted one. In May 1995, as part of the process already devised, the commission issued a paper on the kind of site it would consider for the exhibition. Page had begun to gather together the team of professional consultants, lawyers, bankers, project managers, engineers and site evaluators. The terms of the site guidelines had begun to acquire substance, a sense of reality. Almost imperceptibly the idea of a great exhibition was moving over from an essentially political desire to a potential reality. It had become 'a compelling showpiece celebration' – a distinct move away from the rather educational emphasis of earlier discussions and towards the Jenkins idea of an enjoyable fiesta.

The exhibition was now 'expected to run from 1 January 2000 to 31 December 2000', the first time that a full year's operation was mentioned. A temporary show but 'a lasting legacy' would be required from it. Construction would take 'a minimum of two years, indicating a start date of mid 1997 at the latest'. (Despite everything that was to happen over the subsequent 24 months, construction did indeed begin on the Dome site in mid June 1997.) Some idea of the scale of the enterprise was also attempted here for the first time. The site should cover between 50 and 200 acres, and be capable of accommodating at least 15 million people and up to 30 million in the course of the year. It should be able to hold 100,000 visitors a day, arriving and leaving at up to 20,000 an hour, half of them by public transport (the first move in that direction). Suddenly, here, in proposed figures (much higher than those for which the Dome would eventually be designed), is an indication of just how big they wanted this thing to be. It was, in the words of Jeff Hawkins, then a consultant to the commission, 'a project with no template. It was off the scale of anything anyone in this country had done before.'

The invitations for site proposals produced 61 replies. Four of them duplicated each other and so there were 57 to be considered. By the end of June the 57, of which many were frankly crazy (one had suggested the whole of the Isle of Wight should be converted into a party space, with giant ferries carrying the millions to and fro across the Solent), had been reduced to 20, then to seven and then down to four. The four divided into two groups, one of one, the other of three. The first was the National Exhibition Centre in Birmingham. Because of its size the Birmingham centre was not quite in the top league of European venues. The NEC management saw the Millennium Exhibition, and the grant attached to it, as the perfect vehicle with which to add the extra exhibition space which would bring them over 200,000 square metres, capable of housing the biggest European shows that currently went to Hanover, Düsseldorf, Paris or Milan. The NEC could also offer an established management system, a knowledge of how to handle big events, large car parks, an unrivalled connection to the motorway network and a catchment within two-hours' journey time that was unmatched in the country, as well as a railway station and airport on its doorstep.

The other three shortlisted sites were quite different. Pride Park in Derby; a site at Bromley-by-Bow in Stratford, east London; and the huge thumb of land south of there, around which the river Thames flows in a giant lowland meander, known throughout history as Greenwich Marsh or the Greenwich peninsula: these three sites were all ex-gasworks. Pride Park had been largely cleaned up, but the others remained tainted by the residual poisons from the industrial works to which they had once been devoted and which had become redundant with the arrival of North Sea gas in the 1960s.

At first glance it is hard to understand why these sites might have seemed attractive. The project was already faced with a set of inherent difficulties: a sceptical, hesitant commission whose mind was divided – Michael Heseltine adamant that it wasn't going to be an amusement park, others anxious about the modern relevance of a trade fair; a country that was not particularly keen either way; discussions with the likes of Disney and Lord Hollick's media group MAI, both of which were consulted during 1995, which at least hinted that if the commission had no strong ideas on the subject of an exhibition, and if there was no fierce public demand for one, they ought seriously to consider whether it was something they should be doing at all.

To consider landing on top of this all the requirements imposed by the development of derelict brownfield sites may seem a little foolhardy. Looked at coldly, and with an eye to no more than 'selecting the site on a cost effective basis', as the commission's own May 1995 'Site Guidelines' had put it, then clearly an extension to the NEC, with its obvious legacy, clarity of arrangements and simple cleanness, would have been ideal. The commission papers had talked about the need for excellent transport connections and even of available hotel beds.

Although Derby was on the railway, Stratford was in line for the terminus of the Channel Tunnel rail link and the Greenwich peninsula was to receive its own stop on the Jubilee Line extension, already under construction, none of these sites would, on that basis alone, have been the first choice of site through which to funnel 15 million people or so in the first year of the new millennium.

But there were other forces in play, not least the fact that urban regeneration had come to assume an increasingly prominent part of the Millennium Commission's thinking. The consultative lunches around the country in 1994 had thrown up regeneration as one of the people's clearest priorities. It embraced technological renewal and a refreshed urbanism; concern for the environment and a rebuilding of communities; it would create jobs, often in areas of high unemployment; it was not tricksy or over-specialised – a wide range of activities and people could be brought under its umbrella; and it could be dramatic – big, visible changes could be wrought, creating rich human landscapes in the place of dereliction. These old town gas sites, often near city centres, were ideal candidates. If the millennium was to be about anything, regeneration was as good a label as any.

It was also a longstanding passion of Michael Heseltine, by far the heaviest-hitting of the commissioners, who was beginning to see in the London sites in particular the possibilities for locking the prospective exhibition into a larger-scale enthusiasm of his own. 'Personally, of course, I had a memory of the Greenwich site. Because when I took over the derelict East End of London sites in 1979–80, I was proposing to take over derelict sites in seven London boroughs, five to the north of the Thames and two to the south. There was intense resistance from officials in the Department of the Environment and of course in the local authorities themselves. And in the end I shrugged my shoulders and said, "Well, let Greenwich and Woolwich go." And we didn't do it. And eighteen years later, the site in Greenwich was as derelict as I had allowed it to remain in 1979.'

In 1995 the Stratford site, on which Mark Bostock of Ove Arup, a key figure in the evaluation process, Heseltine and Simon Jenkins were initially very keen, and the Greenwich peninsula both formed part of what Heseltine was calling his 'hot banana', the curved Euro-region which begins at the East End of London, moves out through north Kent and southern Essex and then down through the industrial heartland of Europe to the great commercial centres of northern Italy. It was the big vision – not always endorsed or shared by his cabinet colleagues – into which a millennium exhibition on the Greenwich peninsula would naturally fit, a signal to the future and a coalescence of Heseltine enthusiasms – Europhilia, urban festivals, regeneration, the larger East End of London, trade, glamour, dynamism, the interventionist state – which might have been cut for him in Savile Row. It is not surprising, as the Labour MP Austin Mitchell was to say in the House of Commons, that this project would in time become seen as the 'Hezza Dome'.

Of the two London sites, Ove Arup considered Stratford the better, although there was also a draw towards Greenwich, where Tussaud's was already, with British Gas, considering opening a major attraction on the peninsula. The borough of Greenwich itself, the business lobby London First and the officials of the Government Office for London were all promoting Greenwich as the prime London site. Nothing was settled. Virginia Bottomley had a bet with Simon Jenkins: she thought Tussaud's at Greenwich would get it; he bet Virgin at Stratford.

Once the site shortlist had been established, the question of operator could be addressed. Clearly, the National Exhibition Centre at Birmingham was not only a site but already an embryo operator. Others had to be drummed up. In this, as ever, the commission was again sailing close to the wind. 'We weren't allowed to initiate,' one commissioner now says, 'but we broke the law and went round initiating like there was no bloody tomorrow.'

The no-initiation rule had its virtues. It meant that every project which came off had a local partner, was shaped by local priorities, and had a natural leader to manage it and feel proprietorial about it. Those were real strengths. Without them, it is quite possible that the commission's projects, some of which came in for heavy criticism in 1999 as projected visitor numbers failed to materialise, would have had even more trouble with the national press.

Without those powers, they had to make a great deal of noise 'to stimulate the upsurge of proposals', as Michael Heseltine puts it, but there was another time-consuming problem. One of the commissioners, Patricia Scotland, advised them on the legal risks of short-circuiting a proper process of consideration. 'This,' as Heseltine says, 'is a world of judicial review. We had to take very clear legal advice on how to take our decisions and that doesn't speed them up.'

In July the commission issued its guidelines to operators. Key words and phrases are scattered through the document: inspiration, whole community, fun, potential, vision, twenty-first century. The scale of the ambition is unmistakable: 'The chosen operator must have convinced the Commission that it will deliver the best event of its kind in the world.' Saying that it does not 'wish to prescribe how this would be achieved', it then goes on to do so. Clarity of purpose, scale of enterprise, excellence of design, diversity of 'entertainment, information and experience', universality of appeal and effectiveness whatever the weather: these are the qualities of a successful idea. Organisations were to suggest themselves by mid August and would then be invited to a conference on 23 August 1995, where bidders and potential suppliers would be introduced.

Fifteen organisations responded and the commission met them at the Queen Elizabeth II Conference Centre in Westminster. The idea was to bring together potential site owners with potential operators, to infuse each with the other's skills and enthusiasms. Those who had already been living with this for many months, fired up with the vision of what a spectacular millennium event might be felt that the conference was not a great success. There was a baffling lack of good bids. Jeff Hawkins came away thinking that it had all been 'very low key. There was no spark, no one with the means of delivering something that would blow your socks off. It was all landscape architects, lawyers and accountants, looking more for what they might get out of it than what they could give to it.'

That was not the feeling in the exhibition unit at the commission. They were gripped by the idea that this event had to move outside the envelope to embrace the unprecedented and unexpected. Some of the people at the QEII conference wanted to rebuild the Crystal Palace, to celebrate the arrival of the twenty-first century with a replica of an 1851 structure. That did not set any hearts on fire. 'Even at this stage,' Hawkins says, 'we recognised this thing had to be about the future, it had to open up a great new perspective on how things in the next millennium might be.' No one at the conference was talking in anything like those terms. It felt, Hawkins said, 'a little flat'.

Flatness and vagueness were the least of the exhibition team's worries.

They could do nothing but push on. At the time Simon Jenkins was re-reading the great early twentieth-century novel by the Austrian Robert Musil, *The Man without Qualities*. It too is concerned with the difficulties and ironies of the state deciding to make a huge, unprecedented and celebratory gesture, with the vast afflatus of the government world, and with the problem that was to dog the Dome: content. Diotima, one of Musil's high-minded, bourgeois political hostesses at the heart of imperial Vienna, describes the proposition she and others like her have in mind as

> a unique never-to-recur opportunity to bring into existence what must be regarded as the greatest and most important thing in the world. 'We must and will bring to life a truly great idea. We have the opportunity and we must not fail to use it.'
>
> 'Do you have something specific in mind?' Ulrich [the Man without Qualities himself, the embodiment of the modern ironic spirit] asked naively.
>
> No, Diotima did not have anything specific in mind. How could she? No one who speaks of the greatest and most important thing in the world means anything that really exists ... But if you point this out to someone who happens at that very moment to be speaking of the greatest and most important thing in the world, that person will suspect that she is dealing with an individual devoid of feelings and ideals.

This was the very gap which would come to characterise the relationship between the press – and to some extent the country – and the Dome. It was never quite put in this way, but it was founded on the modern distrust of the large, the officially idealistic and the celebratory. The modern spirit is set against the triumphal and the monumental. Monumentality has become inseparable from pomposity and bogusness. The fragmentary, the natural, the chance, the abraded, the slight and the marginal are the source of validity. And in the light of that, the currency of the modern can only be sceptical, ironic and flip, eating away at all the fat substance of the inauthentic. Vast, near billion-pound state enterprises find those qualities difficult to adopt. The Dome would grapple with this problem until its opening day.

Despite that core difficulty, the process was now unstoppable and the search was on for a vehicle by means of which 'the best event of its kind in the world' was to become a reality. It moved to the next phase in the hands of Claire Sampson. She had arrived at the commission from the most fruitful background that could be envisaged for such a project: she had worked as production manager for the theatre and for both pop and classical concerts; she also had experience in arts administration. She was now head of the Exhibition and Festival Unit at the commission.

By mid September a more detailed invitation for operators to apply for the grant had been issued by the commission. Figures were now mentioned. The grant would be huge, not limited by the £50-million ceiling which applied to other capital projects. Privately, the commission was now talking of something approaching £250 million. 'A sense of ownership and not awe will make it a commercial success; excellence, quality and innovation will sustain its reputation and make it the envy of the world.'

The terms of this invitation to bid danced in and out of the familiar problem: this was something the Millennium Commission was instigating yet it could neither prescribe nor dictate. The commission wanted something that was 'fun, forward looking, innovative and creative as well as giving something back to the nation'. More than that it could not say. But it would 'have greater confidence in an applicant' if a certain set of criteria were fulfilled; it expected 'that the successful operator will develop a brand'; 'it is for the applicant to decide whether the Exhibition needs a landmark attraction' – and so on. All these phrases were designed to conceal a truth: the commission was telling putative recipients pretty much what was wanted from them. The proposal had to be brilliant but it must also be coherent. Vision was not enough. Nor, on the other hand, was worthy competence. This had to be a marriage of genius and deliverability. There had to be individuals involved who could inspire and sell the exhibition, and those who could 'demonstrate the drive, commitment and project management capability to make the exhibition happen'. Operators must show that long and hard consideration had been given to how to bring about a commercial success. Doing the job without it colonising your life would not be sufficient. Any recipients of this money had not only to behave with utter and demonstrable propriety; to marshal creative forces on a world-beating level; to produce CVs showing unrivalled achievement in comparable fields: the exhibition had to matter to them more than anything had ever mattered. In this fierce and demanding tone one can read, more than anything else, the understanding at the commission that commerce, if it was to get involved at all, had to know exactly what was being proposed. This was not going to be an easy ride or 'business as usual'. Huge rewards were available, but only if enormous efforts were made. There was no point in pretending otherwise. The prize was vast; so would the struggle be.

By the last week in October fifteen applications had been made on this basis. Most were insubstantial, failing to come anywhere near the Olympian standards set by the September invitation. Four of them, however, were thought good enough to shortlist. These were MAI, the media and entertainment group led by the Labour peer Lord Hollick; Granada Group plc; a specially gathered consortium of consultants, which had been named M2000, led by Touche Ross; and the design and event company Imagination Ltd, led by the inspirational, inventive, electric and occasionally emotional figure of Gary Withers. These four were then invited to submit full applications for the grant. They were given just over a month to do so. The full commission would consider their applications on 14 December 1995.

The set of instructions which they received laid great emphasis on the necessary popularity of whatever was proposed. 'The Commission's funds come from the millions of people who participate in the National Lottery. The exhibition is for them and for future generations, and the Commission believes that it must be seen by the people as a worthwhile use of their money.' Those sentences are packed with significance. They enshrine what might be called the Reithian culture of the Dome. Like the television and radio licence fee, the National Lottery acts as a voluntary tax on the population, a tax which is not progressive. It costs the same for rich and poor. But the ways in which it is spent are determined not by popular will but by bodies such as the Millennium Commission – or the board of BBC governors – chosen precisely because they are not ordinary. Those bodies, which are the predecessors and the opposite of focus groups, must feel their way towards a middle ground which satisfies the requirements both of the cultural and political elites from which they are drawn, and of the people who have funded the projects and will, in theory, form their audiences.

It is the question the Dome has addressed again and again throughout its life. An instinct towards moral and cultural respectability must be combined with a kind of reaching down to the people's sense of enjoyment. Fun must be had and the 'governors' must try to understand what people very unlike themselves think of as fun, without allowing the fun to erode the cultural importance of what they are doing. The old BBC, and the herbivores of the Festival of Britain, with all the authority of a respect-based culture behind them, had an easier ride. For the Dome in the 1990s, when that hierarchy had been deeply eroded by the anti-authoritarianism of the sixties added to all the populist anti-elitism of the Thatcher years, life would be much more difficult. It was consistently attacked both for worthiness and for triviality, for statism and commercialism, for being both stuffy and silly. It would seem at times either like an attempt to create a Reithian project in a post-Reithian world or, as Roy Strong puts it, 'a Dome for the Dumb, a symbol of the stupidity of the age'.

Those groups and companies embarking on the month-long challenge of meeting the commission's requirements were faced with some pretty austere strictures. 'The Crown will not underwrite or guarantee any of the funds to be made available by the Commission nor will it provide any financial support in connection with the operation of the Exhibition.' It was to be a hands-off relationship. No expenses were to be granted for the costs of making the submission.

The financial proprieties would be strictly observed and the audit trail, when the National Audit Office came to look at the books, would be impeccable. This was public money and nothing must go financially awry. That alone can explain the rigorous conditions imposed. Any operator's proposals for financing the company, for example, should be 'sufficiently developed and robust and have attracted sufficient support and commitment from lenders and investors to satisfy the Commission that there is no material risk on financial grounds of a failure to complete the exhibition to time and specification or to operate or maintain the exhibition in accordance with the requirements set out in this document'. Quite a few of these phrases would, within a month or two, start to ring pretty hollow.

Meanwhile, 'in another part of the forest', as Jennie Page puts it, others were stirring. David Puttnam, the film producer, was moving ever more firmly into the world of Labour politics. At Enigma Productions he had working for him two young Labour policy wonks: John Newbigin, who had been one of Neil Kinnock's speechwriters; and Ben Evans, who had been a researcher for Mark Fisher, Labour's arts spokesman. The relationship between politics and culture had never been particularly high on Labour's priorities and this small Puttnam-led group was looking for ways to push it up the agenda. At first their focus was on the lottery, and on ways in which lottery funds might be spent on more than, or in addition to, the Majorite feel-good causes to which it was currently devoted. It was here that the first ideas emerged for what would eventually become Labour lottery policy: the education-based New Opportunities Fund and NESTA, the National Endowment for Science, Technology and the Arts.

In the autumn of 1995 this group at Enigma turned their attention to the millennium. The VE-Day celebrations had taken place that summer – inevitably a series of military parades dominated by the heroism of the past and the pall of empire – and the idea that the millennium might be more of the same horrified them. 'It reeked of lost empire and conformity,' Evans says. 'And it stuck in our mind as precisely what the millennium shouldn't be.' Some in the Labour Party were already turning towards the idea of 'the young country' and renewal as the core message on which the party and the country should focus. The millennium should not be about dewy-eyed nostalgia; it was a golden opportunity to be forward-looking, educative and enjoyable. It should be memorable for the opening of doors, not the closing of them.

Puttnam began to gather some heavy hitters from the crossover zone between the arts, media and Labour politics. That autumn, meetings were held at Richard Rogers's office in Hammersmith and at David Puttnam's house. Apart from Puttnam, Newbigin and Evans, 'the Group', as they called themselves, consisted of Richard Rogers and Philip Gumuchdjian, another architect in the Richard Rogers Partnership; Melvyn Bragg; Michael Grade; Sir Peter Hall, the city strategist and urban historian, who had been Michael Heseltine's close adviser at the Department of the Environment during the Docklands years; Maurice Saatchi; Alan Yentob; and John Sorrell, chairman of the Design Council. There were other, less central and slightly unexpected figures in this new establishment list: Jocelyn Stevens, Malcolm McClaren, Jonathon Porritt and Bob Harris, deputy leader of Greenwich, whom Ben Evans was also advising at the time, all attended one meeting.

Their worry, as Ben Evans expressed it in a paper for the Group late that October, was that 'the millennium celebrations, of which the exhibition is central, lack vision and clarity of intent'. They sent a paper to the commission describing their ideas of regeneration and celebration, to which the commission failed to respond. In particular, the Group was worried by the quality of those who had applied to become the exhibition's operators. Warner Bros, Disney, Virgin and the Pearson Group had all been approached but had not come through. Should they put themselves forward as potential operators?

During November other figures joined, or at least half-joined, the Group – in particular Lord Hollick of MAI, who already had his own bid on the table, and Harvey Goldsmith, the pop impresario, who had masterminded Live Aid and who was involved with the M2000 consortium. As the deadline approached, these three bodies effectively coalesced under the M2000 banner. With only 48 hours to go, architects and draughtsmen at Richard Rogers Partnership stayed up all night to produce some presentation boards.

The Granada interest had fallen away. They were involved at the time in a large-scale and angrily public battle to take over Forte and they felt unable to take on the millennium at the same time. In effect, then, a shortlist of four had collapsed to two: M2000 and Imagination. Those were the two that were to deliver their material to the Millennium Commission by 5 December 1995 before making their pitches in person on 14 December.

Jeff Hawkins was disturbed by this collapse of interest. 'Without Granada and without MAI as a lead player, absorbed now into the M2000 bid, we'd actually lost investors. They would have brought enormous amounts of money expertise. They were people who had launched products and businesses. There were people there able to draw on all sorts of management and finance resources. The others didn't have that. Or not so much. M2000 were all professional advisers, used to spending other people's money. The only one among them who knew about putting money on the table was MAI. Imagination were also very used to spending clients' money. So you had lost the people who would be the nucleus around which the investor club might grow.'

The M2000 bid had garnered some impressive names. Goldsmith,

Hollick and Rogers sat alongside Bovis, the construction company, Touche Ross, management consultants, Gillespies, the landscape architects, the Reed Exhibition Company, part of the Reed Elsevier group, and Stuart Lipton of Stanhope, perhaps the most powerful property developer in the country. Norman Foster was in the wings.

Their exhibition was to be sited principally on the Greenwich peninsula but with a northern extension at Stratford, the other side of the Thames (which is also, coincidentally, on the Greenwich meridian). The vision was to be labelled 'This Is Where We Enter the Future'. It had some alluring gimmicks, in particular the Ticketron, an interactive electronic ticket which included a mini-computer to tell you where you were, give you information about that part of the site and provide a link between the organisers and the visitors. Special millennial Jubilee Line trains would run between Stratford and Greenwich. There was also to be a large-scale travelling exhibition called 'Shaping the Nation'.

At Greenwich itself the M2000 proposals were a little flat-footed: a lake-cum-ice-rink; a tented circus pavilion; and a network of travelators-cum-escalators which would provide a continuous ride; and an expectation that people would get through about six different experiences in ten hours. No one would have to stand in line for longer than 45 minutes. That in itself sounded too long.

The M2000 bid had been assembled in a hurry. Some of it was scarcely worked up at all and even its most developed aspects were not in themselves impressive. The Innovation Mine, Neighbourhood Earth and the Nation United, for example, would each be housed 'in a unique and stunning interior and will contain exhibits, multi-screen projections of still and moving images plus high quality sound'. On Sundays there was to be 'a Gospel brunch'. It was not inspirational but the track record of those involved, not least for the scale on which some of their projects had been conceived – Live Aid, the hugely successful Broadgate development in the City of London, Canary Wharf, Pavarotti in the Park – would take some ignoring. Harvey Goldsmith and Stuart Lipton were to be the joint chief executives. They promised 'hands-on management'.

The commission had decided that each of the bids should be presented to the commissioners in a room which the competing proposers would be allowed to take over and prepare for the occasion. They were to be given half an hour each, no more, but were allowed to produce any amount of supporting documentation they wanted. The M2000 bid involved a few boards placed around the room and the presentation itself was 'over-long, fumbling, inarticulate and scarcely convincing', according to one of those present. Those involved may not have realised the state of affairs within the commission itself; indeed they may not have understood that a majority of commissioners still needed to be convinced that an exhibition was worth doing at all. M2000 may have been relying on their collective status. That was a mistake.

The Imagination proposal was different. Imagination was a design and event company founded in 1978; it had doubled its business almost every year since its inception. By 1995 it had an admirable record, working for BT, Ford, Cadbury Schweppes, the Natural History Museum, Disney, Andrew Lloyd Webber, Time Warner, MCA Universal, Pearsons and the EU (it had built the EU pavilion at Seville in 1992). By now Imagination employed some 200 people in glamorous offices in Store Street in central London, across many categories: graphic designers, set designers, film, TV and video producers, architects, project managers, showmen, communications experts, theatre and lighting designers, engineers, photographers, model-builders and writers. Each of these skills amplified aspects of the character of Gary Withers, the inspiration behind Imagination, its founder and governing genius.

Withers realised that Imagination would have to make an extra-ordinary impact if he was to redress the imbalance between his own reputation and what he imagined was the heavy artillery lined up against him. He threw his entire workforce on to the Millennium Exhibition bid for a full month, gambling not less than £500,000 on one of the most extraordinary pitches for a job anyone had ever seen.

The Imagination team took over their allocated room and removed everything that was in there. In its stead, they installed a total environment: video screens, a blue shell to the room, elegant steel chairs, a modern table on which even the mineral water was in blue bottles. Withers was acting to a precept of Marshal McLuhan's: 'Everybody experiences far more than he understands. It is experience, rather than understanding, that influences behaviour.' From long practice of pitching to boards of enormous companies, Withers knew the formula that worked.

The pitch lasted 20 minutes, no more than two-thirds of the time allotted. Withers spoke directly to the commissioners, looking them in the eye, without notes. 'The millennium,' he said, 'should breathe a renewed pride and spirit into the nation.' While he had a deep respect for the Great Exhibition, there was little point in creating a bigger 'me-too' version of past glory. The idea was not to make 'a pre-determined exhibition that people go and look at'. That was a dead and old concept, static and retrograde.

Imagination's ambition was to create 'a living and evolving millennium destination'. Withers explained what he meant, enthusing his audience with this ingeniously shaped idea. During 1996 a set of Millennium Spheres or outposts would be created around the country in which regional energies would be focused and stimulated. Most of what would be in the exhibition would originate out there in the country, shaped by the people and not by the metropolitan design establishment. These spheres – physical objects – would travel around the country and finally arrive at the exhibition site itself, where they would be bolted on to ten enormous and glamorous pavilions. Millennium Central was in this way a destination, not simply an exhibition, where all the hopes of the nation could be expressed in an effusion of communal optimism. The company which would make this happen would be called Millennium Central Ltd. Its logo would be a giant blue M.

The Withers idea was as canny as it was idealistic. It short-circuited any bias the commission might have had against a national exhibition, by translating the local into the national during the course of it. It did not feed off a retrospective view of national significance and yet was not indifferent to the past. It did not exacerbate the North–South divide. By beginning in 1996, it created a platform for potential sponsors that was four years long. Withers knew from his own commercial experience that three or four years was usually the minimum to which large corporate sponsors were prepared to commit. Its local roots would create local sympathy (fulfilling precisely the commission's requirements not for 'awe' but for 'ownership'). And because no one knew what a great millennium exhibition was – there was, in the jargon of the marketing business, 'no latent understanding of product' – the four years around the country, as well as providing the sponsor platform, would sell the exhibition itself.

That rationale alone might have been enough to land Imagination the job. But Withers had spared no effort. He realised that he was addressing two audiences: first the commissioners, who would probably be swayed more than anything else by the meeting at which he presented his idea to them; and secondly the commission staff, to whom he needed to demonstrate strength in depth. With a comprehensiveness typical of the man and his organisation, he approached each audience with a separate instrument of persuasion.

The first, shown to the commissioners at the 14 December meeting, was the video of Johnny Pickering. In the small band of distinguished figures without whom the Dome would not now exist – John Major, Simon Jenkins, Michael Heseltine, Jennie Page, Gary Withers, Mike Davies, Ian Liddell, John Prescott, Peter Mandelson and Tony Blair – Johnny Pickering, the only fictional one among them, takes his place.

In the video which Imagination had conceived, written, shot and edited within six weeks, Johnny Pickering is the hero. He is an eleven-year-old boy, living with his mother and father in an average, but not too glossy, middle-class home. The black and white tiles of the hallway floor, lit sharply by sunlight coming in through the window to one side, have a slightly retro feel, as does the innocence and purity of the household. This is not a place where video nasties are ever watched or Gameboys very often played.

The postman rings the bell. 'John Pickering?' He gives him a letter. It is from Millennium Central. 'Mum,' Johnny calls. Mum comes to him warmly: a picture of a proper family, precisely the image of coherence which the current social statistics showed to be under such pressure. Together they look at the letter. Dad is upstairs. 'Peter, have a look at this!' Johnny has been chosen to play his flute in the orchestra for Millennium Central's 'Song for the Millennium'. A big piano chord introduces the song, an adaptation of the 1990s feel-good anthem 'Altogether Now', originally by The Farm, and the tempo picks up. Johnny, dressed in his school uniform, goes with his mum to the headquarters of Millennium Central (Imagination's Store Street offices dressed up for the purpose). It is thrumming with activity, energy and optimism – 'It's all go here at Millennium Central!' Millennium TV is filming a link in a studio. A bank of receptionists fields calls from the nation. Trevor Brooking comes in for an appointment. We hear Andrew Lloyd-Webber casually mentioned in passing conversation. The name Eric Clapton is stencilled on to an equipment case that is being manhandled out of the building. The camera moves around more quickly, the editing becomes sharper. Banners are designed in the trademark blue (it's Pantone 286); moments later we see them unfurled from Imagination's tall steel balconies. Gary Withers himself sketches out a large 3-D M. Enormous earth-moving machines are seen landscaping the site of the future exhibition, where 'everything is going very well': a '20-metre square grid' is being laid. A string quartet made up of young women in black plays in front of Inigo Jones's church in Covent Garden; a Salvation Army band, an all-female choir, and then a group of children, including Johnny on his flute, are all playing the 'Song for the Millennium', which by now has grown and swollen into a big and passionate sound – 'All together now, Across the land ...'

Glimpses of a Millennium Central M with a Welsh rubric, and others with the cross of St Andrew, move in and out of the background, adding layer on layer to the brilliant subliminal structure of the film. The logos of Sainsbury's, Tesco's, BT, NatWest, ICI and BA all make their brief, scarcely grasped appearance. There is not a single word of voice-over. Everything is viewed as if through the wondering eyes of Johnny himself. In the final shot he is going home hand in hand with his mother. The picture they make is somehow reminiscent of the old Start-Rite advertisement of two children walking together through the wood of life. Johnny is wearing a sweatshirt in the now-familiar bright gentian blue. On it are printed the words 'one in a millennium'.

The video left one or two members of the commission close to tears. It had, in a couple of minutes, conveyed a vision of the future in which hope was rewarded and cooperation was the norm, where innocent ambition found communal fulfilment and where the idea of 'a country at ease with itself' and of a dynamic, energised society seemed like a possibility. It was everything the commission had hoped might one day exist presented to them as if it already did.

This was the first moment that a sense of concrete possibility had begun to colour the idea of an exhibition. Imagination's accompanying documents, in five spiral-bound, Millennium-blue, A3 volumes, put an exceptionally impressive skeleton inside the body which the video had sold.

The theme of the exhibition was to be Time itself. Twelve divisions of the exhibition site would focus on different aspects of Time (World, Action, Dream, Future, Past, Discovery, Show, Fun, Our, This, Big and

Free) and the 'brand proposition' would be 'Millennium Central, Your Time, Your Place'. It envisaged a total project cost of £600 million. Of that, the Millennium Commission would be asked to provide £300 million, according to the standard 50 per cent formula. The rest would come from TV/media deals (£45 million), a small European Union grant (£13 million), sponsorship (£90 million), gate money (£124 million after tax) and £80 million as an investment by the eventual owners of the site and buildings. That gave a total of £652 million, with cash in hand at the end of the exhibition of £52 million. This assumed attendance by 10 million people at an average ticket price of £15 for an adult, £10 for a child.

Imagination had already secured the involvement of McAlpine Laing, the construction managers, Buro Happold, the structural engineers, IMG, the sponsorship specialists, Ove Arup, the engineers who were already working for the Millennium Commission on site evaluation, and Major Parker, CVO MBE, the organiser of the VE-Day parade. Merchandising had been designed as well as a mascot, a blue fox with a yellow nose. Striking computer-collaged visualisations and models had been made of the ten glass and steel pavilions. In bad weather 'a translucent membrane roof of Teflon coated vinyl would be stretched between the roofs of the pavilions, supported by braces and tension cables to shelter the central avenue from the weather and provide sunlight during the day'. There, in embryo, the concept of a giant Teflon umbrella covering the site appears for the first time, the seed of the Dome itself.

Even sceptics in the commission were swayed by the extraordinary conviction of the Imagination proposals. As one member of the commission staff puts it, 'When we got the Gary Withers proposals, then I felt, Hell, this could be phenomenal. He understood that the British psyche is basically a village psyche. All you need to do, to make people love it and own it, and think of it as something they have done, is to make it a village fête, but a fête for the nation. You make it very spacy and hi-tech but everyone has got their own place in it. It all becomes very human and very accessible. The first time I watched the Withers video, I was practically crying. I thought this could be so wonderful. At last, somebody with an idea!'

M2000 was told, in Jennie Page's words, 'Thank you and goodbye.' It looked, by January 1996, as if the future lay with Imagination.

CHAPTER FOUR

Testing to Destruction

There was a problem. The Imagination proposal for the Millennium Exhibition was based on Birmingham. Once the spheres had completed their odyssey around the country, they would end up at the National Exhibition Centre outside Britain's second city. That's where Millennium Central would be.

The prospect of Birmingham was viewed with barely disguised gloom in some quarters. The very name seemed to the pro-London members of the government – Heseltine, Bottomley and John Gummer, Secretary of State for the Environment and Minister for London – to bring with it a pall of functional mediocrity. It seemed clear, according to one commissioner, that the task was 'to detach Gary [Withers] from Birmingham and attach him to Greenwich'.

Imagination had provided, in amongst their vast documentation for the Birmingham scheme, a couple of plans showing how it could be adapted to the three other sites (Derby, Stratford and Greenwich). The details were sketchy. The only serious change was at Greenwich, where the two parallel rows of ten pavilions in Birmingham would be arranged into a circle of twelve to fit the nose of the Greenwich peninsula – a critical step, as it would later turn out, towards the conception of the Dome building itself.

Imagination had evaluated the four sites, scoring the NEC 99, Derby 79 and both Greenwich and Stratford 61. Although the gasworks at Derby had been cleaned up, access to the site from the rest of the country was not ideal and could in no way match the advantages of the NEC. The Stratford site had five different owners, was partly in use and was squeezed in the middle into an hourglass – not good for circulation. Access from the rest of the country was also bad. The Greenwich peninsula, although in the possession of a single owner, British Gas, was put by Imagination in the same category. In their mind, the NEC was the obvious candidate.

Imagination also had a long relationship with the Birmingham centre. Gary Withers was an old friend of Barry Cleverdon, the chief executive of the NEC. He had done trade show installations there for many years and the management of the two organisations knew and trusted each other. Withers had emphasised the significance of this in writing to the Millennium Commission:

In developing our NEC proposal, the importance of [their] integrated, established and ready to go operations team cannot be stressed too strongly. The opening date for Millennium Central is fixed. There is no second chance. There is no revised deadline. Any delay in the early part of the Critical Path Analysis will result in extreme pressure at the back end of the schedule.

Birmingham made the exhibition deliverable.

In addition to Birmingham's proven and well-oiled expertise in preparing and running big shows, there was another even more structural aspect to their relationship with the Imagination scheme. The NEC were prepared to commit an initial £50 million in order to create 'a legacy of exhibition space'. A further £30 million would be invested in 2001 out of the profits from the show.

If that commercial willingness to invest and take a risk were subtracted from the equation, an enormous hole in the figures, initially about £80 million wide, would open up. The longer the decision was delayed, the wider the hole grew. The Imagination plan had envisaged £15 million a year in sponsorship for each of the five years from 1996 to 2000, providing a total of £75 million. Ten large corporations could without much strain be persuaded to part with £1.5 million for each of those years out of their annual marketing budget. Without the certainty of Birmingham and without the programme becoming locked on to its critical path – without there being anything, in other words, for anyone to sponsor, the hole in the figures began to stretch towards something more like £155 million. That was a number which came to dominate the financial calculations later in the story. Without Birmingham – or at least without *a* Birmingham, a landowner prepared to take the risk in return for the eventual reward – the plan did not cohere. The predilection both of the government and of the commissioners was against Birmingham and so a substitute for Birmingham had to be found.

There were real arguments against Birmingham. It was massively car-based. When Imagination was asked a set of supplementary questions by the commission in early January 1996, one of the answers it gave was that 45 per cent of visitors would come by car. That did not chime with the mood of the moment. It would have meant making improvements to the A45 and the M42, perhaps involving a whole new lane on the elevated section of the motorway, which would be horribly expensive and would undoubtedly involve a long planning and public consultation process. It might also have been necessary to build an expensive extension to the Midland Metro Line 2, perhaps costing £120 million. In addition to that, the site did not engage with the whole regeneration rationale to which the commission was now wedded. The development would be on a green field next to a wood. Again, that was not the way in which the country was moving. No one knew quite how the huge numbers of visitors to the Millennium Exhibition were going to be accommodated alongside those attending the shows in the rest of the NEC, some of which were already booked.

For certain commissioners, there was a more nebulous and questionable feeling about Birmingham. 'No one in Britain wants to go and spend a day in the outskirts of Birmingham,' one says. Birmingham 'had none of the aesthetic appeal which both Stratford, on the banks of the river Lea, a wonderful riparian site, and Greenwich, in that incredibly dramatic loop of the river', both had. The NEC, whose enormous sheds already had something of the air of a vastly inflated industrial park, would be 'struggling for beauty'. The tourist industry, on this criterion alone, was sure of one thing: an exhibition in Birmingham would not generate the foreign business, perhaps as many as 1.5 million extra visitors, which the other sites might attract.

There were other more technical questions: would the NEC, which was owned, via one route or another, by Birmingham City itself, have been allowed under lottery rules to receive the grant from the Millennium

Commission? At the time it was thought not. (In retrospect, that was clearly an obstacle which could have been overcome. One year later a version of Millennium Central Ltd, owned entirely by a cabinet minister, the Chancellor of the Duchy of Lancaster, on a site which had belonged to a privatised utility, British Gas, and now belonged to a government agency, English Partnerships, would be in line to receive a £450 million grant from the Millennium Commission without anyone saying that government bodies couldn't receive lottery cash.) It also became apparent that the £50 million which the NEC had pledged to invest was probably going to be borrowed. John Gummer, Secretary of State for the Environment, the minister with a controlling hand on local government borrowing, was reluctant to let that happen. The £50 million Birmingham was planning to borrow would have been scored by the Treasury against the Department of the Environment's own central budget. Officials in the department would have to cut £50 million from other programmes. That could scarcely be contemplated. In addition, as Jennie Page says, there was a real question about who, in the NEC scheme, 'would actually take on the commercial risk. Birmingham itself, as a local authority, could not. That was against the law. Birmingham, as the owner of the NEC, couldn't allow the NEC to do so. And Imagination was too small. So, despite first appearances, there was no big backer for the scheme. There was no commercial player.'

Finally, there was a political objection. As Virginia Bottomley put it, 'Ultimately the informal message came back that Members of Parliament from Manchester, Sheffield and Leeds said, "Look, my lot want to have it in Manchester, Sheffield, Leeds." If we can't have it there, London is acceptable but it is certainly not going to Birmingham.'

Both Derby and Stratford had been taken out of the reckoning. Despite Derby's relative cleanness, and the panache with which its bid had been presented, and despite Stratford's advantages, including at one stage a preference for it expressed by both Simon Jenkins and Michael Heseltine, clearly neither would have been a rational choice over the others. It became a two-horse race. Other suggestions remained in the air. The possibility of holding the exhibition in Hyde Park in central London was floated. Plan X, as it became known in the commission, was revived: to disperse the exhibition and hold it on many sites, linked by technology, all across the country.

Those thoughts were in the margin. The main battle was a symbolic one: between the capital city and the second city; between Midlands efficiency, reliability and lack of glamour against the enormous challenge of Greenwich, the historical resonance of that name, and the attractiveness, above all for government ministers, of attempting the undoable. Simon Jenkins is quite frank about it. 'It was a beauty contest, with two contestants. And there is no doubt, on beauty, London was always going to win. But Birmingham had to be kept going as a fall-back. If Greenwich had turned out to be no good, we would have had to give it to Birmingham.' On many occasions during this period, Page and Jenkins both thought Birmingham would get the prize. It was the politicians who found that difficult to accept.

By the beginning of December anxiety in Birmingham was rising. Roger Burman, chairman of the NEC, wrote to Jennie Page: 'We in Birmingham had become concerned by the apparent preference of some commissioners for a London site, notwithstanding the promise of even-handedness held out in the commission's formal documentation.' A correspondence followed in which Virginia Bottomley promised that the successful site would be the one to which the successful operator's bid related.

Clearly, if that formulation had held, the selection of Imagination's bid meant that Birmingham would have been selected with it. That did not happen. Instead, Imagination was divorced from Birmingham and, with the commission officiating at the ceremony, married off to Greenwich. The exact process by which this happened remained obscure for those at the NEC. They felt they were kept in the dark while attempts were made to create a viable bid based on Greenwich; and kept simmering along in case the Greenwich attempt failed. In that they were right.

Through late December and January the Greenwich-based efforts continued. At certain points it looked impossible. On 20 December a scheme was proposed whereby there would be a core exhibition at the NEC, with satellite shows in the four capitals of the United Kingdom. But no one was satisfied with that. In early January 1996 the property developer Stuart Lipton, who had been part of the M2000 bid, was brought on to the scene. Perhaps he could make Greenwich work. He was introduced to Gary Withers, an Imagination–Lipton–Greenwich combination started to look possible, and on 12 January the commission gave its tentative approval to the working up of that idea.

The money for it, though, was not forthcoming. The demands in the press were becoming fiercer. An answer had to be given. By the middle of February something had to break. After a breakfast meeting at Virginia Bottomley's house, in a last-ditch, far from ideal but necessary attempt to quieten the public clamour, it was decided that the whole planning process should be separated from the funding process. In other words, the decision for Greenwich would be made public and definite even though there was no secure financial route for its delivery. The search for the money, however desperate it was, could continue after the announcement about the site.

London in general and Greenwich in particular (or what was always referred to in Birmingham as 'the Woolwich Dock site') were putting in a spectacular lobbying effort of their own. There had been some complex intra-London manoeuvring between Stratford and Greenwich, from which Greenwich had emerged the victor. Sir Bob Scott, who had run Manchester's Olympics bid, had been retained by Greenwich Council to promote their millennial scheme. The council leader, Len Duvall, is one of the capital's most impressive networkers and he was mobilising support throughout the capital and government. Tussaud's and P & O were both wooed as possible commercial operators. The *Evening Standard*, read, of course, by Westminster politicians, was pounding away day after day, week after week, about the ridiculousness of Birmingham as a festival city.

Added to these was the powerful presence of the City Corporation. The City felt under threat. The 1992 Labour manifesto had pledged to abolish the corporation when it came to power. A charm offensive was necessary. The City itself is surrounded by a ring of poor Labour boroughs. Michael Cassidy, policy chairman of the corporation, recognised that the City's ends could be served by making common cause with those boroughs and by showing that the corporation was not 'a fuddy duddy collection of old dotties in medieval dress'. The power behind Cassidy was the knowledge that the City was awash with money. It had well over £1 billion in its coffers, most of it in a fund which since the Middle Ages has been called simply City's Cash. There was no development agency for London and the London Tourist Authority was desperately short of money. The City could obviously play a role.

Cassidy persuaded the Labour London boroughs, including Greenwich, that they could act together. Greenwich's own campaign, which had been running since 1992, was welded with the City's. The business lobby called London First, on whose board Cassidy sits, became a willing ally. The Government Office for London was also closely involved.

On the grapevine, the London boosters started to hear that their city was in danger of missing out. On 'the usual drinks and dinner network', according to Cassidy, people involved in the London bid were meeting Heseltine, Gummer and Bottomley, and being told that although the government wanted the exhibition to come to London, the objective arguments in favour of Birmingham were looking unassailable. Something had to be done.

Cassidy arranged a one-week press campaign, with the grabbing strapline, '£50 million in one week to save the millennium for the city'. London TV stations ran it on the news every evening that week. 'Is London going to do it?' A hotline was set up and pictures appeared on television of receptionists apparently on the phone receiving bids. At the end of the week the City announced that it had raised the £50 million. Cassidy had actually garnered some letters of interest: 'They weren't bankable in that form but that didn't matter.' Simon Jenkins, Virginia Bottomley, John Gummer and Michael Heseltine, Cassidy says, 'were all a great help to us'. The suspicions in Birmingham were based on a reality. The government ministers and those commissioners who were friendly to them were doing their utmost to bring the exhibition to London.

It was proving difficult for London to come up with anything like the money which Birmingham and the NEC had managed to produce. Meetings were held at the Mansion House. Soundings were taken at the Lord Mayor's breakfasts. The representatives of the big clearing banks thought the exhibition would seem 'poor value for money for their own shareholders and customers'. They were national companies and they couldn't see their northern customers backing what looked like a London project. There was a meeting at Imagination. Gary Withers and Michael Heseltine attempted to enthuse some representatives of the banks, in the way the commission had been enthused back in December. It did not work. Eventually, at a meeting of the City Corporation Policy Committee, Cassidy persuaded the other committee members that there was enough money in the City coffers from the rates for them to show their support. It was suggested that the City itself should produce £6 million, on the condition that another £6 million would be produced by the banks. That was put to the vote and it went through. 'They mumbled their agreement,' Cassidy says. It was nothing like enough. The offer of £6 million, with a possible promise of £6 million more, and behind that an even more shadowy £50 million in vaguely worded letters of intent was not going to float any exhibition worth the name.

The selection of Imagination had been announced on 18 January. The Millennium Commission finally chose Greenwich, 'after searching analysis of both sites', a month later, on 21 February 1996. It was agreed at the commission meeting that no one should say anything to the press before Birmingham and its MPs had been told. Virginia Bottomley, chairman of the Millennium Commission, was the first to leave the office in Little Smith Street. An enormous gaggle of TV and the press was outside. The commissioners inside the building were watching the scenes on Sky TV.

'Secretary of State,' shouted a reporter, 'have you made a decision?'

Bottomley said, 'It was a very good meeting.'

'A good meeting for Greenwich?'

'Yes,' said Bottomley, all smiles. 'A very good meeting for Greenwich.'

Two days later Michael Cassidy was invited to dinner with John Gummer at a hotel. Gummer 'was very friendly. He never said London had won, but his whole manner said London had done well.' The story appeared, to the fury of the Prime Minister, Heseltine and Gummer, two days later in *The Financial Times*.

The formal announcement at a press conference on 28 February in the Institute of Chartered Surveyors was frenzied. The Birmingham MPs Jeff Rooker and Robin Corbett heckled Bottomley and Jenkins on the platform. 'It's a stitch-up,' Corbett said. 'It's been a really fair fight,' Jenkins replied. Jenkins and Jennie Page had to declare themselves, respectively, natives of Selly Oak in Birmingham and Coventry. No sign of London bias there.

In Birmingham doubts and anger remained. Michael Lyons, chief executive of Birmingham City Council, felt that, 'Looking back, the whole process seems ill-fated from the beginning.' He was adamant that regeneration was needed in Birmingham too. 'Of course, in the mid nineties the Greater Birmingham economy needed just as much a shot in the arm as Greater London did.' The NEC had over the years consistently delivered jobs and sustained economic activity around it. The accountants KPMG calculated that the impact of a big show at the NEC was a £300 million boost to the British economy.

Lyons felt sore for his city: 'We didn't go to them and say, "Can we play your game?" They invited us to play and they gave us the rules. And then they broke them. NEC spent about £500,000 on the bid. The NEC is owned by this city and, if I were to be crude about it, I would say that £500,000 came out of Birmingham's education budget.'

This difficult and bitter episode needs to be set against the background of a larger national debate. There was, in the early nineties, a feeling of frustration outside London. The government was fairly overtly pro-London. Each city had been awarded a minister. The Minister for London was the Secretary of State for the Environment. Birmingham, among others, was given a junior minister of no great standing. 'We went through a series of ministers for Birmingham without even meeting them,' Lyons says. 'How can you compete by having a Cabinet minister for London and that for us?'

There was, of course, a recognition in Birmingham that government is not a rational process. It is usually a question of hunch and leadership, neither of which fits neatly into a rational scheme. Equally, Birmingham recognises that it is what its chief executive calls 'a prosaic city'. It has always had a strong sense that it has to fend for itself, to find its own future. The NEC was called a white elephant when it was founded in 1973: 'Not an appropriate thing to put in the Midlands,' London voices said. Alongside that is the inherited Birmingham feeling of 'They can go to hell and we'll get on and do it.' Roger Burman of the NEC says quite straightforwardly, 'We haven't been weeping about it ever since.'

Nevertheless, there is something here which smells of old Britain, of an exclusive metropolitan elite and the patronised provinces. 'It was as if we were playing against a team that met in another room,' one leading Birmingham figure says. 'You could never quite get the rules of the game they were playing. It felt almost as if we were working class lads going off to public school and not quite knowing what the etiquette was, what the rules to follow were.' Nicholas Coleridge, the writer, journalist and chronicler of the London establishment world, gave the unspoken view: 'All this stuff about Birmingham being the geographical centre of Britain seems a red herring to me. I mean, Alice Springs is the geographical centre of Australia but the Australians won't hold their millennium show there. So why stage our exhibition out in the sticks?'

According to the site selection guidelines issued by the Millennium Commission the previous summer, any successful site needed to be between 50 and 200 acres in size and capable of handling 100,000 visitors a day, with 80,000 on site at any one time. Both the NEC and Greenwich would meet those criteria, at least after the Jubilee Line extension had been built and the site decontaminated. On two others, though, Greenwich did not match the requirements which the Millennium Commission laid down. 'The site should be available by mid 1996, free from encumbrances and with no obstacles to expedited construction.' Plainly, Greenwich could not comply with that. The ferocious demands made by the commission for robustness of finances had not been met, quite, by the Imagination/NEC bid. For Greenwich, of course, there was no money whatsoever, no operating company, no experience, no planned after-use of the exhibition structures, no personnel and no sponsorship plan.

According to one senior member of the commission staff, 'The site that should have won was Derby: it was flat, it was clear, it was reclaimed. It had been tanked already. What they have had to do at Greenwich had already happened. It was cheaper, it was very accessible and it would have been a huge regeneration input. Why wasn't it? Because it wasn't Greenwich.' The staff member goes on: 'That was my one piece of real disillusion with the commission. Why say that you are going to have a proper competition when you are never going to have a proper competition? If you are going to give in to government over this? If you are going to say, "OK, yeah, we are going to have it in Greenwich?"'

Looking back, Michael Heseltine, when asked whether this story represented 'a hijack of an exhibition by a regeneration project', said, 'There is no way, if I were a Brummie, that I would be persuaded by any argument that took the site away from Birmingham. I have a total respect for that position but it is not the decision which the Millennium

Commissioners themselves took for a range of reasons, including specific problems to do with the Birmingham site but also considering the regeneration factor, the capital city factor. So Birmingham's wasn't the winning position. You were going to offend three other contenders whichever site you chose. There was no escape from that.'

Another minister closely involved in the project later put it a little more starkly: 'I suppose in retrospect it would have been better to say right from the start that Greenwich was the preferred place, rather than going through that charade.' That is the point of view of a politician but Jennie Page denies it. 'The Millennium Commission,' she says, 'had no alternative but to run a competition because of the legislation. It was not a sham and no one first planned for Greenwich. The government did not direct the commissioners.'

The commission was now faced with the most difficult circumstances anyone could have imagined. There were under four years to go. It had an exhibition. Or at least, it had the outline of an exhibition, whose many, rapidly conceived elements had yet to be tested or, in truth, be fully fleshed out. It had a site. Or at least it had a site in mind. The site itself belonged to British Gas, widely acknowledged as a dinosaur, not used to moving quickly, scarcely attuned to the flexibilities and methods of the modern market-place. The land itself was deeply contaminated. The British Gas site as a whole, some 294 acres belonging to a wholly-owned subsidiary called Port Greenwich Ltd, had a negative value. The costs of getting it in shape would be more than the value that process would give it. Those mathematics alone explained why this huge tranche of land, six miles from the centre of London, had remained almost derelict for so long.

The peninsula was as good as inaccessible. After long negotiations with London Underground, British Gas had paid some £20 million – 'a very long £20 million', according to one of those involved – to bring the Jubilee Line extension through the peninsula. It looped across the river from the north bank and back again. The line was still several years away from completion, which was targeted for March 1998. The only major road access to the peninsula was through the Blackwall Tunnel, which was already heavily congested at rush hour. The financial arrangements for the exhibition, so carefully delineated in all the preparatory papers the year before, with so many checks and balances, guarantees and assurances sought, were now in tatters. Imagination, although clearly alive with genius as a design company, was equally clearly not capable on its own of delivering the exhibition. There was no business partner in view for it, no property developer who might be prepared to take on the risk of the exhibition, no operator for the exhibition and no investors to produce the match-funding which the Millennium Commission would require to release its grant.

There was one element to put in the balance: political will. The aftermath of the Conservative leadership election the previous autumn had elevated Michael Heseltine to Deputy Prime Minister. He now sat on a huge number of Cabinet committees, unrivalled except by the Prime Minister in his influence on government. Heseltine wanted this to happen. On the same day as the choice of Greenwich was publicly revealed, John Major announced the formation of a new committee. Heseltine was to chair it and the Chancellor Kenneth Clarke, Home Secretary Michael Howard, Transport Secretary Sir George Young and Environment Secretary John Gummer were to be the members. Scarcely noticed at the time, the creation of this committee 'to oversee the government's role' in the Millennium Festival drew the exhibition even more firmly within the orbit of government.

The four heads of the problem with which they were now faced – the source of finance, making the costs of an exhibition fit the budget, the site and an operator – were deeply intertwined. Investment would only come if an operator looked as if it were going to deliver. An operator would only come if the site looked as if it were redeemable and workable thereafter. And the site would only be redeemed if money and an operating company were there to do it.

Heseltine now persuaded Gummer that he, as Secretary of State for the Environment, should bring in the government's own development agency, English Partnerships, as the property developer which the Greenwich site needed. By early February Heseltine himself had established the groundwork of a deal between British Gas and English Partnerships that would, in time and in theory, deliver the Greenwich peninsula for the exhibition.

That was a major step forward but money clearly remained the key. The hole in the finances which had been opened up by the rejection of Birmingham was £155 million wide, made up in the original Imagination scheme of £80 million equity and £75 million sponsorship. Heseltine set about filling it. Sir Peter Levene, later, as Lord Levene, Lord Mayor of London, was at that time working in the Cabinet Office as government adviser on efficiency. He had come to Whitehall prominence during the Gulf War, when he managed the procurement programme for the Ministry of Defence with widely admired acuity. He was also an old friend and ally of Heseltine's. Levene was set the job of filling the hole.

In mid March 1996 Bob Ayling, chief executive of British Airways, was driving into central London. His car-phone rang. It was Colin Marshall, his executive chairman. Marshall had just come from 'a chat with Peter Levene. Peter's got this extraordinary idea, crazy idea, that the private sector should put on the millennium celebrations at Greenwich.' Levene was on the hunt for the money.

Ayling told Marshall that although he had a lot on his plate, he would go and see Levene. They met in Levene's 'little eyrie he used in the Cabinet Office'. As Ayling came in, Levene said, 'Have I got a proposition for you!' Levene was offering Ayling a £200 million grant from the Millennium Commission. ' "You match it," he said to me, "in the form of commercial revenue and any surplus profit goes to the enterprise." I said, "OK, we'll have a look at it, Peter, but no promises." '

Ayling's light, relaxed and optimistic reaction had various sources. The idea of having a millennium event of real global scale in London was immensely appealing, first because he is a Londoner, of at least five generations, and proud of it. He also thought the country was in need of a spectacular event. And thirdly, it would be good for the travel business because people would come to London to see it.

He asked Carl Michel, in charge of business development at BA, to see Levene, 'get the real facts and find out if we can make a business out of this'. Although Michel reckoned that a possible 1.5 million extra foreign visitors might come to Britain because of the exhibition, perhaps half of them by BA, a massive boost to their revenue stream, everything else looked bad. After two weeks Michel reported back: 'It was a death-trap from the point of view of the business.' He had no view on whether it would work eventually. It was difficult to tell. But what was certain and clear was that the number of unknowns was huge. No one really knew much about it. How much was it going to cost to clean the site? Who was going to own the site? What was the site going to look like? What was it going to be for eventually? There was no final scheme for a building, beyond the Imagination 'boxes'. There was no idea of the content, apart from a few conceptual suggestions. Nobody knew how many people in Britain would be attracted to it, or how much they might be willing to pay.

'A business,' Ayling says, 'can cope with one or two variables. We put on a new service to somewhere and the variable is how many passengers we can get. We know we can fly aeroplanes, we know aeroplanes work, we know how much the price of fuel is, we know everything we need to know, there is only one variable. But this was different. Everything was variable. That's why it was a death-trap. And that's why we said no.' At the beginning of May Ayling went back to Levene and told him that British Airways could not act as the operator for the project.

It was not an unexpected reply. During that spring commission staff and their consultants were already recognising that the whole private enterprise route was, according to Jeff Hawkins, 'looking pretty dodgy'. James Winterbotham of Lazards the bankers in particular realised that with no planned end use, with no idea of what to do with the structures when it was all over, it became very difficult to know what to build in the first place. You could make a decision on whether an exhibition would work in a structure intended eventually for something else (whose viability had already been established). If neither short-term nor long-term use was known, as was the case here, everything became too loose to decide. No property developer could be drawn into the net. Simply put, the benefits of the huge Millennium Commission grant were more than absorbed by the risks of an exhibition on the site. Risk remained even after all the grant had been taken into account. There was no way business would look at this.

By then, Jennie Page and Simon Jenkins had already discussed the possible outcomes. 'We said to each other,' Jenkins remembers, ' "This will be done either by the government or by a government company. The risk is too great. But we have got to go through the motions because of the law and the ideology." ' The no-initiation provisions of the Lottery Act and the free market ideology of the Conservative government, harried as it was by its own right wing looking for any deviation from Thatcherite purity, meant that they had to stick with the idea of a private sector vehicle. Undeliverable as it seemed to Ayling, Jenkins, Page and even Levene, for whom 'a back of the envelope calculation showed it wouldn't work', the private sector route had to be tested to destruction over the course of 1996.

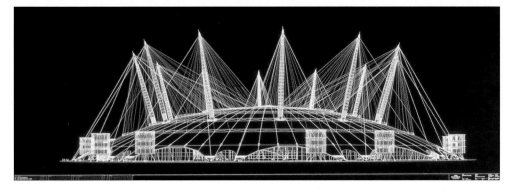

Above: The Dome, the cap of an enormous sphere whose geometrical centre is 300 metres below ground level, was in many ways a response to indecision, an enormous cover for something that had yet to be defined.

Above: In October 1997, Jennie Page, Chief Executive of NMEC, is flanked by the engineer Ian Liddell of Buro Happold and the architect Mike Davies of the Richard Rogers Partnership. They are standing inside one of the twelve masts from which the Dome was to be suspended.

Left: The foot of one of the masts is lowered towards the apex of the four-legged pyramid on which it will rest. Held there by the tension in the cables it supports, the spike rests in little more than a pot of sand.

Bob Ayling
Chairman

Jennie Page
Chief Executive

Liam Kane
Managing Director

David Trench
Site and Structures Director

Ken Robinson
Operations Director

Jeff Hawkins
Programme and Projects Director

Claire Sampson
Production Director

Sam Chisholm
Executive Committee Chairman

Michael Grade
Litmus Group Chairman

Left: Key players in NMEC.

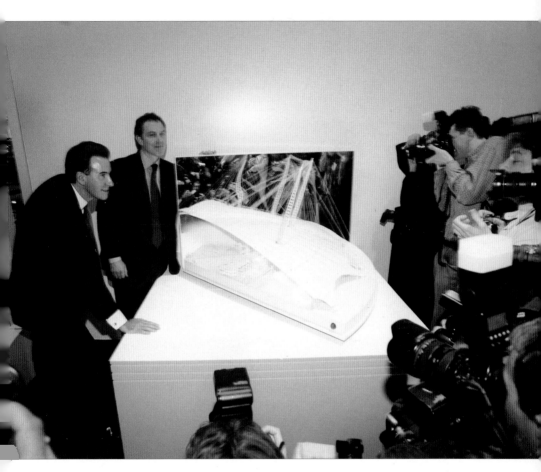

February 24 1998 Launch at the People's Palace on the South Bank. Peter Mandelson and Tony Blair face the press across a quarter-model of the one object for which they had most been vilified over the previous months.

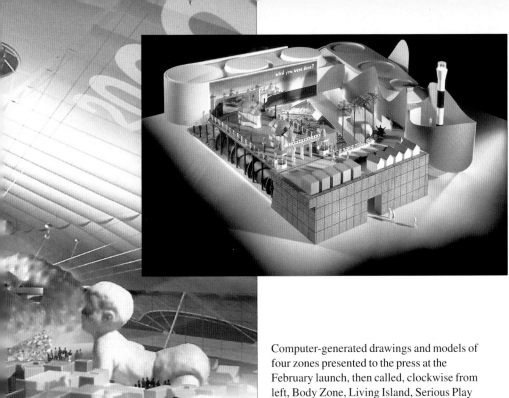

Computer-generated drawings and models of four zones presented to the press at the February launch, then called, clockwise from left, Body Zone, Living Island, Serious Play and Spirit Level. At this stage more show than substance, only Living Island would appear in the Dome in anything like this form.

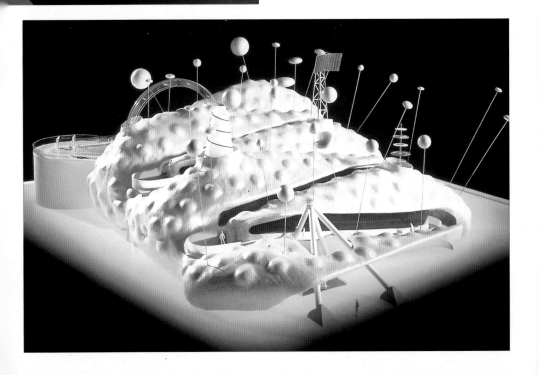

Left: By October 1997, the twelve masts were up and the giant concrete ring beam to which the cables would be anchored had been installed around the perimeter. By March 1998, the steel structures for five of the Dome's 'core buildings' to house the restaurants and loos were underway.

Above: Greenwich Peninsula, Spring 1998: the emergence of something from nothing, the image of regeneration.

Below: March 1998. The cable-net complete. Never more than at this point could the Dome be seen, as its architect Mike Davies described it, as 'an evanescent building, an anti-monument, light in everything it does.'

Above: March 1998. The first of the Teflon coated panels are installed on the vast, tensed cable-net of the roof.

Below: May 15 1998. The view from the world outside. The roof panels begin to move down to ground level.

Not until that December, when all options had failed, did the government and the commission finally accept that the state had to do this itself, and that the Dome had to be nationalised. It would be a long and gruelling road to travel to get there. In retrospect, Michael Heseltine said, 'There are people for whom state activity is the be-all and end-all of life. But that's not the way the government at the time or my commissioners, my fellow commissioners, actually believed it was the way to proceed. If it had been up to me, I would have done it in the French way. I would have said, "We're going to do it," and we would have done it. But that's not how things happen in this country. That's not how we do things.' The eventual irony, of course, was that under an agreement reached between Michael Heseltine and Tony Blair early in 1997, brokered largely by Simon Jenkins and Jennie Page, that turned out to be exactly the way they did things.

Meanwhile, in the slough of 1996, all the hydra's heads needed tackling at once. Alongside the Levene campaign to drum up money, British Gas, the owner of the Greenwich peninsula site, had to be persuaded to think that the only sensible thing to do was to sell their land to English Partnerships, the government's property development arm. In that lay another intractable. English Partnerships (EP) needed approval from both the Department of the Environment and the Treasury.

The usual Treasury tests of value for money were applied. Would any government investment here pay the sort of dividends that were required? Would it pay them quickly enough? Was this something which could have justifiable priority over other regeneration projects in other parts of the country? The answer to all those questions was the same: no.

They were asking for more money, more quickly, than the Treasury rules allowed, with no certainty that the exhibition would even go ahead: the officials decided to call a halt. Sir Andrew Turnbull, then the Permanent Secretary at the Department of the Environment, later at the Treasury, asked for what is called 'a Ministerial direction to commit funds'. It is a signal that civil servants consider the level of expenditure excessive and the value for money unacceptable. It is a request, in other words, to be formally and openly overruled. It is not unheard of, but it is rare. John Gummer, as the relevant minister, issued the direction, and EP was committed. Gummer had come under pressure from Heseltine to do so. Heseltine himself thought that EP was log-rolling. 'You never know,' Heseltine says, 'whether a statement by a government quango that they need more money is true or just bluff to get more from the Treasury. What you know is that there is always more money than you are told. One doesn't fall for that sort of stuff. When you are Deputy Prime Minister it happens to you every day of the week.' Despite ministerial pressure, the negotiations between the privatised utility and the development agency were interminable. In November 1996 a sale price of £20 million was agreed and the deal was actually done in February the following year.

The Peter Levene project to make the scheme financially viable was entering new territory. The funding gap of £155 million, combined with the Imagination plan for twelve pavilions on the theme of time, produced a figure which was to loom over the Dome for the rest of its life. By 21 May 1996 Levene had come up with a simple plan: £12 million sponsorship for each of twelve pavilions would almost provide the necessary money. Imagination was asked to adapt its scheme so that each pavilion would be a vehicle for each of the twelve main sponsors. Here the Levene-Heseltine imprint on the exhibition was becoming more sharply defined, clearly steering it away from Imagination's original themed conception towards a rather more conventional, if high-razzmatazz, trade fair. Imagination, which was to produce more than 50 scheme variations, of which 20 were detailed, responded professionally to these demands, even if reluctantly and expensively. The total cost of their and their consultants' work over the eighteen-month period from October 1995 to March 1997, when they finally withdrew, exhausted and drained of enthusiasm, was £7.9 million, including VAT where applicable.

An enormous team of consultants was employed keeping the show on the road. KPMG, the accountants, McAlpine Laing, the construction managers, Buro Happold, engineers, IMG, the sponsorship specialists, W. S. Atkins, the engineering and construction conglomerate, Colin Buchanan, transport consultant, ERA, experts in visitor numbers and flows, Gardner Merchant, the site operations specialists, were all attempting to give substance and measurability to the idea of an exhibition at Greenwich. Imagination and commission staff were also trying to draw together this enormous effort in a situation which, financially and politically, was still as mobile as it ever had been.

The other key players, the Richard Rogers Partnership of architects, had been brought in by British Gas. They had first been approached in December 1995. British Gas's 294-acre land holding on the Greenwich peninsula formed part of over 1,000 acres of derelict land in the borough. This, in turn, was part of the wasteland which Michael Heseltine, in one of the most symbolic moments of late twentieth-century British urban history, had seen from his aeroplane in 1973 en route to the site of a possible new airport on the east coast:

> Pressing close against the clamour of the City's square mile lay the emptiness and hopelessness of hundreds of acres of deserted docks, wharves and warehouses ... There were all kinds of committees, reports, discussions, but beneath me stretched this appalling proof that no one was doing anything effective. Everyone was involved. No one was in charge.

On the ground in Greenwich the pain was palpable. At the turn of the century, on those 1,000 acres, there had been 150,000 jobs in manufacturing. The Woolwich Royal Arsenal alone employed 80,000. By 1992 the total number employed in manufacturing in the borough had sunk to 6,000. Male unemployment was 30 per cent in the worst wards. On some estates it rose to double that. Following the devastation of the East End, a consequence of the death of the docks, containerisation, and the enormous transformations in all industrialised cities the world over, Greenwich had sunk into poverty and dereliction. 'We were losing the equivalent of a coal mine a year,' Bob Harris, deputy leader of Greenwich, says. Infant mortality rates were high and rising. Eighty per cent of the public housing stock was in disrepair. Five hundred Greenwich businesses went bust in 1992 and 1993. Unemployment grew by 10,000.

This was the environment into which the Richard Rogers team found themselves invited. It was far from foreign territory. For many years Rogers himself, his partner Mike Davies, and Philip Gumuchdjian had been working on large-scale schemes for the regeneration of inner cities, the reviving of sites which had been abandoned but could again become part of the dynamo of the city. Rogers had already put to the M2000 group his idea of the revived Thames, the glittering thread along which the festival might be strung.

That had come to nothing, but now British Gas had invited them to bid for the masterplanning of its site. In March 1996 the Richard Rogers Partnership (RRP) had been awarded the contract. British Gas had already been through two masterplans for the peninsula, one with Terry Farrell in the 1980s, another with the Llewelyn-Davies landscape architects in the early nineties. The arrival of the exhibition and its money clearly meant that yet another plan had to be conceived.

Mike Davies was the RRP partner in charge of the project, assisted by his fellow director Andrew Morris. They have been a team for eighteen years. Davies is the most inspirational figure to have worked on the Dome. Amid all the tangled processes in which the project had become mired, Davies arrived with a combination of vision and largeness of spirit. Richard Rogers himself describes Davies 'as warm, generous, immensely broad in his range of interests, but intensely focused on the task in hand'. He is an enthusiast and an idealist. In the sixties, as a co-founder of Chrysalis, a multidisciplinary design and architectural practice, he experimented with inflatable buildings and insulated suits in the Arizona desert, as well as the Pepsi-Cola pavilion at the Expo in Osaka in 1970. After that he joined Richard Rogers and Renzo Piano to build the Pompidou Centre in Paris. He is a painter, a rock-climber and a yachtsman. He fought ferocious battles at intervals during the project but remains almost universally admired and loved on the job. Claire Sampson, in charge of the production of the zones and events in the Dome, says that 'the entire project would not have succeeded without Mike. He has been literally invaluable.' Cliff Smith of the McAlpine Laing joint venture says simply: 'He is a great man. It is marvellous to have worked with a man of such vision.' Local residents were wildly anxious about the effect the arrival of the Dome on their doorstep might have on their lives. When their worries were exacerbated by some insensitive wording on planning notices issued by the council in late 1996, which seemed to threaten demolition, they were reassured by the grace, charm and humanity of the architect who came to speak to them.

Little of that is known about Mike Davies. What is known is that he is interested in red. His yacht is red, his car is red, its seats are red, the face of his watch is red, his hair-tie is red and his felt-tip pens are red. The pictures he paints are red. He is 'exploring the colour'. In the 1960s it was purple. Davies's prediction, as the millennium approached, was that it might be yellow next.

On arriving at the masterplanning job, Davies drew up a checklist:

Negatives
1. Peninsula chosen by Mill Comm over NEC
2. Site owned by private company
3. Site polluted and needing remediation
4. No infrastructure on site
5. No clear budget or guaranteed green light
6. No planning permissions
7. No real client body or operational client
8. Huge underground foundations/artifacts [the stumps and half-sealed pits of the South Metropolitan Gasworks]
9. Dubious river wall [it was collapsing in parts]
10. No identity – the middle of nowhere.

Positives
A. London Borough of Greenwich waving the flag
B. Imagination and their consortium retained inc. Buro Happold and McAlpine
C. BG/EP select RRP as masterplanner + legacy champion
D. Jubilee Line station committed on site
E. Amongst the grime, a great site
    – over a mile of river front
    – on the meridian
    – big enough for 1.25 million sq ft exhibition
F. A committed and enthusiastic minister – Michael Heseltine on the Mill Comm
G. A powerful Mill Comm Accounting Officer, Jennie Page, with lots of corridor experience and heavy handbag in the wings.

It was a fair summary. Mike Davies had been here before. In 1984 RRP had been masterplanners for the Royal Docks on the other side of the river, and elements repeated themselves. First, the scale was vast – Davies is intensely alert to the romance of the situation, the enormous vistas, the sense of the world ocean on the doorstep, with 'Sea Reach One', as mariners call it, leading out from the docks down to the estuary and the world beyond. But there were no local structures, no 'urban fixes', no existing nuclei. He quotes Pierre Boulez: 'It is difficult to react to nothing. There are two problems: how do you start and how do you decide you have finished?'

The task was to give shape to a vacuum. And in a vacuum, as Davies says, 'all you can be guided by are your own beliefs'. Briefly put, the beliefs of the Richard Rogers Partnership are 'in a balanced community and a rich environment'. The moneyed monoculture of Canary Wharf across the river was the antithesis of what RRP had in mind.

That brief slogan scarcely encompasses the rich cultural background of the RRP practice. Davies sees a dialectical process at work. The sixties love-affair with technology led to a seventies backlash, towards life-drawing and the elemental form of traditional built spaces, in which solid mass and a rich shadow life – 'the Greek village aesthetic', he calls it – seemed all-important. Out of that sprang the post-modernism of the eighties, the slick ironies, in which there was 'no language to the shadows' – for Davies an unsatisfactory nowhere for architecture or culture.

The nineties were not like that. They saw, he feels, 'a marriage of things which had been separated: science and art; the power of technology and a subtle sensibility'. This was optimistic. People were no longer subservient to the machine; the machine was back in its place. The best buildings no longer dominated the people that used them, but were adaptable, malleable, gentle and generous towards them. It was that humane philosophy of the built environment which shaped both the planning of the peninsula and the design of the Dome.

The peninsula itself had few of those qualities naturally. It was enormous and ugly in its hugeness. It almost always felt wintry there. There was no land higher than 200 feet between here and Helsinki. The easterlies bit at you. It was as if there was no city here and never had been. It was a fragment of northern Europe moored in a loop of the Thames; as a regeneration project it is far more satisfactory when seen on the map than when felt on the skin. These circumstances prescribed one thing above all: shelter. Davies settled on creating for the masterplan what he calls 'a river shoulder', buildings which would turn their back to the driving north-easterlies, like a man in a storm hunching his coat against the wind, and thereby forming in their lee, facing south-west, towards the warmth and the sun, small, human-scale courts in which a comfortable life could be led. According to Davies, it was like erecting a shelter in Siberia.

If that largely dictated the site's east–west profile, the north–south relationships were more complex. English Partnerships and British Gas of course recognised that the expensive area would be at the nose of the peninsula, surrounded by the loop of the Thames and near the tube station. That is where value could be maximised, and where the valuable properties could be built. British Gas at the time had a £1 billion portfolio of land, some of which would never realise any profit. They had to make money on the better sites if they were to break even overall, as was their intention. The further south down the peninsula you went, the cheaper it would become.

Problems leaped into view. First, the idea of a redevelopment in which class and money differences were to be built into the physical structures, although commercially important to the landowner, was scarcely appropriate in any millennial vision of a regenerated society. Secondly, although various schemes were floated, it was eventually felt that the exhibition itself would also want to occupy the high-value tip of the peninsula. Would British Gas and English Partnerships be happy to see the plum section of their site occupied by this vast cuckoo, mopping up the most valuable land they had? That concern alone meant that for many months to come, English Partnerships would insist that the building to house the exhibition must be considered as temporary.

It was a situation rife with ironies. The exhibition was to be closely identified with the idea of regeneration. The only rationale for it being on this site at all was for the regenerative flood of money and improvement that would come in its wake. But the government agency which was acquiring the site to house this great organ of regeneration came to view the exhibition itself as an obstacle to the very end it was intended to serve. Apparently blind to the public resistance to the idea of such an expensive structure being temporary, English Partnerships would continue to insist that the Dome was no more than a squatter on the 'high quality and high density mixed development with a strong commercial element' that would eventually appear there.

Davies was adamant that the masterplan would 'envisage one world, not three'. A 25-acre park along the centre of the peninsula (a French designer, Michel Desvignes, was retained as the landscape architect) would unite the linear site, along which everyone could walk and ride; it would be an axis for heterogeneity, a spine for egalitarianism.

Parallel to it, and wrapping around the whole site, the RRP architects were keen for the whole river edge to be part of the public space. The 'Malibu syndrome', in which huge rich houses hog the water access, ghettoising both themselves and those whom they keep out, was not to be repeated here. Vistas and openness were to be protected. Exclusivity was not millennial.

The Rogers architects worked on the masterplan of the peninsula for six weeks before meeting Gary Withers and his team at Imagination in May 1996. Their 'Circle of Time' arrangement of twelve pavilions and a circular arena mapped straight on to the radial footprint of Mike Davies's masterplan on the nose of the peninsula. Withers presented the latest version to the commission on 16 May. They liked it but when everything was taken into account the figures were absurd: it was coming in at about £1 billion. That was 'not playable', as one of those present at the meeting expressed it. Such a huge cost stretched the funding gap to something like £400 million. Imagination would have to shave about £250 million off the scheme and to do that it was clear that something radically different had to happen.

Two factors came together. Each of the twelve pavilions was costing in the region of £1,500 per square metre. Their expense was partly explained by their need to be genuinely robust structures which could keep out the cold, wet, windy Thames-side weather. But the prospect of that very weather was also giving the designers problems. What would it be like for everybody walking between the pavilions? Not very festive, nor very regenerated.

From the beginning, the mutual stimulus and sense of interlocking enthusiasm between Imagination and the Rogers team had been exciting for them all. Time was ticking and the Millennium Commission was giving them little feedback, beyond the huge budgetary hole that was clearly the heart of the problem. The two companies were left alone to sort out the design. 'We closed ranks,' Mike Davies says. In a series of informal meetings over the famous shortbread and tea to which everyone is always treated at Imagination's Store Street offices, the two teams bore down on the question of how to house the exhibition, a humming concentration of some of the best design minds in the world, the intensity heightened by the isolation and by the scale, urgency and intractability of the problem.

No answer emerged. Richard Rogers and Mike Davies sat amazed as Withers wheeled through a virtuoso presentation of the predicament they were in. Despite the brilliance, it became clear that tinkering with the earlier pavilions would do nothing to solve it. As Davies and Rogers left that first meeting, they agreed that whatever shape the separate pavilions took, they were always going to be too expensive.

Something had to give. Withers and Alex Ritchie of Imagination, together with Rogers, Davies and Philip Gumuchdjian of the Richard Rogers team, had all talked of fabric pavilion covers, inflatable pavilions, outdoor ride pavilions, smaller pavilions and cheaper contents. None had seemed to offer the lever necessary to turn the problem on its head, but they all felt that this was the area that might contain the seed of the solution.

There were fewer of them at the second meeting: Withers, Davies and Gumuchdjian. Davies himself had decided that temporariness was the key: proper pavilion buildings might be too permanent. In Imagination's Store Street offices there is a tall and dramatic atrium roofed with a fabric cover. Was the answer above their heads?

At moments like this some delicacy is needed. According to Philip Gumuchdjian, 'Mike was hesitant to suggest to Gary that they might enclose a large chunk of territory. Clearly it was the next thing to say, but you're just reluctant to do that, so I broke the ice.' Gumuchdjian said, 'You've got to make something large, something enveloping.'

'Yes,' said Davies to Withers, 'I think we need to address shelter on a large scale here, some huge environmental cover.' It was 22 May 1996. The idea could not have emerged without Imagination's problems and context. And in their original submission the year before, there had been talk of 'a Teflon cover between the pavilions'. But this was the first mention of anything like the Dome. An exciting moment for them. 'How about a bloody great cover,' Davies said, 'something with guts and scale that fits the peninsula, something huge.'

According to Davies, no drawings were done the moment the idea emerged. He went back to the RRP offices in Hammersmith and the next day he made a whole set of sketches of the Dome in his red felt-tip pen. It was 'a very large mega cover', in Davies's words, perhaps an inflatable, or a frame structure, like an umbrella with stiff ribs. It would certainly keep the weather off – Richard Rogers calls it 'the giant umbrella' – and it would be very cheap, perhaps £400 per square metre, a third of the cost of the earlier pavilions. A day or two later he was back at Store Street with the sketches – drawings of huge festive structures with forests inside them and flags fluttering from the masts.

An excited huddle. 'We all knew at a glance,' Davies says, 'that this was a new approach which still respected the principles the Imagination team had laid out. It would save hundreds of millions of pounds, months on the programme, could be started soon, without knowing the detail of the content, was at the right scale for the site, could provide an incredibly spectacular shelter for most of the exhibition and give it an unmistakable identity. It worked!'

Withers, Ritchie, Rogers, Davies and Gumuchdjian had all been at the birth of the Dome but it was Withers who made the next and definitive step: to involve the engineers. Ian Liddell at Buro Happold was known to them all as one of the most inventive engineering imaginations in the world. 'Brilliant, odd, sometimes difficult,' one of the architects described him, 'tenacious to an idea, abrasive, but you can accept the abrasion because you are going to get the brilliance.' 'Fax this to Ian now!' Withers shouted. Twenty minutes later they were on the phone to him, discussing the Dome. The concept had begun its move towards reality.

The idea of the Dome is a perfectly natural step in the succession of work that the Rogers Partnership has done over many years. In some ways like the Pompidou Centre and the Lloyds Building, and even more precisely like Massy Autosalon in France and a scheme for a dome prepared for Stuart Lipton in the Royal Docks in the 1980s, it is a building which makes its own structure dramatic, celebrating the very way in which it exists. Engineers call it 'an assisted long span structure', the assistance coming from the visible cables suspended from the masts. In the original sketches the long spans took the form of hard, narrow, sprung filaments.

That began to change as soon as Ian Liddell started to think about the problems. Liddell is another of the central figures in the life of the Dome. A sparky and competitive symbiosis developed between him and Davies. 'The concept and engineering idea,' Davies says, 'are so strongly linked that they are inseparable. The idea and the fabric are one, and in achieving that, the economy of means is phenomenal.' Although the elements are enormous – a London tube train could drive down the middle of each of the masts – the effect of the building is one of gigantic naturalness, a moored and tethered cloud. 'It has a presence from its scale and from the simplicity of its statements,' Davies said. 'I wanted to have a public route up on to the roof of the Dome, so that they could all be up there in the middle of immensity.' Health and safety reservations meant that was never possible.

By 5 June the Dome was ready for its first public outing. Sir Peter Levene and Michael Heseltine had reached a critical point in their attempts to sell the exhibition to British industry. Two weeks earlier, in mid May, the commission had been due to approve their grant of £200 million for the exhibition. But the sponsors had not materialised and the budget still had an enormous hole in the middle of it. Sir Peter had been forced to ask them to delay their decision for six weeks to give him more time for a final push.

Invitations were issued to an event in the Cabinet Office. Press and public interest was running sky-high. There had never been anything like the media crowd outside the steps of 70 Whitehall, the entrance to the Cabinet Office. A policeman from Number Ten, around the corner in Downing Street, was summoned to make an alley for the businessmen to get through the crush from their cars to the door.

In a room usually devoted to dusty meetings of ministers and officials, Imagination created one of its trademark bonanza environments; the place was unrecognisable behind its modern hi-tech Millennium skin. Thirty-five leading figures in British industry were invited. The vast majority came, 'their mood', according to Bob Ayling, 'one of curiosity and disbelief'. British Airways, the British Airports Authority, British Aerospace, British Telecom ('the Big Bs', as corporate sponsorship specialists call them), GEC, Hanson Energy, Sainsbury's, the City Corporation, Rolls-Royce, Siemens, Swatch, ICI, the clearing banks, Smiths Industries, Reuters, McDonald's, the Stock Exchange, Woolwich Building Society, BP, Shell, the Society of Motor Manufacturers, Marks

& Spencer, the Post Office, AMEC, London Electricity, BSkyB, Glaxo, Zeneca, Granada, SmithKline Beecham and Samsung were crowded into the room – so many of Britain's most powerful executives that much of the elaborate Imagination room-dressing was invisible. Levene was already there with Ayling and Page. Ayling remembers, 'We had one or two of them asking, "What the hell is this all about?" '

Heseltine came in, beautifully groomed and at his most presidential. Virginia Bottomley was behind him. The Deputy Prime Minister gave a hard-hitting pitch. 'It wasn't quite as crude as "Your Country Needs You",' one of those present remembers. 'It was talking up the spectacle of a grand scheme, the value to the country of having something that was really eye-catching from a world point of view, a showcase for British culture, a landmark for people to move from one millennium to another.' But there was a little more edge to it than that. Behind it lay the implication that if only the industrialists in the room had the will and gumption of their predecessors, Heseltine would not have to be up there goading and encouraging them. They would be coming to him, urging government to get involved with something British industry itself had the courage to believe in. On top of that, the sponsorship they were being asked to come up with could not be used for advertising. Although each pavilion would have a theme related to the sponsor's industry, there would be no direct commercial benefit here. This was a matter of national duty.

Major industrialists are not used to being addressed like this and it did not go down particularly well. It was 'arm-twisting'. One deliberately avoided coming to the meeting. 'If I had gone I would have had that great hairy thing bearing down on me and my pocket would have been picked,' he said.

Richard Rogers and Mike Davies then described the Dome and Gary Withers the idea of the exhibition. He played the Johnny Pickering tape – 'a rallying cry to the essence of the idea', as Davies describes it. It impressed even this hard-bitten audience: 'To get people that worked up in two and a half minutes is a rare thing.'

A host of questions followed. Sir John Egan of the British Airports Authority asked, 'And who's going to have the retail franchise?' 'When someone dared to ask who would underwrite the risk of cost overruns, he was brusquely slapped down by Hezza,' another executive told *The*

Financial Times. 'Hezza said only that the private sector would not be asked for more money and that other details were not our business.' Questions were then asked about the management structure – 'Which is where I was landed in it big,' Bob Ayling remembers. 'Somebody asked, "How's this going to be run?" Michael said it was "going to be run by a company limited by guarantee and Bob's going to be the chairman."'

This came as a complete surprise to Ayling. He was considering it but 'the fact that it was going to be said at the meeting was not what had been agreed. There was no chief executive hired or appointed.' The Millennium Commission had not awarded its grant. The negotiations over the site between British Gas and English Partnerships were mired in disagreement. The very existence of this Cabinet Office meeting was a symptom, despite the constant and repeated public denials, of the acute financial difficulties facing the project. But for Ayling, this was now a public commitment.

The funding hole had now stretched to £195 million. To fill it, the target was £150 million in sponsorship and £45 million from other commercial ventures. In the weeks after the Cabinet Office meeting Levene and Heseltine badgered the industrialists for letters of intent. Interpreted optimistically, the corporations responded with £99.95 million of 'indicated support'. About half of this did eventually emerge in some form or other as sponsorship for the Dome and its national programme. At this time there was said to be another £49 million of 'potential support', of which virtually nothing was to come good.

The finances were, looked at coldly, in crisis. These letters of intent carried no guarantee whatsoever. Not one of them was an irreversible commitment, even though British Airways and British Telecom had said publicly that they would put money into the exhibition (both with caveats: no more than £6 million from BA; a high proportion of the BT money to go on their national programme, not to the London exhibition). Sceptics pointed out that both companies were in heavily regulated industries and were not going to run counter to the government's wishes if they could help it. The same could be said to apply to the clearing banks and building societies, whose chairmen, during these weeks, had two meetings with Eddie George, Governor of the Bank of England. George gave them the impression 'that he was very much on Hezza's side'.

Even if all these letters of intent had been reliable and definite commitments, a central element was still missing. Nowhere was there any form of final guarantor. No company had offered to take on the risk and fund the cost overruns if the whole project went haywire. For the commissioners, there was no basement to the scheme. Despite the card-houses being built in the Cabinet Office and the Imagination schemes which were continuing through a near endless sequence of evolutions, there was a vacuum at the heart of the project. The desire to make it all happen had no foundations.

On 18 June Michael Heseltine cut this knot. It was the first concrete step towards nationalising the Dome. He had been bounced into it. A report to the commission by James Winterbotham at Lazards had been leaked to the BBC. Winterbotham pointed out what everybody knew: the money was looking impossible. Heseltine realised immediately that any offers of sponsorship would evaporate if the core viability of the project, even with the sponsors' money, was in doubt. Heseltine spoke to the Prime Minister and the Chancellor, Kenneth Clarke – 'Of course I cleared it with Ken and John.' He then announced that the Millennium Exhibition would be bailed out if it incurred substantial losses. The government would not meet any additional costs, but if necessary – and it was seen at this point as no more than a contingency – the funding life of the Millennium Commission would be extended beyond 31 December 2000, when it was due to be wound up, so that it could receive further money from the National Lottery.

That assurance had to be firmed up for the commissioners. At their meeting on 17 July they said to Heseltine that they were still worried about the money. If the hoped-for sponsorship and the projected revenue from visitors failed to materialise, the commission itself, they feared, would be called on to make up the difference. This was the latest ripple of a longstanding anxiety about the Dome project: the hungry infant in Greenwich would begin to oust their own treasured fledglings from the nest. Central government, with its central scheme, would deprive the regions of funding for their own projects. Heseltine repeated to them the assurance he had made publicly three weeks before: there would be no government money, but an extension to the funding life of the commission, if necessary. The money that would flow during the extra year, perhaps £250 million, would be dedicated to cost overruns on the Dome, nothing else. It marked another stage in the marginalisation of the commission. The extra money would come through their books, their chief executive would be the accounting officer responsible for the way in which it was spent, but the commissioners would have little say in the matter. The commission had become the *poste restante* for the money, little more. Despite all the elaborate formal structures, the Dome was now in fact what it had been in essence for a while: a government project.

Even though the Lottery Act allowed the government to make changes of this kind 'by order', Heseltine had experienced some difficulty in persuading the Chancellor, Kenneth Clarke, that it should be done. No order was, in fact, made. Heseltine's assurance remained no more than that and, as such, was vulnerable to revision. In the eyes of the most hard-headed of commissioners, official advisers, potential sponsors and members of the Shadow Cabinet, the Dome's finances remained as flaky as they had ever been.

Meanwhile, actions had to be taken and structures created if timetables were to be kept. Nobody could wait for the money before deciding how it was going to be spent. Throughout the spring and summer Imagination had made repeated pleas for 'a client' to be produced – a company which could make demands of them, with which they would discuss their ideas and engage on the creative process. The commission was not allowed to be that company and so, slightly oddly, Imagination itself had stood in as a virtual client for its own scheme. It was a situation no one was comfortable with. Jennie Page realised that 'Millennium Central Ltd', the company envisaged by Imagination the year before, had to be divorced from Imagination itself and become active in its own right. Ayling was to be its chairman and a chief executive was sought. But that repeated phenomenon on this project, a closed logical loop, prevented the immediate creation of the company. Millennium Central could not exist as a private sector company, trading in the real world, without staff to create the business plan. The staff could only be taken on if the company had the backing to pay them. And the backing would not appear without a business plan for the investors or sponsors to judge it by.

As a route out of this impasse, a shadow Millennium Exhibition Unit was created within the Millennium Commission. It was to be the 'interim client'. This whole elaborate process was what Simon Jenkins would later call 'the testing to destruction' of the private sector route. It is a strange vision: an ideological position being taken up ('private enterprise knows best'), applied to an impossible end ('celebrations of the kind no business would undertake'), exposed to the winds of reality ('as a business proposition it is a death-trap'), and allowed to slowly wither and die on the vine.

Even the interim client had an interim director. Chris Peckham was seconded from the personnel department at British Airways while BA's headhunters searched for a permanent replacement. By September they had found Barry Hartop, at the time chief executive of the Welsh Development Agency. He saw his task as twofold: to get planning permission for the Dome; and to create a business plan which would work. The deadline was the Millennium Commission's meeting of 11 December 1996. The shadow of the millennium itself was already falling over the programme. Unless steel for the vast cable-net structure of the Dome was ordered at the beginning of January 1997, the final deadline would be missed.

Hartop had been to see Ayling, Marshall and Heseltine. 'It was the first time I had been offered a job by a Deputy Prime Minister. When I said I would like to think about it, he said, "Well you either do or you don't, there isn't much to think about."' Hartop surrendered.

By 28 October the planning application had been submitted by W. S. Atkins in their name. It was important to persuade the inhabitants of Greenwich that something good was arriving on their doorstep. The genius of Gary Withers was wheeled on and 60,000 flyers were distributed. In a string of public meetings around the borough that autumn the Dome team touted their wares: the charmingly persuasive and mage-like figure of Mike Davies, who appeared, one resident said, to have learned by heart the borough's street plan and traffic system; the reassuringly managerial presence of Hartop, coolly concentrating on the practical matters in hand; and Withers, the creative genius. He built 'a silvery cocoon, a wonderful capsule, so you went from Greenwich, from outside, into this capsule where an utterly seductive model of the Dome greeted the visitors'.

Although Greenwich continued to be anxious about the effects the exhibition would have on its traffic, the borough was able to impose a whole series of conditions and required side-benefits in return for the planning permission. This has meant a river of money flowing into

Greenwich, a total of £26 million of benefits from the Dome to the local population. That helped to allay many of the suspicions. Hartop's progress on that side of his brief was without critic.

In the drawing up of the business plan things were not quite so easy. Hartop, as he later came to realise, had not understood the situation he was entering when he took the job. Only slowly did it dawn on him that 'whereas there had been a viable option up in Birmingham, to make the NEC a European centre, taking it away from Birmingham removed the fundamental private sector rationale. It could only work if you could sell it on. As soon as you couldn't sell it on, the structure of the whole thing was filled with holes and anomalies. I think from the moment it moved to Greenwich, it became impossible for a private sector company to run this project.'

What Hartop calls 'disconnects, unjoined-up writing' began to enter the process. Political demands were pushing the commission in one direction; commercial requirements were pulling the embryonic Millennium Central in the other. In these circumstances drawing up the business plan for the December commission meeting presented Hartop with a number of problems. At the centre of it was the ideological fantasia: a private sector company which required everything to be underwritten by the government. In October, according to Hartop, it 'began to look a bit silly. If everything had to be underwritten by the government then it might as well not be in the private sector. What did private sector mean in that context?'

Worries were spreading about the outcome of the December meeting. The number of consultants was proliferating. One close observer at the time thought the exhibition unit had turned into 'professional advisers heaven. Advice is always partial, in both senses: each adviser sees it through his particular skill set.' Some commission staff felt that Hartop wasn't getting the strategic control fast enough. There was 'no helicopter view'. He was thought either not ready to or not capable of overruling his advisers. There was no one in the exhibition unit who could bang heads together sufficiently hard. It was said to be 'a ship with 20 rudders'.

The hand which Hartop had been dealt was immensely difficult. Apart from the finance, the site was imposing its own demands and logic. As Jeff Hawkins explains: 'If you keep putting more visitors on the site to get more revenue, it is actually costing you more in facilities. Bigger isn't necessarily better. You've got to find the optimum amount.' The amount of revenue required seemed to demand 100,000 visitors a day. But 100,000 visitors a day meant that the company would have had to pay for a second entrance to the tube station. The entrance paid for by British Gas would not accommodate the visitor flows. But the cost of the second entrance to the tube station removed all the extra revenue generated by the extra visitors for whom it was built. Anything more than some 35,000 a day wouldn't work on site. But 35,000 visitors a day wouldn't generate the money required.

Those tensions and pressures were a product of the situation, not of the people in charge of it. No one in Hartop's position could have done any better. Nevertheless, schemes were being drawn up within the commission, and without his knowledge, for a completely different approach to the problem. 'I was focusing on making the project work,' he says. 'You know: what's the building look like, can we put it together, what's it going to cost, how's this going to work, will it all be up on 31 December '99 and how are we going to organise it? I don't think anyone was talking about nationalising the company at that time. I wasn't aware of anyone devising the public sector outcome at the time.' But they were.

Page and Jenkins had seen it coming in January or February. By August, before Hartop's appointment, it was clear to Hawkins and Claire Sampson that they would have to decide what would happen if the private sector solution was unworkable. 'It was hardly an if,' Hawkins says, 'because it was just not going to happen.'

The first huge object in the landscape that had to be prepared for this nationalisation of a private company, the first time a private sector entity had been taken into public ownership since the 1970s, was Michael Heseltine. Sir Terry Heiser, ex-Permanent Secretary at the Department of the Environment, advised on the extreme delicacy of this situation. The question was: how to devise a structure which took the Dome into public ownership, could nevertheless receive a lottery grant and still convince Michael Heseltine that, in this, there was no alternative.

The core argument to Heseltine, presented to him in a paper that October, hinged on the question of risk. The levels of uncertainty on the Dome, as Ayling and everyone else had recognised, were not suited to the private sector. Those levels of risk, the argument went, are what the public sector normally has to carry. It carries them because the private sector doesn't. The private sector says it likes risk but it only likes risk it understands. A risk it doesn't understand is a government risk. The Dome of its nature is a government project.

Heseltine was seeing Simon Jenkins, Jennie Page, Gary Withers and consultants more and more regularly. After 24 October he saw them every day for an early morning meeting, sometimes at 7.30, more often an hour later, with the various parties disposed around the three vast white sofas and one or two upright chairs of his Downing Street office. Politically, as a born interventionist who believed in the vitality of the enterprise culture, he was split down the middle. He didn't want the state solution but, given the force of the arguments, he had to accept it. The question remained in the balance until Barry Hartop and his team presented their business case to the commission in early December 1996.

The presentation was in two parts. The first, to Jennie Page and her own team of consultants, took place at the offices of Norton Rose, the commission's lawyers, on 7 December. Page assembled her team of advisers across the table from Hartop: Norton Rose, Lazards, SEMA Consulting on hers; Touche Ross, KPMG, Gardiner & Theobalds on his. The exhibition unit was to make its case and then the commission team would have a chance to ask questions on the detail. From the start, according to one of those present, 'it felt bad, a bad day'. Kazia Kantor, the finance director, and Barry Hartop were not as one. They had different views on different issues, 'and Barry wasn't capable of saying, "Shut up, I'm chief executive."'

More than that, though, a certain dullness seemed to hang over the presentation. There was no passion or commitment. It was as if they were treating it as a job. Jeff Hawkins read it as 'one of those body language meetings where people move further part. They did not rally round and support one another when they had made a duff point. A good team rallies round, creates diversions, looks after each other. There was none of that.'

Page was not happy. The business plan was not working. She turned to Hawkins. 'Have you got anything to ask?'

'That,' according to Hawkins, 'was the signal. That's when you start taking it apart.'

The unkind, revelatory questions were asked. For example, certain evening events would, according to the plan, generate a substantial income; these had to be separately ticketed. But the builders of the site had not provided a section where separate admission could take place. The predictions of huge sums of money to be brought in by corporate hospitality were based on the premiss that anybody giving any form of corporate hospitality in London that year would decide to do so in the Dome. It was a collection of detailed separate bits, with over 100 pages of spreadsheets, but with no coherence or interrelatedness.

More disturbing than any of these failings was the sheer size of the budget. It included overall costs of £724 million, with a projected income of £705 million. But those costs did not include corporation tax, interest, inflation, or contingencies, which in the worst case would take the budget to £1,137 million. That left a potential deficit of over £400 million, a joke. Nobody said much on the commission side.

In his own defence, Barry Hartop says, 'You are picking up in September this project which is beset with difficulties. Three months later you are delivering a business plan. Nobody in the United Kingdom has ever done anything as big as this. You can't go to Coopers and Lybrand and say, "Have you got a couple of people who can tell me how to build a dome?" Here we were talking about spending £500 to £700 million in a project no one could grasp the size of. All one could do was hint at the levels of certainty and uncertainty. That's all one could do.'

The commissioners held their meeting on the 11th. It might have been a launch pad for the exhibition. The cut-off date for ordering the steel was less than a month away. But it was the very opposite. Commissioners who had always been against it repeated their opposition. Those in favour were downcast. The crisis which had been building all year now had four clear elements to it: the budget was in shreds; the people who were meant to create and run the exhibition had not delivered; the energy and verve of Imagination had been drained and suppressed by the turmoil of the year – to the point where Gary Withers no longer wished to be involved; and politically, the Dome, as a result partly of Heseltine's vigorous promotion of it, and in the increasingly harsh shadow of the approaching election, had come to seem like a Tory project: big, bloated, indifferent to real needs, out of touch and grandiose. It was a year since Imagination had first moved and stirred them all with Johnny Pickering. At the beginning of December 1996 it looked as if the best thing to do with the Dome was to kill it.

CHAPTER FIVE

Near-Death Experience

It couldn't have been worse. This was the Dome's Year Zero. Not only were the details difficult and chaotic, not only had disenchantment entered some of the key relationships on the project, but the entire environment in which the Dome was struggling to survive had become poisoned. Hanging over it in December 1996 was a political crisis which had been deepening steadily throughout the autumn and early winter. And it had been coming out in the press. Most of the Millennium Commission's secrets were appearing in the newspapers, particularly in *The Financial Times*.

The lack of confidentiality meant that the ballooning budget had become public knowledge. Details of a letter from Gary Withers to Jennie Page appeared in the *FT* on 25 September, a couple of days after he had written it, in which Withers guessed the total cost might now be heading towards £1 billion. There seemed to be no ceiling to the expense, and the base-line guarantee for the potential costs of the exhibition was not in place. Michael Heseltine's commitment on behalf of the government – that the funding life of the commission would be extended – had yet to be formally approved by his Cabinet colleagues. They too were giving off-the-record briefings to the effect that their approval would not be forthcoming 'this side of an election'.

That election was now no more than a few months away. Labour was miles ahead in the polls. Compared with the beleaguered Tories, the Labour Party had the air of government about it. As everyone was coming to realise, the key question was not whether Heseltine could persuade the Conservative government to underwrite the Dome but whether the

Labour Party would commit themselves to its future. Would they, as the next government, go on with it or cancel it?

In this, as in everything, Labour was far from monolithic. Different sections held radically different views. Jack Cunningham was the shadow spokesman on National Heritage. His lack of interest in the brief had from the start, even to Labour policy wonks, been 'quite apparent'. In particular, he shared with a majority of the party a dislike for the Dome. It was a Tory project. It was in London, when Cunningham's own allegiances were firmly in the north of England. It was apparently indifferent to social needs, was extravagant and seemed woefully organised. On 28 October that year the *Guardian* called the Dome 'a synonym for national incompetence'. Was that really the sort of thing a Blair government would want to sign up to? In response to the Withers letter, Cunningham publicly warned the commissioners that they 'should have a firm grip on the costs' before committing any lottery money.

This, reasonable as it was, and reflecting precisely what both the commissioners and the Tory ministers privately thought themselves, nevertheless struck a new note. Until then, Labour had kept shoulder to shoulder on the exhibition. Virginia Bottomley, Secretary of State at the DNH and chairman of the commission, recalled a conversation with her opposite number on the way to Michael Heseltine's June presentation at the Cabinet Office. 'I spoke to Jack Cunningham on the phone in the car, and he said, "I'll give you all the support I can, Virginia. What can I do? Indeed, I'll go and speak to BNFL."' Sellafield, British Nuclear Fuels' reprocessing plant, was in Cunningham's constituency. (The idea of BNFL sponsoring the Living Island zone in the Dome – they had been approached, of course, along with all the other utilities – would lurch up again in 1998, giving palpitations to the environmentalists working on it, but nothing came of it.) Now, though, in the pre-electoral polarisation of positions, his subtext was clear: Labour rigour, seriousness and control set against Tory muddle, sloppiness and incompetence.

On 29 October the Cabinet committee dealing with the millennium approved the Order in Council by which the funding life of the commission would be extended for a year. It was what the commission had been waiting for but it was too late. As Simon Jenkins wrote privately on 4 November, 'The guarantee from HMG is not worth the paper it is written on. Labour has to sign up to it.'

The Conservative ministers could sense the power ebbing from them. They were no longer able to determine the future of the project. The combination of the date of the millennium, deep into the next Parliament, and the current state of the polls meant that, in this, they were not completely in control. It did not feel comfortable. Both Bottomley and Heseltine felt that Labour weren't playing fair. Cunningham and Michael Montague had agreed to the Heseltine plan during the summer. Now it was being questioned. What could explain the change?

Heseltine maintains that 'The matter had been taken out of Cunningham's hands, centralised in Blair's office and exploited for all the political runs they could take it for. Michael Montague was a busted flush. The New Labour establishment had disowned him.'

As one might expect, that version of events is denied by Labour ministers, who point simply to the objective difficulties of the Dome project at the time. Any reasonable person would at least say you had to go carefully here. In the heightened circumstances of the run-up to an election, there is no reason why both accounts should not be true. Labour was both genuinely anxious about the funding, structure, management, content and deliverability of the Dome and saw in that an opportunity to paint the Tories as unfit for government. The two positions were not incompatible.

There were further strands to the Labour position. In late October, at a party in Richard Rogers's house in Chelsea, Rogers himself and Bob Ayling spoke to Blair about the project. David Puttnam had also been in touch with him about it. Others working for Puttnam were talking to people in Blair's office. The idea of a new, rebranded Britain had already taken hold in the heart of New Labour, carrying on where the thinking of the Puttnam–Rogers Group of the year before had left off. If New Labour meant new hope; if this, as Blair had said in his party conference speech, was 'a young country'; if the river Thames could be seen as a string along which the regenerative pearls of Richard Rogers's vision of the new London could be strung; if the belt of poverty in east London was to be broken; if one wanted to believe in the future; if one wanted to say something about Britain not only to British people but to a wider audience, presenting the country in a different perspective to the world, then what better vehicle could you look for than the Dome?

These were some of the elements in the air as the commission itself heard and rejected the Barry Hartop budget and business plan on 11 December 1996. The wider atmosphere only served to tighten the screws. On the day of the Hartop débâcle Cunningham wrote to Bottomley:

> Whilst I want to see the project proceed, I cannot agree to unlimited further expenditure on it. The business plan makes huge assumptions about income. It would not be prudent or proper stewardship of the people's money to agree to an open-ended commitment to further Millennium Commission funding.

This was not something Bottomley found helpful.

The following day, as Cunningham met both Blair and Rogers, Heseltine began to face up to the crisis. The political circumstances were as catastrophic as could be conceived but solutions had to be dragged out of the ashes. 'It wasn't a happy experience,' Heseltine says. 'The thing was fragile. I could see unless we got a firm grip the thing would disintegrate and I wasn't prepared to see that happen if I could do anything about it.'

On the morning of 12 December Michael Heseltine held an emergency meeting in his Downing Street office. The place was packed, the sofas filled, people standing against the walls. Members of the Number Ten policy unit, other ministers, Simon Jenkins, Sir Peter Levene and Hayden Phillips were all there. The decision which had been in the air for the previous ten months or so to move the Dome company clearly and openly into the public sector was once again mooted. Jennie Page had been prompting Heseltine in this direction for some time. Since Heseltine's commitment in June that the government would underwrite the exhibition, it had been *de facto* in the public sector. This was strange and unlikely territory for a Conservative government. No one was surprised that Michael Heseltine was reluctant to enter it or to accept that there was no alternative.

It was a period of intense and debilitating uncertainty. No one could be sure what would happen or how. There were solutions that had been thought of and all of them had been endlessly discussed: slash away at the budget; move Jennie Page over to become chief executive of Millennium Central (MCL, the new Dome company); take that company openly into public ownership. But the route towards those solutions was far from clear. A fog of complexity hung over this battlefield. The commission itself had mixed views. There was a danger of the Dome dying in its own coils.

Bob Ayling, the proposed chairman of the Dome company, had to tell Barry Hartop that his role on the millennium project was over. It was not a pleasant task. Ayling felt sympathy for Hartop. He had previously, at Unilever and elsewhere, been a successful executive and it is doubtful whether anyone could have squared the innumerable circles confronting the Dome. Ayling 'told Barry it wasn't to be. He took it extremely well. He was realistic. He is a very realistic man.'

Ayling was also keen to know what Jennie Page herself would make of transferring from the commission. He hardly knew her. They met over a bottle of wine in Brooks in St James's. He wanted to judge three things: Did she want to do it? Could she do it? And could they work together? His assessment was that 'she didn't have any experience of running a big private sector enterprise. She didn't really have the experience of running a big project. But she had four things which impressed me. She clearly wanted to do it. Secondly she had energy. And she had intelligence. And of course she had good knowledge of how Whitehall works. That was clearly going to be useful.' He offered her the job. She felt profoundly uncertain about it. No one else knew as much about this project as she did. She knew she could not contemplate remaining in the commission and watching while someone else struggled with its complexities and turmoil. She felt she had to do it but she didn't know if she wanted to do it. There was no way that she could commit herself without greater clarity in the situation. Solutions to the multifarious crisis had to be found first. And she would apply herself to finding them.

All five aspects of the crisis – political, organisational, administrative, creative and financial – were still overlapping. It couldn't be tackled piecemeal. Its very intractability consisted of the inter-tangling of its parts. What in various parts of the press was called 'the uncertainty', 'the shambles', the 'chaos' and 'the squanderama' were all eating away at the public standing of the Dome. The bad press, which had started when the first lottery grant were given to the Churchill family for Winston Churchill's state papers, intensified over the Greenwich/Birmingham crisis and become habitual during the funding fiasco of the summer, now was ratcheted up another few notches. Asked about this tangled mess, Cunningham repeated his mantra: no blank cheques. Although Labour's front-bench spokesmen were now receiving briefings from their relevant permanent secretaries, and Cunningham was seeing Hayden Phillips, Bob Ayling and Jennie Page on a regular basis, Heseltine 'could get no answers out of him. It was always: "We'll let you know, we'll wait and see, and God knows what."' On 19 December, Cunningham said, 'I've had no discussions with the government since last week. Our position remains that numbers have to be more sensible for us to accept the plan.'

Bottomley's frustration boiled over. 'Just before Christmas I rang Tony Blair's office and said, "This is beyond a joke. There has never been political divisiveness in millennium celebrations. My concern is to act in the national interest, which is more important than party political divisions. Please call your dogs off. And get them to settle."' They didn't.

The commission team went in over the Christmas period at the end of 1996 to try and tackle the budget. It was the second of the ruined Christmases which punctuated the life of the Dome (1995: the choice of Greenwich or Birmingham; 1996: this five-part agony for the commission, combined for the Buro Happold engineers with a headlong rush to complete the designs and drawings for the masts and cables; 1997: a desperate struggle to bring in the first sponsors and first zones; 1998: the fall of Peter Mandelson; 1999: the impending millennium). In 1996 the task was straightforward: to see if there was a way of producing a business plan that did not cost a billion pounds. To do, in other words, what the Hartop team had failed to do.

They stripped out the Hartop plan. The target they settled on, almost arbitrarily, was £750 million. To reach it was, as Jennie Page described it, 'a real hack-and-destroy process'. Using the same September 1996 prices, the budget they came up with reduced costs to £583 million and revenue to £523 million. If a large but necessary contingency of £193 million was added, the total budget came to £776 million and the total shortfall to £253 million, a figure interestingly and suspiciously close to the £250 million which the extra year's funding for the Millennium Commission would provide.

The new indicative Page budget for MCL, in other words, was relying on that money. It had previously been seen as a fall-back in the event of cost overruns, only to be used if necessary. Now it was an essential part of the budget. Page had hacked and destroyed but she had also provided herself with a large swag-bag to see her through the hazards ahead. This was more than a paring down of the Hartop plan. It was a complete reframing of the budget.

It was the status of the contingency that had changed. Both the scale and the lack of definition of the project at this stage were almost overwhelming. No one even knew if the site was safe. There was talk of 30 unexploded Luftwaffe bombs buried there. The risks of construction on this scale were unknown. Because the exhibition was to be so huge – the Dome itself covers 20 acres, the other structures 130 acres, the site 180 acres – even a small variation on a per area cost would have vast repercussions on the budget. A rise of £10 per square metre put £6.5 million on the bill. A drop in on-site spending of £1 per visitor took £12 million off the revenue. The budget was designed to say to the Millennium Commission, to the government and to the opposition: this is the scale of what you are confronting, this is the scale of the risk. If this is what you want to do, this is what you have to consider spending. Don't start unless you are prepared to finish.

The extent and variety of risks were listed nakedly enough:

- getting brand right
- securing sponsorship
- getting content right. MCL depends on creative talent to provide 'wow' content within a limited budget
- programme tightness and complexity
- open to 'blackmail' by contractors
- site environment problems
- dependency on third parties – English Partnerships, London Underground, Highways Agency, London Borough of Greenwich, Millennium Commission, Government

That Himalayan range of risks lay behind the enormous contingency of £193 million. It was almost exactly a third of the core budget costs.

Quite clearly, the budget they had come up with was ragged. Much of it, inevitably, was based on guesswork. The huge contingency implied as much. But there was still time to adjust and refine it. This was little more than a lifeboat budget, a demonstration that the project did not have to be a £1 billion-plus, out-of-control balloon. The January 1997 budget showed that rigour could be applied to the Dome. The commission was the first of the target audiences. They had turned down a £1 billion Dome. They could, this budget said, have a £750 million Dome. It was, initially, their call.

On Monday 13 January 1997 the new budget was submitted to the commission and they accepted it. Michael Montague was not able to attend. He was in Hawaii. The following morning the budget went to Jack Cunningham. The day after that, Wednesday 15 January, it was discussed by the Shadow Cabinet. Gordon Brown, the Shadow Chancellor, refused to give any kind of endorsement to the Heseltine plan, which envisaged another year of lottery money for the Millennium Commission, the very money on which the Page budget relied to cover its contingencies. This treasury-style rigour, alongside Cunningham's own distaste for the Dome, was enough. The Shadow Cabinet rejected it. Cunningham announced that they would only let the Dome go ahead if Labour could review it on coming into office. But the critical dates on which orders had to be placed for the steel masts of the Dome, the steel cables that would form the cable-net structure, and the roofing material were all now only a couple of weeks away. If the go-ahead was not given now, there would be no Dome in time for the millennium.

On the following evening, Thursday 16 January, Heseltine saved the Dome – at least for a few hours. Jennie Page had spoken to him on the phone from Hayden Phillips's office. She had told him the terms on which she might become chief executive of MCL. 'I am not prepared to take the risk of the opposition arbitrarily pulling the rug. You have to get them to say they won't do that.' Heseltine then went to see Blair in the leader of the opposition's office in the House of Commons. It was a perfectly courteous and civil encounter but the Deputy Prime Minister had been made to wait and the time was cut to 25 minutes because 'two business leaders were waiting'. This was the opposition as government, government as opposition. Power was draining away from the Tories. Heseltine conceded everything the Shadow Cabinet wanted, including the right to a full review in government, an unbreakable lid on the overall budget (i.e. no guarantee on limitless cost overruns) and a commitment (despite the structure of the Page budget) that the £250 million contingency would be used only for unforeseen costs. Afterwards, Blair was asked by a reporter if he was surprised at Heseltine coming to him cap-in-hand. Blair twisted the knife: 'Yes, I suppose it might have looked odd,' he said, 'that he was coming to us in this way, as he makes so much in normal circumstances of asking us, "Where's the money coming from?"' This was ritual humiliation.

After the meeting that Thursday evening everything at last looked as if it might work. The long, ruptured story which had its roots in the decision to reject Birmingham a year before was perhaps now heading for resolution. Blair was on board, Cunningham was on board. Heseltine and the commission were on board. Gordon Brown had his safety net in place.

The recognition that Millennium Central had to be in the public sector had now taken hold in everyone's mind, including Michael Heseltine's. The actual mechanism by which a public sector company could receive a lottery grant had been the subject of private discussions since mid summer. In simple terms, no part of central government, such as a government department, could receive any grant from the lottery. That was a principle central to John Major's concept of 'additionality'. It was a principle not explicit in the Lottery Act but it had been implied when debated in Parliament. Lottery money was not to go pouring back into the usual hungry governmental mouths. Staff and consultants at the Millennium Commission had been tangling with a whole series of possible structures. What if the government were to own a holding company – which itself could receive no grant – but the holding company were to own a subsidiary operating company? Would that subsidiary be allowed to receive a lottery grant? The treasury solicitors thought not. The Holdco/Opco structure, as it was called, wasn't going to help them, at least not in such a straightforward way.

It was another impasse, but its solution was critical to the continuation of the project. Perhaps if Millennium Central became a straightforward quango, it could happily receive the grant. After all, the British Museum and the Tate Gallery were both government-owned institutions (while not part of core government functions) and they received large lottery grants. But that was no good either. Millennium Central, dependent as it would be on enormous amounts of private sector sponsorship, as well as being a flagship for a Conservative government, had to show a friendly and suitable face to the private sector. A quango wouldn't have done that. The company was to be ambivalent in its role and purpose and so had to be amphibian in its constitution. The answer which was finally formulated in this agonised period between the December 1996 commission meeting and the following January was known, to the tight circle of Millennium Commission staff addressing this question, as 'Jenco'. The limited company established by Imagination in the autumn of 1995 was now to become a new and strange kind of hybrid. It was to be a private company, registered under the 1985 Companies Act and subject to the rules of that legislation. At the same time it was to be a Non-Departmental Public Body, subject to the rules covering government organisations. It was both a commercial and a public body. It was to have two shares. Michael Heseltine didn't want to be the shareholder – nor, as a Millennium Commissioner, could he have been – but he didn't want any other Secretary of State to be shareholder either. A search through government was made and, in the words of one consultant then advising the commission, 'Roger Freeman, Chancellor of the Duchy of Lancaster, was wheeled out of the shadows'. He was to become the first shareholder of the new Millennium Central, although, like the others who would come after him, he was made to sign a share transfer form, which would remain with the DNH made out to the Secretary of State, but undated. No one was risking the farce, should the shareholder fall under a bus, of his widow owning the Dome.

But there was still something missing. Bob Ayling, chief executive of British Airways, and the putative chairman of Millennium Central, could not accept the deal which Heseltine had done with Blair.

Ayling could see well enough from Jennie Page's budget that the extra £250 million would cover the costs but he feared that the directors of the company could still be exposed to overruns for which they would be personally responsible. He couldn't set up the company on those terms. MCL could not ratify the Blair–Heseltine deal.

Later the same evening Simon Jenkins rang Heseltine. 'We can't deliver. We've got no bankable guarantee and without a bankable guarantee we've got no board for the company. Ayling won't wear it.' Heseltine was incensed. He had expended a mass of political capital in yielding to Labour's demands, would be taunted in the press for it and now apparently it had been to no avail. If Gordon Brown would not agree to a Labour government underwriting any potential cost overruns, Ayling was refusing to take the Dome forward. The Dome was dead. 'I think we've lost it,' Heseltine said on the phone.

Jenkins told Heseltine that there was no way around the problem unless Blair could persuade Ayling himself that the new government would give an open-ended guarantee – precisely the point which New Labour's concerns for tight control of finance would not allow them to concede.

The following morning, Friday 17th, it was clear that the Blair–Heseltine deal was dead. The various parties had dispersed: Heseltine to Manchester, Blair to Sedgefield and Ayling with his wife on a wedding anniversary trip to Rome. Page and Jenkins were still in London. Alastair Campbell and Jonathan Powell were in Blair's office in Westminster. It was the day of the faxes. Campbell faxed over to the Millennium Commission the draft of a press release which he hoped might satisfy Ayling. It was too vague. Ayling in Rome faxed back his verdict: he couldn't deliver a board for the company on the basis of anything that was vague. From Manchester, Heseltine raged down the telephone. Faxes went back and forth.

According to Ayling, 'Julia didn't think it was a particularly good use of our precious time in Rome that I was talking to Jonathan Powell about the Millennium Exhibition.' But it had to be done. 'They were asking the sensible questions, the questions any normal person would ask. What are we doing this for? How much is it going to cost? What's it going to look like? How many people are going to come? What sort of impression is it going to give? They just wanted to get hold of the idea in a perfectly normal way. They didn't have an angle on it. They dealt with it very straightforwardly.' They may have but they clearly still needed reassurance on those fundamentals.

It seemed to them all a kind of lunatic geometry. Simon Jenkins was struggling to agree with Blair's office in Westminster, and with Blair himself in Sedgefield, the text of a letter which Ayling could send for approval to Heseltine in Manchester before releasing it to the press. It had been announced that a statement would be made at 2 p.m. that day but the time came and went without an agreement. Over the whole scene hung the echoes of Gordon Brown's litany of the need for a prudent budget. Campbell drafted a briefing note to Blair which reopened all the issues of cancellation or drastic downscaling of the exhibition which Jenkins, Heseltine and Page had thought closed by the Heseltine–Blair agreement the previous day.

By six o'clock that evening there was total collapse. Nothing had been or, it seemed, could be agreed. The Dome's life was stuttering towards its close. Jenkins and Page decided that they had to go to Blair's office themselves. It was dark. Powell and Campbell were there to meet them. Blair was on the phone. 'Heseltine has delivered his government,' Jenkins said to Powell. 'Now we need yours.' Blair himself had drafted a letter from Ayling to Heseltine but this one was no good for Ayling either. Yet more drafts were faxed to and fro. None worked because none faced up to the nub of the issue. The key point now was Labour's refusal to guarantee the budget beyond the £250 million that would come from the Heseltine scheme, by which the Millennium Commission's funding life would be extended for a year. Without that extra commitment, the Dome wouldn't happen.

This was the crisis. On the phone from Sedgefield, Blair said quite openly that he could not go beyond the terms agreed with the Shadow Cabinet. But Blair himself clearly had to take a decision. Would the glamorous, enlivening potential of 'the young country' now be given its own theatre, a showpiece for what new Britain might become? Or was he to accept the principle that budget rigour mattered more than anything else? Was the Dome, in other words, to succumb to the austerity and sense of responsibility which marked off New Labour from the muddle and flatulence of an exhausted Tory administration – qualities which had come in the public mind to characterise the project itself? Or was it to be the vehicle to a new future? This was not a conflict between Tory and Labour, nor between new and old Labour, but between the two defining qualities of New Labour itself.

On two separate lines at the same time, Blair in Sedgefield was speaking to Page in Westminster and Ayling in Rome. Page described to him the difficulties that would arise from going ahead with the company, only then to find that Labour might cancel it almost immediately for a perfectly intelligible electoral advantage. Ayling repeated his need for a bankable guarantee. It was now about eight o'clock at night.

Simon Jenkins told Jonathan Powell that Blair needed to make 'an enthusiastic commitment'. Enthusiasm was an important quality. It put an emphasis on the positive, whereas a naked 'review' would in itself be undermining. They put the point to Blair in Sedgefield, who then made the decision. They would go ahead with it, subject to review. Jenkins said to Campbell and Powell, 'This is your first act in government.'

Jennie Page then rang Claire Sampson on the mobile phone – she was waiting in the commission's office in Little Smith Street – and the three of them went and drank champagne in the St Ermine's Hotel in Caxton Street. The atmosphere was scarcely very festive. Nervous exhaustion had now sunk them into the depths of gloom. The Dome, again, had squeaked through. Ayling believed he had a qualified commitment from Blair not to close the exhibition either before or after the election. Although there was some ambiguity hanging over the question, this was a form of underpinning and this was the go-ahead. It meant that Jennie Page could take the job.

The following day the DNH issued a statement to the effect that the exhibition would go ahead. Describing the ugly heart of the wrangle, the civil servicese put it like this:

> The Government had discussed the Millennium Commission's plans in detail with the Opposition, who had expressed enthusiasm for the proposed Exhibition at Greenwich and indicated that, if elected to Government, it would want to review all aspects of project delivery to ensure that it was cost effective and properly implemented and came within its existing budget.

The wording of that statement is ambiguous. 'All aspects of project delivery …' What did that mean? Did it mean they might still cancel it? Or was it just a question of getting the money right? Jenkins felt he knew the answer. For him, Blair was locked on to the project and there was no possibility of the Dome being cancelled. As he saw it, there was no ambiguity. The Dome was now going to happen.

On Tuesday 21 January 1997 Jennie Page 'picked up three cardboard boxes and left the commission'. She took with her Claire Sampson, who had been head of the festival unit, and her magnificent and intensely loyal PA, Cherie Williams. They had worked together since Page was at

English Heritage. 'Other people spend an hour with her,' Williams says, 'and come out looking as if they've gone ten rounds with Mike Tyson. I get it month after month. I've told Jennie I should have nine resignation lives. Sometimes she goes on and on and on and I just say to her: "Jennie, go away and let me finish one thing, will you?"' Williams wouldn't work for anyone else.

She had to start hiring senior staff. 'I knew I needed immense competence and drive and also a take-it-or-leave-it attitude.' These could only be people at the top of their profession, successful, immediately available, and probably with their own businesses. She had already spoken to David Trench, the immensely powerful jam-busting project manager who had delivered the British Library after years of chaos and indecision. Would he come on? Of course he would. He had commitments to the library for a couple of months, but from April he was the Dome's.

At a performance of Cirque de Soleil in the Albert Hall, Page had also talked to Lord Montagu of Beaulieu, whom she knew from English Heritage, of which he had been chairman. Ken Robinson, one of the country's leading experts in the operation of visitor attractions, had been managing director of Montagu's leisure businesses and was now a consultant with his own companies. Montagu suggested Page got in touch with Robinson. They knew each other already. Would he join? Robinson felt that his entire professional life had been preparing for the Dome – 'this wonderful, wonderful animal', as he calls it. He had been to the Festival of Britain as a boy from Battersea and, like Mike Davies, had been utterly inspired by it. This was his chance to do the best thing in his business ('it's not about entertainment, it's about inspiration') that had ever been done. He joined.

Jeff Hawkins, who had been close to the project for eighteen months, gave in his notice at SEMA Consulting, a leading French firm of management consultants, and also joined the team. Apart from Bob Ayling and the board members, these few people were Millennium Central, the company building the Dome. They had taken their cardboard boxes down to offices in Old Broad Street in the City. It was a temporary base for the client team, a gloomy and depressing set of rooms, taken on by W. S. Atkins, the firm which in various forms had been effectively running the job on the ground, working both on the regeneration of the

Greenwich peninsula and on getting planning permission for the Dome. Here Page and her team contemplated the task in view.

Some aspects could not have been improved on. They had on board the Richard Rogers Partnership and the engineers Buro Happold. On 17 February, after the necessary competitive tendering process, they were to be joined, as construction managers, by the McAlpine Laing Joint Venture. This alliance between two of the country's leading construction firms was to be the bedrock on which the exemplary development of the site was to be laid. Bound together by David Trench into a contractual tripod with Buro Happold and Richard Rogers, all three were committed to 'target-cost contracts'. If the job came in under budget, they would all share a bonus. If it was late, they would all suffer the penalty. Trench's term is 'shared pain and shared gain'. On construction jobs, blame is often the source of delay. This system, which is solution- and not problem-based, diminishes the tendency to blame. Trench backed it up by running a very tight and light project-management system. The existing team of project managers from W. S. Atkins, which he found on his arrival, was soon slimmed down. The complex demands of the job, which would mean a great deal of overlapping design and construction, as well as an unremitting schedule, would only work, Trench felt, if people and organisations did not stiffen up. There had to be very little letter-writing and a lot of 'face-time' between key players from all disciplines. Trench also insisted that the engineers, the architects, the construction managers and the many heads of the client should all share the same office on site. Andrew Morris of RRP and Bernard Ainsworth of the McAlpine Laing joint venture were given the job of delivering David Trench's aspirations. Fluidity, candour and teamwork were all.

If that was the good, there was a great deal that was challenging. Page and her team had to set up a company and start the recruitment of other senior commercial, financial, marketing and communications staff. It was difficult to recruit such people until after the election. Nobody who was already booked into a big job, with pension rights, share schemes and the rest of it, would come. MCL also had to produce a more robust business plan; find permanent offices (in fact they moved twice before May); negotiate the terms by which the Millennium Commission would give them their grant; conclude the lease on the 180-acre exhibition site with English Partnerships, an organisation which, according to Page, 'at that stage turned out to be almost as difficult to deal with as British Gas and was treating us as if we were a third-rate banana-importing company'; face the fact that Imagination had come to the end of the road and were no longer in a position to undertake the entire design; look for a new rationale on which the design of the content might be based; begin to think about the way in which the exhibition would actually work on the ground; prepare for the review which the new government would conduct; place the orders for the steel and roof-covering; and establish systems by which the building would be built. All this in the space of three months, and with their future life uncertain. 'January to May 1997,' Page says, 'was difficult.'

Away from the frenzy of the political arena, down on Greenwich peninsula, it was in some ways an equivalent world. The place was being cleaned up. If you were looking for metaphors, the buried history of the site could scarcely have been more articulate. It had, in its time, been both a bleaching field and a vitriol factory, a rhubarb farm and a giant gasworks, a marsh over which the highest tides effortlessly washed and a place where the more celebrated criminals, once hanged, were shut in iron cages and left, quite literally, to twist in the wind. Bleach, vitriol, rhubarb, gas, structural ambivalence and the gruesome display of the famous dead: anything that might happen at Westminster had been prefigured here. Now, as the final gesture, it was to be cleaned and, in the technical phrase, 'made good'. Bugsby's Marsh: Regeneration Central.

The clean-up, which British Gas was legally obliged to perform, had begun in July 1996. The whole place looked like a battlefield. There were walls right across the site. An old gateway into the gasworks remained, isolated, across one of the entrances. London Underground was excavating the vast 'box' in which the tube station would be housed, a hole as large as the Canary Wharf tower laid on its side. There was an ancient branch railway line leading into the site and a bridge over it. Locating yourself was a near impossibility. Workmen would get lost for an hour at a time. Up at the northern end, where the Dome itself was to be built, and where the most hideous of gas-cleaning processes had been housed, keeping their fumes as far as possible from the people of Greenwich, the smell was now almost unendurable. Deep underground there was a tarpit, lime kilns and other toxic capsules. You couldn't walk about there without a mask. All the employees of Edmund Nuttall Ltd, the firm engaged to do the decontamination, were wearing disposable anti-toxic suits. This broken, post-Armageddon landscape, tainted with the sense of polluted abandonment and bustling with these armies of busy, masked, white-suited operatives, looked like the aftermath of some terrible nuclear accident. All visitors had to pass through a decontamination unit, putting on overalls, gloves and boots. All vehicles on the contaminated site were allowed off it only once they had been cleaned.

Problems were multiplying here too. Dealing with the overlapping requirements of British Gas, the Environment Agency, English Partnerships, the Highways Agency, London Underground and Millennium Central, every one of which had its team of consultants and advisers, was never going to be simple. Often it was difficult for these consultants to get an answer out of their own agencies. Decisions could never be definitive. Everything always had to be referred back. There was in particular a coordination meeting held every week at the Rogers office in Hammersmith. Sometimes more than 30 of these consultants, architects, planners and engineers would be crowded in there. Essentially, they were aiming to address the tangled mesh of needs and requirements for the exhibition, for Millennium Central, and for the masterplan of the peninsula for English Partnerships. Who was to pay for the infrastructure? Which infrastructure could be considered common to the two projects? Which was uniquely for one or the other? Should the requirements of one override the needs of the other? Percentages of commonality varied from place to place.

It was, according to Peter English, an independent construction consultant working for the firm of W. S. Atkins, who in turn were working for MCL, 'a dreadful meeting, a muddle between the exhibition, 'MEX', as we called it, and the masterplan. There were too many people.' W. S. Atkins were there in three or four guises: as the Project Implementation Team working for Millennium Central; and as engineers to EP and to British Gas and to the Highways Agency, who were just starting to plan the reconstruction of the ventilation system for the Blackwall Tunnel running under the site. The Richard Rogers Partnership had its architects and its own landscape consultant. 'Wednesday afternoons at RRP went round and round and round,' English says. The Environment Agency, for its part, was refusing to accept that British Gas was doing a satisfactory job cleaning up the poisoned earth. Millennium Central's own engineers,

Buro Happold, wanted to know what the ground conditions were like so that they could design appropriate foundations. A long wrangle over access and means of payment for the investigators ensued. It was symptomatic of the sort of difficulties these multi-agency projects involve. British Gas owned the site, with W. S. Atkins as its engineers, and was using Edmund Nuttall as the remediation contractor. Millennium Central couldn't investigate somebody else's land. But they needed to if the timetable was to be preserved. Eventually, British Gas agreed to be contracted by Buro Happold so that the ground investigation company, Wimtech Environmental, sub-contracted to Nuttalls who were themselves contracted to British Gas, could carry out the work needed by Millennium Central. But all this only if the Millennium Commission – at this point the source of all money for the embryonic MCL – paid Buro Happold who would then pay British Gas, before they paid Nuttall who would finally pay Wimtech. The complexities of conditions underground were effortlessly matched by those above it. As winter turned towards spring, the clock moved onwards: the millennium was now 1,000 days away.

Back in central London, it was no better. Millennium Central were locked in an argument with the Millennium Commission over the terms of their grant. It may seem farcical now but it was passionate then. The very terms which Jennie Page as chief executive of the Millennium Commission had been proposing for the grant to Millennium Central, she now, as chief executive of Millennium Central herself, violently objected to. Bob Ayling was on her side. 'The terms of grant were ludicrous,' he says. 'Ludicrous! They were based on the idea that we had come along and there was a grave risk that we were about to abscond with the money. The opposite was true! We'd been asked to do this by them, but the terms were based on the idea that we were untrustworthy. That was outrageous.' Page made fierce objections to Mike O'Connor, previously her deputy and now her successor at the commission. He felt mangled in the process. Ayling stood by his chief executive: 'I supported her. It would be impossible for us to do the job if we were hamstrung with the conditions of grant as they were originally proposed.' Sir Hayden Phillips at the DNH poured oil on the waters, promising that while the terms could not differ from those imposed on other grant recipients, there would be no pedantic or obstructionist interpretation of them. The way it was resolved was that MCL agreed to work on an open-book basis. A Millennium Commission auditor would sit in their offices and do a continual audit. If they had issues to raise, they could raise them as they went along. This arrangement was in fact never taken up. Instead, any issues were discussed at monthly meetings. Staff at the commission felt they were in a difficult position. Page had left, taking with her Claire Sampson and the commission's lawyers, Norton Rose. No one who remained knew much about the project. In addition, the uncertainty cast by the coming election meant that everyone was treading extremely carefully. An incoming government would need to find an antiseptic level of hygiene around the Dome and the letter of the law had to be stuck to. Given the unique and arcane status of the new company/quango, the actual nature of that law was not easy to grasp. What looked from MCL like an acute bout of paranoia during negotiations lasting six weeks was in truth little more than the rigorous observance of proprieties in a difficult and confused situation.

Millennium Central – later renamed the New Millennium Experience Company – was the child of the marriage between the Millennium Commission and the genius of Imagination. Formally, its only relationship with the commission was to receive from it the lottery grant of £449 million, of which £50 million was for cash-flow purposes, to be repaid in 2001. But the very scale of that grant and the central place of the Dome and its national programme in the country's millennium celebrations meant the company was always going to be intimately supervised by the commission, by the DNH and by ministers. That intimacy took the form of a supremely involuted piece of quasi-state organisational architecture. It embodied all the modern requirements of a public–private crossover not by taking some aspects from one side and some from the other but by taking all aspects from both. It was both a quango with a shareholder and a private company owned by a government minister.

That duality imposed some horrible strains: 'The company accepts entirely its public accountability responsibilities within the framework of government guidance,' Jennie Page wrote in something of a cri de coeur in 1998. 'Nevertheless it is pulled between the requirements of baring its soul to meet demands for information and of operating in the commercial world where release of detailed budgetary information is not the norm.' Throughout the life of the Dome public and private pulled at them in a slow and relentless form of medieval torture. It was life on the millennium rack.

As for the supervision and reporting system for the Dome within government, the diagram looked like the nervous system of a lobster.

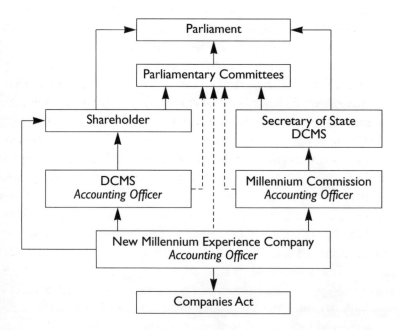

The accounting officer at the company, i.e. Jennie Page, had in one direction to answer to the demands of the Companies Act. In the other, she had to answer both to the accounting officer at the Millennium Commission (in other words her successor there) and to the company's single shareholder, in some cases via the Permanent Secretary at the Department of National Heritage/Culture, Media and Sport. The accounting officer at the Millennium Commission had to look to the Secretary of State at the DNH/DCMS. All five individuals had to answer to the relevant parliamentary select committees, and both the ministers involved – the shareholder and the Secretary of State – had to answer to Parliament itself.

In one way in particular the time pressures of an immovable deadline, the expectations of an acute commercial performance and conformity to the standards of propriety in public life made the Dome company's existence nearly intolerable. Both in procuring material and in hiring staff they couldn't, as a private company could, simply source the goods or hire people they liked the look of. According to European Union rules, any work involving a construction contract had to be advertised in the Official Journal of the European Community. Even on those contracts where OJEC did not have to play a part, a long-winded rigmarole had to be followed. If, for example, the Dome wanted a senior manager of an essential process, they would ask around. A person would be identified. The shareholder or the chief executive would meet him. He would look suitable. He would be needed on the project. But then the selection performance would begin. A headhunter would be necessary. A long list of headhunters would be produced. They would be interviewed. They would submit tenders for the job. A Dome committee would evaluate them and at last a headhunter would be selected. Then a job description for the post would have to be drawn up and advertisements placed. Applications would come in and they would be sifted. A long list of possibles would be prepared and a shortlist whittled out from it. There would be second interviews. A job would be offered and then negotiations over the contract could begin. Eventually, several months after the person to do the job had been identified, he could begin it. And that is a simple version of the story. At least once in the history of the Dome the official selection process failed to deliver the candidate who had been identified in the first place and much of the process had to be repeated.

One of Jennie Page's great gifts is her ability to manage this modern, profoundly supervised world of public accounts without becoming bogged down by its demands. Jeff Hawkins, programme and projects director on the Dome, oversees contracts and timetables across the whole range of this enormous job. He describes Page's approach: 'Jennie would say, "Right, I need some accountants. Run me a competition now and I want it done by four o'clock. I want to know availability, CVs and fee rate."' This approach was calculated to appeal to the providers of the service. 'Anyone would bite your hand off to do that,' Hawkins says. 'There's no need for a big sales pitch from them, it's competitive and they know we'll buy that day. For them, it's a cheap sell. "I want this. I'm serious. I've got the money. All I want from you is this: What are your standards? How do you do it? Who's going to do it? How much is it going to cost?" They'll respond to that.'

Despite the vigour of approach, at times it felt as if they were living in a maze of interlocking demands, each agency, department or firm of consultants as clamorous as the next and each, in its desire to know what was going on and how the money was being spent, interfering with the very processes whose efficiency it was meant to be supervising. It was not surprising, in this context, that the Dome began to develop a habit of reluctant communication and busy impatience with many of those who wanted to know what was going on. Hidden beneath the skin, there was a never-ending tension between urgency and accountability. Inevitably, in the face of a hostile press, hatches were battened down. No one on the Dome wanted to say much.

The old questions of purpose and content were still painfully alive. The relationship between Millennium Central and Imagination was now on its last legs. Mutual dissatisfaction had come to colour it. Imagination remained endlessly frustrated by the absence of a client making definitive requirements. Millennium Central now felt that the theme of time and its subdivisions originally proposed by Imagination was not standing up to the tests which reality was beginning to impose on it. With his focus on the questions of practical deliverability, Ken Robinson, the Dome's operations director, was ruthless with many of the proposals on the table. 'The good thing about being old and grey,' he says, 'is that you no longer care what anybody thinks about you. You just say what you think is right.'

Imagination's proposals had reached the stage where there were now 60 different features in the Dome. Each of the twelve masts had five different attractions clustered around it. Robinson rejected the entire scheme. 'Being in the Dome is going to be like eating fruitcake,' he says. 'Five to six hours in the Dome is likely to tire people out. And they are only going to come once. Are you really going to say to them, "Here are 60 incredible things. You're going to be able to see eight or ten of them"? No, you're not. People who come must get to the majority of what there is to see. If you come here you see it, you get it. And it has got to be in comfortable circumstances. Seventy-five thousand people is a nonsense. It has got to be half that.'

The implications of this thinking were: fewer, bigger things, perhaps ten zones; a limited number of tickets; and advance booking so that whoever came would be sure of getting in. Rigour, tightness, a grip being got: the entire project felt different with Robinson on board. For Imagination this was difficult. 'Gary was the seminal father of the whole project,' Robinson says. 'He dreamed it, he knew it, he talked it, he persuaded people. Without him it wouldn't have happened.' Imagination's method of working was to deliver a total package to a client, from first sketchy conceptions to the full operating glory of an event. Here, they were becoming embroiled in the most multiple-headed organisation anyone had ever come across. Ken Robinson was imposing whole new sets of alien demands. He wanted to get rid of many treasured aspects of the Imagination scheme. His vision was not a free-flow, go-where-you-want exhibition, but 'centred on a number of exhibits that were linked by timed tickets. There would be no queuing and you would just move them around the Dome, a to b and b to c and c to d.'

Robinson went on holiday to the Galapagos. On the same yacht ('a very upmarket thing with lackeys', in Robinson's words) was George Russell, chairman of Camelot, the lottery operators. Over dinner Robinson suggested that the Dome's pre-booked tickets, the biggest ticketing exercise ever conducted, should be sold through Camelot's high street lottery outlets. 'Your licence will be coming up in 2000,' Robinson taunted him. 'It will be a jolly good thing for you to do.' As a result, that is precisely how most Dome tickets will be sold.

On Robinson's return, Withers had come up with something new. Imagination was to withdraw from most of the project. Robinson's zones could be designed by others. But in the centre of the Dome would be the most extraordinary structure yet proposed: the Drum. An enormous, open, cylindrical theatre would occupy the heart of the Dome. It was the size of Trafalgar Square and almost as tall as Nelson's Column. Inside it the banks of seats would themselves be mobile in several dimensions. Each section of seating could independently rise and rotate around the central arena. The audience would be taking part in a huge automated ballet as part of the show it was watching. The Drum itself was made of a ring of towers, each of which would put out wings towards its neighbours when a show was to be performed, totally closing off the central space. At other times the wings would be withdrawn and the separate towers would surround a central piazza with cafés – the Dome's equivalent of street life.

It was, once again, a moment of great excitement. Given that Gary Withers was worn out and depressed by the turn things had taken – he would suffer an acute bout of shingles later in the year – it was an astonishing response.

The architects from the Richard Rogers Partnership loved the idea and it was later to form the basis for the concept of the Central Show. Jennie Page and Claire Sampson had now come to the conclusion that the contents of the Dome had grown too big for one company. No one design outfit could encompass the necessary breadth and depth. Besides, now that it was in the public sector, it would have been wrong to put one company in charge. To reflect the multiple vitality of the country, the Dome needed to be multiple and vital itself. The project was too big, they insisted, for Imagination on its own. Both Page and Sampson had struggled for a long time to persuade Gary Withers that he might become the creative guru at the heart of the Dome, supervising a family of designers and guiding them towards a coherent conclusion. That suggestion, which would largely have divorced Withers from the company he had created, was one he couldn't accept. He *was* his company; it was an indissoluble marriage.

Nevertheless, Imagination grappled with Robinson's new demands. Following this bold evocation of the possibilities for the heart of the Dome, Claire Sampson wrote an operational brief for an almost free-standing project, in which all Imagination's remarkable energies could be concentrated.

At the same time the search was now on for a new basis on which the contents of the Dome could be justified and organised. It was perfectly clear that an incoming Labour government would ask: What is in it?

Maurice Saatchi had been talking to Bob Ayling. Ayling was worried he didn't have the right people in place. Did Saatchi think that Bill Muirhead, a partner in M. & C. Saatchi, might be interested? He did. A few days later Muirhead, on his way back from a game of squash in his club in Pall Mall, met Ayling coming the other way in a Soho street. Ayling had been receiving an award. Muirhead was heading back to the chic white minimalism of the M. & C. Saatchi offices in Golden Square.

Ayling said, 'Ah, just the person I've been looking for. What are you doing? What are you doing now?' They walked back together to Ayling's office in Berkeley Square. It was like something out of an Edwardian novel.

Ayling outlined the project. 'He wasn't anxious,' Muirhead says, 'but he was concerned that the whole thing was going to come off the rails.'

'I wasn't,' Ayling says. 'There weren't any rails for it to come off.'

Things moved fast. During the meeting Ayling rang Page, Page spoke to Muirhead and fixed a date to see him: 7.30 the next morning in the Old Broad Street office. Meeting the core Millennium Central team, Muirhead was struck by one particular aspect of the situation. 'Nobody seemed to really know,' he later said, 'apart from this piece of architecture and this site, what it was about.' When he asked them what it was about, it seemed to him that nobody could answer that question. In the light of all the preceding history, that sketchiness about the contents was perfectly intelligible. It was the natural outcome of everything that had happened before. Only to those coming in from outside was it surprising.

After the meeting, on 3 February 1997, Muirhead wrote to Page. 'The millennium desperately needs a focus. It needs to be explained simply what it is, what it means for people.' Expert views are partial; they see what they are trained to see. Muirhead told Page that she had to create a communications department, doing PR, media relations and advertising. And they had to do some market research. What did this thing mean to people? What did they expect from it? What would make them come?

Various luminaries of the advertising and live event world were immediately involved: Paul Twivy, Peter Miller and Mike Lockett of WCT Live, an event organisation company. Muirhead went to see Gary Withers at Imagination. Withers seemed 'very depressed and low, feeling cynical about the whole thing and that he had been shafted. He had invested so much time and energy and now it was in pieces on the floor.' Muirhead considered the presentation he was given by Withers at Store Street 'impressive but lacking in substance. You didn't come away thinking "wow". It was like a Chinese meal. You love it while you're eating it but you come away hungry.' Muirhead's reaction wasn't surprising since much of the original creative content had been removed by the new team at Millennium Central leaving a gaping hole at the heart of the scheme.

Muirhead did what advertising people do: he began to look for a simple, universally recognisable truth about the product, on the basis of which the entire superstructure of selling it could be erected. What, here, was the heart of the matter? He talked to Jeremy Sinclair, his co-director at Saatchi's. Sinclair mentioned Stonehenge. 'If you watch people going up to Stonehenge and watch them going away from Stonehenge they seem to walk straighter,' Sinclair said. That was good, an oblique thought, connected obscurely and underground to the question of the millennium. Visit this and come away better. Walk taller or be moved in a way you haven't been moved before. Was this a fruitful avenue?

Sinclair, Muirhead and Page sat and talked about how to bring the focus to bear. Market research cannot be done on the basis of 'What are you thinking about at the moment?' Ideas and suggestions have to be put to people and tested. It was those ideas and suggestions which were being developed here. In March they were tested on various groups by the market researcher Alastair Burns. His confidential report to Millennium Central, delivered at Imagination's offices in early April, gives an extraordinary and original glimpse of Britain in the mid 1990s.

It was far subtler than the kind of newspaper poll which asks simply, 'What do you think of the millennium?' His focus was threefold: brainstorming sessions with 'trendsetters' (designers, clubbers, musicians); opinion-formers (businessmen, writers, academics); and community leaders (religious and charity people). To each of them he made various propositions, on the basis of the Muirhead–Sinclair–Page discussions – what advertising men call 'stimulus materials'. Long talks were held with eight 'cradles of opinion'. The idea behind these groups was that people when surrounded by their usual friends and companions are more likely to tell the truth than if confronted singly by a researcher or in front of people they don't know. Peer pressure short-circuits waffle and boasting. The community groups were: members of two football teams in Edinburgh; foreign tourists also in Edinburgh; mothers with young children in Farnborough; retired people who were members of a photography club also in Farnborough; church members in Oldham, both Roman Catholic and Anglican; factory workers in Swansea; scientists in Windsor; and schoolchildren from a comprehensive school in Greenwich. These were followed by six long interviews with the heads of big businesses around the country.

The sophistication of the method paid off. The answers Burns came up with stepped outside all the normal, well-worn attitudes to the millennium. In time they would come to play a governing role in shaping the Dome.

Some groups were scarcely responsive. The scientists were completely disengaged and not thinking about anything except their work. The Greenwich schoolchildren were deeply disenchanted, disconnected and cynical. The Swansea factory workers were nostalgic. 'When you were younger,' one of them said rather beautifully, 'the years were endless, but now the year is gone, three years, a month is nothing.' Another: 'There's always hope because we wouldn't be here otherwise, everybody lives in hope. Things have got better through the years. It's just that we can't see it …' There was very little perception, even among the religious communities, that this was a religious festival. It was clearly to be a shared and communal event, not owned by any one section. Proprietorial attitudes shown by any group would diminish it. Burns found that across all these people, negative attitudes were virtually missing. It was evidence for what politicians were endlessly saying: that the negativity of the press – what Heseltine bitterly calls 'the background of carping, sniping and misrepresentation against which this project had to struggle, a classic example of this country's death wish' – was not commonly shared.

Instead, two strands appeared. 'Tonight we're going to party like it's 1999,' the artist previously known as Prince had sung and the message had gone home. It was going to be the blast of the century. But beyond that, when people were dangled for a while in front of any of the large 'soft millenarian' ideas which lay behind the simple change in date, another attitude became apparent: this was a milestone in time; its natural scale was not national – a strong feeling against anything jingoistic emerged – but global; and it should of its nature have something unifying at its heart.

The tone was surprisingly gentle and generous: 'We're celebrating for the future generations in a way,' explained one of the businessmen. 'We are saying that we have played our part in making this world.' 'Yeah, but what happens after the party?' said one of the Greenwich schoolkids. Burns asked his interviewees what, if the word 'millennium' was an acronym, the letters would stand for. 'Making Involving Lessons Learned Enabling Normal New Interesting Universal Memories', one answered. 'Mothers and fathers Is being there Living Love Emotion Never giving up New beginning Important Understanding Men women and children', said another. This was a whole new note being added to the thinking about the Dome: tolerant, cheerful, optimistic, emotive, serious and responsible. It was not the millennium itself that interested people – what was it but an artificial point in time? – but what the millennium might bring about. It was not a focus or a target but a vehicle and a pivot, linking all the expectations of party with all the soft-millenarian ideas that were in the ether. It shouldn't belong only to London, let alone to the East End; it must be deeply and intimately involved with a national programme spreading across the whole country; it mustn't be dominated by Christianity or the royal family, and it mustn't be overtly British. It must say to people, in the words of the advertisement that M. & C. Saatchi came up with the following year, 'Imagine what you can do tomorrow'. That concise and stirring formulation – linking inner worlds and outer, vision and action, today with the future – was the clarion call. (By the time the advertisement appeared, over Christmas 1998, the 'you' had been turned into 'we', a soggier, more communitarian pronoun, which weakened the challenge while, in theory, toning down the presumption.)

Instead of either phrase, though, Jeremy Sinclair at M. & C. Saatchi settled on 'It's time to make a difference', a line which, as the journalist Rowan Moore would later say, would have been 'boring as the local election slogan of the Liberal Party in 1974'. The brilliance of the Burns research in identifying some of the underlying assumptions and aspirations of the age probably mattered more than the blandness of the formulation into which it was eventually distilled. The blandness may even have been, as Jennie Page maintains, an advantage. Bland doesn't box you in or close off any options.

The 1997 general election could now be no more than a few weeks away. Labour's own private polling was coming up with the same answers as Millennium Central's research. Hope was what everyone wanted, a more generous future, the sense of things getting better.

The review promised by the new government would soon be upon them. But the question of the content, not only what it would be but the entire conceptual framework around which it was to be arranged, was still up in the air.

Alongside the Saatchi/Twivy/Burns enterprise Jennie Page had been running meetings with writers and strategists at the commercial event company WCT Live, which for years had been involved with the subtle art of staging political conferences and launching commercial products. Martin Newman, a cerebral figure given to lapidary statements, who was not particularly happy with the kind of work he had been doing and would in time become lead content editor of the Dome, was employed there as a writer. He saw the Dome as a great and exciting opportunity. His boss, Mike Lockett, coordinated 'a mind-mapping exercise' in WCT's offices opposite Buckingham Palace. They had a 'war room' in the basement with an enormous wall-board. On the left, the combined MCL and WCT teams wrote up everything the Dome might aspire to – 'all the reinventing the nation stuff', as Newman puts it. On the right were all the practical difficulties – Newman cites 'the IRA and morgues in the Dome'.

It was a brain dump, pure catharsis for the team. The crowded circus in their heads could be pulled out on to a huge white board with marker pens. The technique itemised the problem. It didn't solve it. There were endless lists of themes on one side. On the other, they now had 'Time to make a difference'. Looked at unkindly, both aspects were unappealing: bald, worthy and generic on one side; muddled, massive and uncertain on the other. It was the situation of The Man without Qualities brought to a knife-point.

All of them were working on this, fully aware that a coherent rationale was required before the new government's review. Various tools seemed useful.

Martin Newman recalled an idea from Alexis de Tocqueville, the great French Liberal political theorist whose *Democracy in America* had appeared in the 1830s. De Tocqueville had maintained that you could measure the state of health of any society by asking whether the majority of people in that society were 'fearing to fall or hoping to rise'. This was the de Tocqueville thermometer and, according to it, Britain in the mid 1990s was ill.

It was one of the clarifying moments. If the Dome was to be viewed as an advertising campaign, as was the natural tendency of the people Page was consulting over this, what were they going to measure in the target audience? The de Tocqueville thermometer provided the measuring tool. The Dome could act as a kind of social yeast. If people in Britain had failed to rise at the end of it, then the whole exercise would have failed.

Breathtaking as the scale of that ambition might be, it nevertheless felt like a step out of the morass.

This idea of a measurable psychological legacy dovetailed with another. Staff at Millennium Central and members of the WCT team were tearing their hair out over the content zoo. For months they had toyed with the idea that the exhibition might be about 'who we are, where we live and what we do'. That slightly facile formulation now acquired a greater prominence. Combined with 'Time to make a difference', plus the de Tocqueville thermometer, this three-part division of human life – into the individual, the social and the environmental – seemed like a way out of their problems. Even if later this scheme would seem capable of being about anything, at the time it felt like a lifeboat, three areas to think about rather than 'Welcome to the *Encyclopaedia Britannica*'.

The election was in the offing. Page had refined the budget, the orders for the steel and roofing material were in, with break clauses in the contracts if Labour decided to cancel the Dome. The period of uncertainty would soon be over. What no one on the project quite grasped was that the Dome was about to face its fiercest test.

CHAPTER SIX

New Labour, New Dome

A ny review had to be done quickly. The Dome's own programme was already imposing its discipline. If the show was to be open by the millennium, the contents had to be in and testable by October 1999. Their installation had to begin a year before that. The skin had to be finished by June 1998, the cable net by March; the masts had to be up by the previous October. The huge, tapered, steel lattice-work cylinders had already been manufactured and were lying in the yard of Watson's Steel Ltd in Bolton. They were to be delivered in six sections – to be fitted together on site – which would have to start arriving at Greenwich on 4 August. The foundations needed to be ready for them. Pouring of the concrete for those foundations had to begin on 7 July. The foundations themselves, because of the atrocious ground conditions on the peninsula, which would have settled by up to 30 centimetres when heavy loads were applied, needed to rest on driven piles. That piling had to begin on 23 June. The contract for the piling could be placed no later than 6 June 1997. That was the date by which the new government had to make up its mind. After the election it had little over four weeks in which to do so.

Signals coming out of Labour during the campaign, for those who were reading them, were not good. Only a week before 1 May, the day of the election itself, Blair announced the diversion of lottery funds away from the kind of elite projects to which the Tories had devoted them. The spin highlighted the £12 million for the Churchill papers and the fortune given to the Royal Opera House. 'It's the people's lottery,' Tony Blair said. 'It should address the people's priorities.' The new projects were:

information technology for schools, homework clubs, a fund for healthy living and NESTA, the National Endowment for Science, Technology and the Arts, 'a national talent fund'.

No direct criticism of the Dome was involved, but for finely attuned ears in the embryo Millennium Central this was a slewing of the agenda away from perceived extravagance and showiness and towards health, education and community projects. What, if you looked at this through narrowed eyes, were the implications for the Dome in that?

Dawn broke on 2 May at the People's Palace on the South Bank in London. Labour had won by a landslide. Neil Kinnock and many others wept. Eighteen years of Conservative government were over. On Saturday morning Chris Smith, who had held the Shadow Health portfolio, was made Secretary of State at the Department of National Heritage.

Over the weekend Smith 'surveyed the whole portfolio. Clearly one of the things that required urgent attention was a review of the position on the Dome.' Within a matter of days he started to receive letters from 'one or two captains of industry who wrote to me to say that this is not something we would want to support'. John Newbigin, who had worked for Kinnock and David Puttnam and was now a special adviser to Smith, puts it a little more forthrightly. 'They said that they wouldn't, and we shouldn't, touch it with a barge pole.'

Smith gives a characteristically balanced and managerial account of the dilemma: 'At that stage it looked like a building in search of something to put inside it rather than a cluster of activities that were looking for a suitable building. The question then was: Did we have enough time and did the people running the show have the imagination to make it good?'

There was a delicate question here. In January it had been obvious to Jennie Page, Simon Jenkins and Bob Ayling that Tony Blair was keen on the Dome. They had all emerged from those conversations convinced that Labour might review the project, its budget and style, but would not cancel it. Page and Ayling had joined the company, others had been hired and some £20 million had been committed.

Now, however, the scope of the review seemed to be drifting a little wider than that. The announcement during the election campaign about the 'people's lottery' had blurred the edges of what lottery money could be devoted to. Health, education and community projects were clearly areas to which central, tax-funded government expenditure would be going. The original principle of additionality, by which lottery funds were to be used in addition to, not instead of, the money that came from the tax system, had been eroded. A question now hung in the New Labour air: if that was the case, why shouldn't the money earmarked for the Dome be applied to other projects more congenial to various ministers' own agendas? It would now become clear that not only delivery, implementation and budget on the Dome would be subject to review. Its very existence was again in question.

The review had several parts. The Millennium Commission itself took on Bovis, the construction company, to analyse and evaluate the business plan which Jennie Page and her team had now produced. At the same time Chris Smith asked both John Newbigin, his political adviser, and Clare Pillman, the DNH official who had been overseeing all parts of the millennium brief, to look at the whole question. For her in particular it was not easy. For months she had been 'the champion of the project' in government. Now she had to take a step back and take a long, cold look at what it represented. 'I was given a very even brief,' she says. 'Ministers required a good, objective piece of official advice. I knew where the bodies were. I was one of the few people who could give it. But it wasn't easy. I couldn't be as open with Jennie as I had been.' For Page herself, the virtual exclusion from the process, although understandable according to the way government works, was nevertheless an unpleasant and uncomfortable experience.

The fourth leg of the review was by far the least formal. Peter Mandelson, now Minister without Portfolio, had a roving brief across the whole of government. He had not previously had much involvement with the Dome question. During the January crisis he and Blair had spoken about it once. Blair had put it to him that it would be no good for the opposition to be blamed by the public for pooping the party. From a Labour perspective, it seemed that this was precisely Heseltine's tactic – to make it look as if Labour was responsible for the Dome's abandonment. They wouldn't fall for that.

Now, though, in government, a decision that went beyond pre-electoral manoeuvring had to be made. Blair had been clear that, intuitively at least, he felt that the Dome could be good for the country. Going on with it, as well as avoiding the opprobrium of killing it, would give them the opportunity to be associated with a project of enormous scale and prominence. Mandelson's own agenda meshed with that. There were several dimensions to this. He was profoundly aware that his maternal grandfather Herbert Morrison had been in almost the same chair in the post-war Labour government. Mandelson was riding high on the triumph of the election he had masterminded, but now, like Morrison, had no direct departmental responsibility. Papers discussing the Dome began to emerge from both the DNH and the Treasury and to circulate through the red boxes of the ministers on the Home and Social Affairs Committee, of whom Mandelson was one. As the deeply questioning and sceptical tone of those papers started to become apparent, Mandelson turned his attention towards the project. Policy advisers, including Ben Evans, James Purnell and Peter Hyman, worked through the questions with Mandelson in the Cabinet Office.

Part of the New Labour government culture was a macho requirement for bigness, toughness and action. In the light of that, the careful consideration of all the options by Chris Smith looked cautious. 'Chris was clearly sceptical about the whole thing,' one enthusiastic Labour minister says. 'Dealing with the question was turmoil for him. The review was framed to come up with a negative answer.' The sort of questions it was asking were: What are the reasons we should abandon this? How should we remodel it or scale it down? For those in the new government who were keen on the Dome, the alternative proposals looked too modest. The whole approach, this gung-ho Downing Street group felt, 'lacked self-confidence.'

It was not quite as polarised as that implies. Everyone acknowledged there were some real questions to be asked. Smith is quite open about it. 'I was cautious certainly. Quite a few of my cabinet colleagues were virulently arguing that we should not go ahead with this. A number of others, of whom Peter was most obviously one, were arguing that we should go ahead. That was the balance of discussion. I was the setter of the scene. David Puttnam was arguing very strongly at the time for an educational purpose. I was quite strongly in favour of that. I think that if it could be put forward as something that was largely focused on educational ideas and issues then that was something that could be put forward as a social legacy.'

This kind of thinking did not meet with much enthusiasm either from Mandelson or from the Dome company. 'Chris Smith and Co. wanted the sort of exhibition that gets put on by the Central Office of Information,' says one of its staff. 'None of their suggestions took on board the fact that something the scale of the Dome could never have been done without enormous commercial backing. And no substantial company would have been interested in anything overtly government driven.'

Puttnam and Newbigin were also speaking to Blair. Blair was still as interested as he had ever been. An inclusive national celebration which looked to the future; a celebration of creativity and genius; something that would be the biggest and best in the world: those were all 'boxes Blair could tick as part of the project' on which he had been engaged for years. But, in a thought which would find its echoes the following year in discussions with sponsors, he emphasised to them how important it was that it shouldn't be too much of a government enterprise. It had to be national, 'a UK thing'. Too crude a Labour or government branding on it would kill it. Of course, there was a recognition that if it was a success, it would be 'a huge mood statement and a fantastic run-in to an election campaign'. But if it went wrong, if the economy was taking a downturn, or if it rained all year, 'Ah ha, fifteen hospitals please.'

The political advisers at the DNH started going through the Dome's business plan. As a result of the long and ruffled history by which the plans had reached their present state, what they found looked bizarre. Everywhere, the numbers seemed to them sketchy or 'fudgy'. 'It was,' Newbigin says, 'like being in the souk in Marrakesh.' It also looked as if the whole process was back to front. As Newbigin says, 'They were hiring the art director before writing the script.'

This approach, as one might expect, was congenitally unfair. 'People assume ideas of perfection which are totally unreal sometimes,' Bob Ayling says. 'Life is a muddle. When you are trying to put together a show as quickly and as ambitiously as we are trying to put together Greenwich, there will be muddle and you just have to accept that.' The people at the DNH didn't.

A measurement of uncertainty had been conducted by Millennium Central in January and in May:

Risk in January	*Action by May*
CEO to have clear authority	Page appointed
Strong individual to manage consultants	David Trench appointed
Public sector accounting puts project at risk	Still at risk
Strong marketing director required	Bill Muirhead advising
Strong management of contingency funds	Page has them
No slack in programme	Construction manager chosen. Key tenders let for steel and roof fabric. Construction programme on schedule. Creative programme critical
Consider developing fall-back position in case of late opening	To be developed by end August 1997
Capital budget contingency inadequate	Raised
Marketing budget inadequate	Raised
Risks on commercial revenue	Additional sponsorship opportunities identified through sponsorship in kind. Provision for 15% shortfall in sponsorship and 25% shortfall in operating revenue
Visitor spend too high	Projection lowered
Visitor numbers too high	Two-session system adopted

Still, though, Chris Smith's scepticism was mounting. He was not essentially against a Dome. He wanted something at Greenwich – not extravagant and not merely a theme park, but something with a serious core which would reflect the very reasons for which Labour had just been elected. The plans as presented to him seemed fragile and gappy. His scepticism began to turn into alarm.

Jennie Page herself came under some fierce scrutiny. Ministers in the new government did not know her well and she found herself having to address some sceptical audiences both at the DNH and in the Mandelson group. She was tested on all sides. Pillman and the officials at the department were focusing on the process – the management, the difficulties in hiring people and the scale of money involved. The politicians were anxious about the outcome – would the Dome company deliver and if so what? Newbigin, with Puttnam and his experience at Enigma Productions behind him, was anxious about Page herself. She seemed 'like a production manager, rather than a director or even the producer of a film. You had to ask, "Where was the creative drive here? Where was the vision?" '

On all sides, the review was a deliberately intolerant process. It aimed to test by hostility. For the Millennium Commission, Bovis were seen, according to Jeff Hawkins at Millennium Central, to be doing 'an immensely professional job, picking over the figures in the way any of us would. They looked at things fairly. We had forgotten about business rates in the plan. They pointed that out. Touche Ross were looking at the leisure aspects. They criticised our revenue projections as over-optimistic, which was pretty rich because they had been part of Barry Hartop's team the year before and they had predicted double our number.' Niggles aside, though, the professionals, on both sides of the fence, were fairly content.

It was the political anxieties that were mounting. The sponsorship situation, largely governed by the political uncertainties hanging over the project, remained exactly where it had always been: nothing whatsoever signed up. Imagination's travelling spheres, which had been intended to stimulate local enthusiasm for the exhibition, had now been cut from the national programme, 'to be replaced by using the media extensively', as the plan put it. The budget was still very large. All this concerned the Labour government.

The progress of the multi-headed review was beginning to slip. The sixth of June, the critical date for placing the piling contract, came and went. Jennie Page placed the contract all the same. She had to act as if the future were certain. There was nothing else she could do. Isolated from the processes of government, she and her team could only await the verdict. Jeff Hawkins prepared a plan for closure, the winding up of the company and the cancellation of contracts. A two-page paper on content was prepared and delivered to Peter Mandelson. Telephone call after telephone call was made around Whitehall to try and find out which way the wind was blowing. 'This project,' as Page says, 'would not have happened without the mobile phone.'

On 10 June Page was asked to come to Downing Street – as she thought to give a factual briefing to the Prime Minister. It was to be a small meeting, perhaps with one or two people from the policy unit there. She walked into the room to find herself confronted by Blair, Mandelson, Chris Smith, Peter Hyman, Hayden Phillips and Alastair Campbell, all lined up on the far side of the table. It was something of a bullpit for which Page was scarcely prepared. She was exposed to a difficult, probing and combative set of questions; she found herself resorting to the civil service language she despises.

Rumour had it that cancellation of the Dome had become one of the options. Now it became clear to Jennie Page that the rumours were true. Cancellation was on the table. Clare Pillman defended the terms on which the review was being conducted. 'We would have been utterly failing in our duty in reviewing this thing,' she says, 'not to have considered what other things you could do with this money. To test your hypotheses, you are looking at what else would create a national focus. Not "Shall we spend it on hospitals and schools?" But, given that this was meant to be a significant national focus for the millennium celebrations, was this the best way to achieve it?'

Page emerged from Downing Street shattered and appalled. That, she thought, was the death of the Dome. Unknown to her, she had made a dazzlingly good impression. Her sheer toughness under fire, particularly from Mandelson, her courage as the big beasts on the other side of the table tried to break her, her intelligence and knowledge of detail convinced them that if the job was to be done, she could do it. 'I meant to be aggressive,' Mandelson says. 'I wanted to test her, to see how she would perform. And it was a good performance, not conclusive, otherwise there would have been no continuing drift afterwards. But she gave a good enough performance. She has a very good presentational technique. It generates confidence.'

Blair couldn't make up his mind. Gordon Brown, the Chancellor, and Alistair Darling, Chief Secretary to the Treasury, were firmly against. Chris Smith was uncertain, not ready to jump either way, sceptical, feeling his way in this complex political situation. David Blunkett, Education Secretary, and Frank Dobson at Health were both against. Charlie Whelan, then Gordon Brown's press secretary, was briefing against the Dome and hinting that there was an anti-Dome alliance between Brown and John Prescott, the Deputy Prime Minister, lined up against the pro-Domeists Mandelson and Blair. That wasn't true. The situation was far more fluid than that and Prescott in particular resented being corralled in this way.

Time was slipping by. Blair's attention was on the immensely complex and technical details of his first EU summit as Prime Minister at Amsterdam. The date at which piling had to begin, Monday 23 June, was now approaching. Page rang the Millennium Commission, Hayden Phillips at the DNH and Mandelson to remind him of this date. She would have to get the pile-drivers in by then, come what may. If the government then decided to cancel the project, they would look pretty stupid. They were facing zero hour and they had better realise it.

Gez Sagar, the newly appointed head of Press and Parliamentary Affairs for the Dome, went to see John Prescott in his office in the House of Commons. Sagar thought he was going for a one-to-one meeting with the Deputy Prime Minister. When he got there, he found 'an array of civil servants', including Andrew Turnbull, then Permanent Secretary at the Department of the Environment, Transport and the Regions. Turnbull was known to be highly sceptical about the Dome and, as Sagar made his presentation to Prescott (he had worked for him in the past and knew him well), Turnbull and the other officials questioned him seriously and closely.

Prescott himself was sceptical about both the mood and the content of the show. Was it to be Disney? Or Alton Towers? Or an Expo? Was it a theme park? Would it have rollercoasters? 'We didn't have much language at the time,' Sagar says. 'It wasn't any of those things but it was more difficult to say what it was.' He talked about the great exhibitions of the past, the need and opportunity to mark the transition into the next millennium, the realistic nature of 12 million visitors as a projected total. Prescott remained fairly unimpressed.

Sagar turned to the questions of regeneration and transport – all nearer to Prescott's heart. Making use of the thinking that was current within MCL at the time, he described the role of the Dome in 'moving the centre of gravity of London to the east'. He floated the possibility of making the building permanent. He explained how the exhibition might demonstrate to the country as a whole that a great event could rely entirely on an integrated public transport system. He showed how the Dome, and the wider Thames-side development of which it was a part, could lay the foundations for a permanently viable river-boat service on the Thames. The officials continued to interrupt and challenge him. Prescott remained non-committal. Although, after the event, what Sagar calls 'black briefings' would come out of the DETR about his own performance, and although he couldn't know it at the time, Sagar had in fact struck home.

On 13 June NMEC representatives met Chris Smith and his advisers at the DNH. It was now clear that Smith was sliding further and further away from the Dome. He didn't like it. The Dome company's people were cagey in return. They were well aware of the rudimentary state of the contents. The view at the DNH was increasingly that a show about time was a conceptual vacuum. It was not, it seemed to them, a show about anything at all. The Saatchi/Burns/WCT redrafting of the governing ideas for the exhibition had scarcely stiffened into cartilage, let alone a bony skeleton with any flesh on it. Smith and others at the DNH came to one conclusion: there was no content.

Newbigin said, 'Tony can't see it. He can't see why he should take his children to it.' This was apocryphal: Blair had never mentioned his children in connection with the Dome. But Jenkins took it up. 'OK,' he said, 'I'll do it. I'll write to the Prime Minister to tell him what's in it for his children. But I don't want it going through you. I'll only do it if it goes in his box in exactly the form I write it.' Chris Smith agreed.

That weekend Jenkins wrote what became known as the 'Euan letter', named after Blair's eldest son. It was, in many ways, an act of the imagination, describing in some detail a long list of contents for which there were ideas but little substance. It was a vision of what Jenkins desired for the Dome, the exhibition whose existence he had nurtured now for three and a half years.

The Prime Minister
10 Downing Street
16 June 1997
Dear Tony,

I understand you are eager to know what will make your children want to go to Greenwich. Let me tell you.

Greenwich will be the world's one big Millennium celebration. The site is acquired, the Rogers Dome designed, the Foster station under construction. German, French, Italian and American planners all concede Britain's leadership here. Every child, including many from abroad will want 'to see Greenwich in 2000' and tell it to their grandchildren. Such events are milestones in a nation's history, but also in a child's life.

He went on to describe 'the forest of lasers radiating from the Dome, pointing around the nation'; the Drum show in which the children would see 'the story of life and the story of Britain, compressed into the most thrilling images'; the 60 pavilions in the remainder of the Dome on the theme of who we are, where we live and what we do. 'Many of the pavilions already have sponsors or are in discussion.' (That, it could safely be said, was an overstatement.) There was to be a virtual reality safari through the human body; a Frankenstein show on science and its misuses; a pavilion on British accents and dialect; the future of religion; the frontiers of play; the 'Trouble with Travel'; and British genius now. 'Every Victorian machine said, "Shown at the Great Exhibition". Every new one should say, "Shown at Greenwich".' Planetary Home Care would be 'a visual image of the earth's environment'. Home from Space would allow visitors 'to walk in space and see earth as others see it'. The young Blairs would enjoy a virtual reality tour around the Home of the Future and experience a century in the life of a tree and of a gnat.

I have tested these ideas on my own children [Jenkins concluded], from the theme tune to the Dome, from the river trip to the website, from the space walk to the food chain. I promise you, Greenwich is a future that will work. It will be Britain's proudest creation and proudest boast in the year 2000.

Yours sincerely
Simon Jenkins

The letter went into Blair's box on 16 June. By then, though, the Dome had been outflanked. The draft of the fairly hostile and parallel report which had been prepared by Bovis for the Millennium Commission had been submitted to the DNH. It had then been circulated around Whitehall without first giving Jennie Page or her team a chance to see it or comment on it. It looked as if the current was running against them.

The Millennium Central team scrabbled to catch up. They had to find a copy of the report and attempt to mend the gaps. It was all in the tone. According to Hawkins, the colour of what was said was rigorously negative: 'They've missed this. They're not very good, are they? They are not as good as they think they are.' It was a spike. Page and Hawkins were 'bloody angry'. Memos went screaming to Hayden Phillips at the DNH and to the commission. 'We weren't just going to roll over and play dead,' Hawkins says. 'If we're going to go down, we're going to go down with all guns blazing.'

Although the Page team didn't realise it, the political geography was shifting. The report on the Dome which Chris Smith submitted to the Home and Social Affairs Cabinet Committee carried no recommendation. 'If the decision had been solely for me to have made,' Smith says, 'I would have said, "Let's go ahead with an exhibition at Greenwich but let's make it a little less extravagant and a little more focused than the original conception, focused on something like the educational theme." But that wasn't something I deliberately tried to press on government. I said, "We have three options. We go ahead and here is what we have got to do if we are going to make it work. Or we pull out completely. Or we go for some sort of less grandiose scheme and here's the sort of thing which you can think about." It was perfectly clear to me that, with such a significant decision affecting so many government interests, my proper role at this point was simply to tease out the facts and lay out options for my colleagues.' In the high-machismo world of New Labour newly in government, that neutrality was not thought impressive by Dome supporters. They saw it as indecision.

Once again the Dome was approaching a life-or-death moment. The Ministerial Committee on Home and Social Affairs (HS) consisted of Mandelson and most of the Cabinet, excluding the Prime Minister. John Prescott was in the chair. There was, according to one of the ministers present, 'a headlong rush to condemn the Dome'. It was 'not a priority, it was a white elephant, it was a gigantic amount of money. Surely it could be put to more socially useful purposes?'

The Home Secretary, Jack Straw, argued to keep it on. He had been to the Festival of Britain. A nation needed something like this from time to time. Then Mandelson spoke. First, he said, Parliament had agreed to celebrate the millennium. It was desirable and useful to the country. It would provide a national focus. It would bring the country together. Secondly, it would project strength and confidence in Britain to the world, and would quite clearly be a showcase for a Labour government. And thirdly, to cancel it now, which would throw some £25 million down the drain and would show that the government couldn't rise to the occasion, would mean that the symbolism would work against them. There was no explicit talk of electoral significance for 2001, however implicit that might have been.

Prescott summed up. The subject was to be kept open. It was to go to a full Cabinet. This committee would report to Cabinet which, as most of the Cabinet was on this committee, meant in effect that they would report to the Prime Minister. In Cabinet and in this committee there was a clear majority against.

The Cabinet was on 19 June at 10.30 in the morning. Blair had been studying the Euan letter the day before. He was impressed but not convinced by it. Its slightly airy covering of conceptual vacuums was apparent. 'It revealed to the government,' one minister says, 'that MCL had not actually been holding anything back. There wasn't anything to hold back.' Blair was under pressure to make a decision. Mandelson had passed on the warnings from Page about the timetable. Blair knew he had little support in Cabinet to speak of. Jack Straw was for it, but not passionately. Mandelson continued to impress on the Prime Minister the need to force a closure of the issue. Any more drift and the thing would go off track. They couldn't end the week without a decision.

On the Thursday morning of the Cabinet Blair and Mandelson were due to meet at nine o'clock to discuss the issue. Together, they and the Number Ten policy unit would reach the point where Blair could finally make up his mind. It was his decision and could be no one else's. At 8.30 Mandelson got a call to come and see Blair in the Downing Street flat.

When Mandelson arrived, Blair was getting dressed. He couldn't see a way to a decision. He wanted to start the discussion immediately. They talked as he dressed, batting back and forth all the anxieties over the lack of content, the lack of national focus, the budget, the sponsorship, the thinness of the management, the temporariness of the building, the national mood, Gordon Brown's concerns – all this set against the opportunities the scheme would offer them if it was well done. A gamble: high price for failure; huge prize for success. At nine they went downstairs. They had fifteen minutes before the weekly bilateral pre-Cabinet meeting between Blair and Prescott.

At 9.20 the Dome's future was still unresolved. Blair was told that John Prescott was waiting. Encouraged by Mandelson, Blair said, 'Bring him in. Let's hear what he's got to say.' According to one of those present, Blair said, 'I don't know what to do about this Dome.'

Prescott: 'Throw in the towel? On this? What do you think people would say about that?'

Blair: 'So you think we should go ahead?'

Prescott: 'Yes I do.'

Blair: 'OK, we will.'

It was a matter of seconds. If Blair knew he had Prescott on side, then the objectors – Blunkett, Dobson and Brown in particular – were outflanked. The Cabinet began at 10.30. Discussions of all the other matters went on and on. Page was waiting anxiously in the Millennium Central office in Buckingham Palace Road, playing with Cherie Williams's Tamagotchi. Then she was summoned to the Cabinet Office to wait in a committee room – it had been Heseltine's white-sofaed office – for the verdict. Hayden Phillips was there, as was Rupert Huxter, Mandelson's private secretary, Clare Pillman and John Newbigin. 'We waited and waited,' Jennie Page says.

Towards the end of Cabinet Blair had to leave for a service in St Margaret's, Westminster. Prescott took the chair. One after another members of the Cabinet spoke against the Dome. 'John then pushed for it,' one minister remembers. 'Tony wants it,' he said. Then came the critical moment. Brown spoke. He had seen how things were falling out and in the light of this now proposed a conditional yes. The decision was made.

Over the previous few days discussion had already taken place between ministers and within the policy unit in Downing Street over what conditions the government might now impose on the Dome. The go-ahead would now be given to the Dome as long as it met five new criteria. In their published form these were:

- it would result in no extra burden on the public purse
- its content would entertain and inspire
- it would be a truly national event
- it would provide a lasting legacy
- the management structure of the operating company would be strengthened.

Each condition was code for an implied anxiety: the budget seemed flaky, the contents virtually absent, the national programme feeble, the temporariness of the Dome indefensible and the current management in need of strengthening. Apart from that, it seemed like a good idea. It was these terms which would give the Millennium Commission the surety it needed to award its full grant of £449 million to the Millennium Experience.

At 12.45 Blair came back from St Margaret's. Mandelson told him of the decision to go ahead. Jennie Page and Anji Hunter, the Prime Minister's assistant, had already discussed what might happen if the answer was yes. Blair had to go to Denver the following day. If he was to announce it himself, it had to be that afternoon. Mandelson, Purnell and Hyman all urged him to go down to Greenwich himself.

An immediate announcement at Greenwich and the idea that Peter Mandelson should be the shareholder, which had been a suggestion made to Blair by Jonathan Powell, were both sold to Chris Smith on the phone. Jennie Page, using her mobile in the Cabinet Office, 'which you would usually get hung, drawn and quartered for because of the security stuff', rang Bernard Ainsworth of McAlpine Laing, the construction managers, to tell him 'to expect an important visitor'. Blair, Mandelson, Smith and Prescott went down in their government cars. The press were waiting. 'These plans require a leap of faith,' Blair told them. 'It is not the easy thing to do. It is the bold thing to do.' Jennie Page and Claire Sampson didn't arrive at Greenwich until after the ministers had left. They had been stuck in traffic. Press reaction was fairly muted. It was another day in the life of the Dome. Blair had said yes, but what else had changed? Earthquake at Greenwich: not many dead.

The relationship between the new government and the Dome company began very much as it continued. At a relaunching press conference on 26 June Peter Mandelson, the Minister without Portfolio and the new shareholder of the company, had answered a question about sponsorship and the fees payable to IMG, Mark McCormack's group. Since the previous summer they had been charged with raising sponsorship for the Dome, which they had failed to do, largely because of the political uncertainties hanging over the project. Mandelson's venturing into this territory did not go down well with the MCL board. Mandelson was told, and accepted, that all commercial decisions and their announcements had to be made by the Dome company and not by him. Nevertheless, there was a real ambiguity here. Mandelson had been replying to a direct question about sponsorship from a *Daily Telegraph* journalist. The very fact that he was being asked demonstrated that, on this project, there was no clear dividing line between 'political' and 'commercial'. In this semi-quango, this publicly owned limited company, charged with the greatest national celebrations ever seen, financed in part by the private sector and in part with public lottery money, the political was the commercial and vice versa.

There was, of course, a backlog of disquiet on this subject. At the very first meeting of the MCL board in the BA offices in Berkeley Square the previous February they had discussed the terms of the grant from the Millennium Commission and the Treasury-approved memorandum controlling Millennium Central as a quango. Bob Ayling had already spoken to Hayden Phillips about the problem of government control. The Permanent Secretary had assured him that, despite the apparent strictness of the terms, the company would in fact be given considerable latitude in the management of its own affairs and that government departments would not interfere with the company's business more than was necessary to ensure proper accountability.

It was an inherently spiky situation. MCL's pushing for operating room was combined with an insistence that if this were a private sector company, reliant for almost half its income either on sponsor companies or on the spending of visitors, it could not be at the beck and call of government. There were the makings of a soreness here which the events of the coming months did little to alleviate.

Mandelson came round to the Dome offices. He said he wanted to speak to everybody. The staff gathered in the boardroom and he talked to them quietly and with charm. He wanted to 'draw a line under the awfulness'. They would change the name and relaunch the Dome. They could trust him. He knew a bit about relaunching organisations. He'd done it twice with the Labour Party. Once it had flopped but the second time it hadn't. 'We might have dithered and delayed,' he said, 'but we are in for the duration. Roll up your sleeves. Here we go!'

This amalgam of exhortation, confidence and confessed-to fallibility, on the back of the huge prestige of the election victory, disarmed many of those present. Mandelson, good at the political arts of remembering names and asking how people are, at home in the world of politicised show business in which the Dome was operating, well connected in a variety of different spheres, an acute and productive critic of scripts for commercials, designs for exhibits and press strategies, felt to many of those in the company like 'a breath of fresh air, the first time that you had the big commitment from a big public figure who understood and was on your side'.

For the whole of his tenure at the company, from June 1997 until December 1998, this appreciation of his qualities would sit alongside the more structural prickliness endemic in the situation. Here was an energetic minister busying himself with the microscopic details of a company which, in one part of its identity, was meant to be independent of government. Yet here too was a company in receipt of an enormous lottery grant and in whose fortunes the fortunes of the government itself were deeply embroiled. For Mandelson in particular, the entire project was drenched in political anxiety. He had done a great deal to persuade Blair to back the Dome. He had to deliver it. A failed Dome would be the symbol of a failed government. As all those involved came to realise, the downside was far greater than any political advantage that might accrue. Success might well be met with a cynical 'So what?' from the press and country. Failure would bring a thundering 'I told you so.' As they came under increasingly heavy press attack, in the context of a desperate need for sponsorship to make the whole scheme stand up, it is scarcely surprising that tolerances were thin and arguments frequent.

There was already a company called New Millennium Ltd. For a new name, that was the ideal choice: simple, to the point and clear. The directors of the company demanded £50,000 for the name. They were offered £1,500, which they turned down. Instead, Millennium Central acquired two potentially desirable shelf companies: New Millennium Exhibition Ltd and New Millennium 2000 Ltd. Mandelson liked 'new' ('True to New Labour it was always going to have new in it') but didn't like the word 'exhibition'. 'Experience' was better because it was people-based. And so, *faute de mieux*, on 2 July the company became an ugly mouthful, 'The New Millennium Experience Company Ltd'. By the end of the year it was calling itself NMEC in corporate literature and press releases, pronounced 'Enmec' in conversation. That was preferable to 'Enemy C', because that invited the joke, 'If they are C, who are Enemies A and B?' Millennium Central might, as they had been promised by senior figures in London Underground, become the name of the stop on the Jubilee Line. (It didn't because 'North Greenwich', was already embedded in the complex and fragile software operating the line and its trains. To change it would have cost several million pounds and would add another layer of risk to the programme.)

At about four o'clock on 23 June 1997, the Monday afternoon after the Cabinet decision had been taken, the first of the 8,000 piles went in, precisely on schedule. Eighteen rigs poured on to the site and began to drive the piles into the Greenwich earth. Not all the contamination had been purged from the polluted ground of the old gasworks. Much of it was now sealed in with clean crushed stone, laid over the whole site in a carpet 45 centimetres thick. The lower boundary between that clean 'engineered fill' and the contamination beneath it was marked with an orange 'warning demarcation layer'. Anyone digging on the site would know when to stop, or at least when to adopt the necessary protective measures. Above the fill would be a vapour membrane made of sheets of heavy-duty, heat-sealed polyethylene, themselves held in place by a layer of sand. The Dome was shielded as much from the nature of the ground below as from the weather above.

Because of these conditions it was important that the piling brought as little as possible of the spoil up to the surface. For this reason most of the piles were 'cast in situ' on a 3-by-3-metre grid. A hollow steel tube with a detachable tip is driven into the ground. This is then filled with steel reinforcing rods and concrete poured in over them. The tube is then withdrawn, leaving the concrete of the pile to go off in situ. All 8,000 were installed within a remarkable thirteen weeks, driven to an average depth of 11 metres on to sustaining layers either of gravels or London clay.

Where the southbound carriageway of the Blackwall road tunnel ran under the site, the Highways Agency insisted that piles could not be driven or vibrated into place. The piles were also required to go very deep, on to layers beneath the tunnel, to avoid any possibility of loading the tunnel structure itself. Here, and in a 67-metre-wide band running across the site in which the Highways Agency planned to build a third road crossing of the Thames, cast in situ piles could not be used. Fat corkscrew augers were employed to extract the soil and the concrete pumped in as they were withdrawn. At ground level beams were then installed over the tunnel on which any structures could rest. The contaminated soil was trucked away to registered sites, most of them in old brickworks in impervious clay in the Midlands.

At last construction of the Dome itself could begin. Since it had first jumped out at Mike Davies and Gary Withers over a year before, the building had gone through a series of evolutions. Davies had initially suggested stiff ribs to the umbrella but the engineer Ian Liddell of Buro Happold had immediately changed that to a cable network – far cheaper, simpler and easier to manage. The first concept also had a 400-metre diameter but that, they soon realised, would not fit comfortably on the peninsula. Another early suggestion for two rings of masts, an inner of twelve, an outer of 24, would, it was felt, not provide the internal clarity of space required. A single ring of masts was retained, made taller to accommodate the stresses the masts would have to carry, and moved outward to create a huge central space. Finally, the very straightforward early scheme whereby the Dome roof came down to the same level around its entire perimeter, and was fixed there with raking ground anchors attached to the end of the paired radial cables, very much like a circular marquee, did not feel right. The Richard Rogers architects wanted a scalloped edge. Each pair of radials, rather than coming down to the same level, would be gathered at the edge by big catenary cables anchored to 24 reinforced concrete anchor blocks.

The very effect which the Dome now produces – its complex mix of monumentality and lightness – is the result of that change. At those 24 points it touches the ground with no more than its fingertips, giving a sense of openness and delicacy – millennial qualities. But at the same time, because of the forces concentrated there, the anchor blocks themselves need to be of a heroic scale. The steel fabrications attaching the various cables and stays to the blocks are almost Victorian in the relish with which they approach their task: immense in substance, precise in function, and somehow full of wit in their toy-like vastness. Nowhere is the beauty and charm of the Dome more apparent. 'Here,' the building says, 'look what I'm doing.' There is no deceit.

The Dome, with its huge span, draws on bridge technology. The twelve masts can be seen as six pairs of diametrically opposed towers with six giant but delicate suspension bridges strung between them. Nested together, these six bridges create the cable net which is the structural essence of the Dome. The white fabric panels are scarcely more than cladding. The cables in the net perform five different functions: the radials, in 72 pairs, aligned along the radii of the Dome, create the huge span of the building; the circumferentials, in seven rings, keep the paired radials evenly spaced; the hangers suspend the radials from the masts, one hanger attached to every point where a paired radial and a circumferential cross – each mast supports each of the six paired radials in seven different places; the thick catenary cable which brings the net down to the anchor blocks; and the giant backstays, also coming down the anchor blocks and like guy ropes holding the masts in the correct position.

As a building, it dramatises the engineering by which it works. Glyn Trippick of Buro Happold explains: 'The more you try and tighten the radial cables, the more they try to pull down and straighten, the more they stress and tighten the hanger cables. You are tensioning the radials against tension in the hangers.' The tension in the hanger cables arrives at the top of the mast and effectively attempts to squeeze the mast. Any long member or strut when compressed in this way will want to buckle under the stress. Hence the shape of the mast. The wider something is, the less likely it is to buckle. Anything that is fixed at both ends is most likely to buckle in the middle, just as a ruler does when squeezed. So the mast has to be cigar-shaped, fattest where it is most likely to buckle.

'This wasn't a puzzle, we weren't playing a game with anyone,' says the engineer Ian Liddell. 'We just wanted efficiency. There is an inevitability on a structure like this and that has a satisfaction in itself. The structure is the building. Everything is engineering. It appears simple. The trick is knowing it is going to work.' That is the sense in which the Dome is an act of the engineer's imagination: a necessary fusion of the aesthetic, the functional and the daring needed to make the biggest roof in the world.

It is best engineering practice, because it is cheaper, easier and more efficient, to use the smallest amount of material you can to do the job. Where fatness is required, as it is in a strut that won't buckle, you must spread your material as wide as you can. That is why the masts are not solid but a lattice-work of steel tubes – in effect a tube of tubes – welded with horizontal members to keep them correctly spaced. They are the shape their function demands, repeating not only the 1951 Skylon, but the struts of le Corbusier's radical modernist pavilion at the great Paris show of 1937.

Having decided on this shape of mast, and having reduced the amount of steel to the minimum, you design a mast that uses steel tubes which you can buy off the shelf. Both the vertical and horizontal tubes in the Dome's masts are standard sections, easily and cheaply available.

The actual geometry of the building was decided by a combination of practicability in putting it up and usefulness of the space created. Too shallow a Dome would have made the margins inside difficult to use, the exhibition structures having to crouch under the canopy as it narrowed to a shallow gradient towards the edge. Too steep a dome would have been wasteful and difficult to put up. The comfortable shape of the canopy is the result of a balance between a curve that is steep enough for peripheral exhibits to fit and one that is not too high in the centre. The height of the masts was then calculated to achieve that geometry. The resulting shape is a very shallow slice off the top of a sphere which has a diameter of 700 metres and a theoretical centre 300 metres below ground. All the masts point towards that centre, both the twelve main masts and the 72 perimeter masts. The two sets fall on the surface of two cones, one steeper and narrower, the other shallower and broader. The tips of both cones are at the theoretical centre of the sphere.

If, in some ways, this rationality points to the Dome as a classical building, multiple in its symmetries and with a Euclidian foundation to its forms, it is also in many ways the heir, curious as it might sound, to the gothic tradition. The explicitness of its structures – the way in which you can clearly see at every point how it works – is a gothic quality: its cables and masts are the modern versions of the flying buttress and the clustered pier. The Dome does not conceal its means of existence. It has no facade. It is self-exposing and self-explanatory, a radial cathedral in modern gothic.

Why, you might ask, are the masts so high? In part there is an aesthetic reason. Mike Davies compares their 100-metre-high, 17-degree outstretch to a huge celebratory flinging of arms into the air. The Van Gogh cornfield yellow in which they are painted, a late decision, is also part of that impulse, as is the red aircraft warning light with which each of them is crowned at night. The legal requirement was for three lights, not twelve. The Dome's masts are its crown of glory.

But, as Ian Liddell says, 'Engineers are ruling the roost here,' and there is a good functional reason for their height. If the masts had been shorter, the hanger cables would have been shallower and, to produce the same vertical lift in them, the force needed would have been much greater. A reduction of 20 metres in the mast height, according to Glyn Trippick, would have doubled the force on those cables. The cables themselves would have begun to thicken out of all proportion. Everything is coherent. The need for tightness in the radial cables, to make a cable net that was quite stiff, lay behind both the height and the shape of the masts.

The Dome had to be designed for the worst possible conditions. If a hurricane blew, the uplift effect of the wind over the roof would tend to raise it by up to 3 metres. That would be a problem at the point where the masts penetrate the skin: it would have been almost impossible to keep such a mobile joint waterproof. To control the movement, the engineers introduced tie-down cables, attaching the cable net to the bottom of the masts. But those cables inside the Dome would have got in the way of the exhibition. To avoid that conflict, the foot of each mast was raised on to the apex of a 10-metre-high four-footed pyramid.

Outside those pyramidal feet is the most hidden aspect of the building.

Part of the enormous tension overhead ends up squeezing down on to the legs of the masts' quadrupod bases. Other parts of it are brought to earth in the beautiful anchor blocks, with their huge vertical anchors driven 25 metres into the clay beneath them. But the pull on those anchors is not entirely vertical. There is a strong horizontal component to it, straining inwards towards the centre of the Dome. That is held by a huge concrete ring beam, which stretches around the whole perimeter of the building, a kilometre long and 8 metres wide, but only 60 centimetres thick. 'You think it is just a floor, but it's one of the things that are holding the Dome up,' Glyn Trippick says.

If there was a heavy snowstorm, the weight of snow on the Dome could approach 3,000 tonnes. Fabric structures – this would happen to the roof of the Olympic Stadium in Montreal in January 1999 – occasionally fail when the weight of snow or of 'ponded' water on them builds up to the point where the fabric tears. The shape of the Dome roof has one natural advantage in this. Where it is flattest, at the top, the segments of cloth are at their narrowest. As the span of the fabric increases, so does their slope. But there was a hazard. The circumferential cables, required to separate the radials, whose natural tendency would be to bunch together next to the masts, usually lie in the same plane as the fabric. If this happened here, there would be a danger of making a small dam against which any run of water would build up, precisely the ponding that had to be avoided. Liddell got round this problem by raising the circumferential cables on cable rings three, four and five above the level of the paired radials on stiff steel posts he called 'wishbones', connecting the top of each wishbone to the neighbouring nodes with criss-cross wires as a means of bracing them.

Engineering applies safety to leaps of the architectural imagination. The very apex of the Dome's roof now came under Liddell's scrutiny. Originally, there had been plans for a huge disc, 10 metres across, with 144 holes along its perimeter, to hold the radial cables. What if the steel disc broke? The entire structure would collapse. The quadrupods had been designed so that if one leg failed, the mast would stay standing. If one of the hangers or radials broke, the Dome itself would not collapse. But with this central disc there could be no safety belt. It would not do. Liddell replaced it with a 30-metre-wide cable ring, made up of twelve 48-mm cables. If six of them broke, the others would hold the Dome. 'It would be like a jet flying on two engines,' Liddell says. 'Not marvellous but not catastrophic either.'

Within the central ring a stiff arrangement of ventilation louvres was installed. The 35,000 people and the vast amounts of electricity used by the exhibition – a 48-megawatt capacity in a new tunnel under the Thames – would generate huge amounts of heat. Using precisely the ventilation principles of a Mongolian yurt, the Dome would be able to open holes at the apex of its roof to let out the hot air. The problem of ponding at the peak of the fabric roof would also be avoided. The ventilation panels were designed with a radial slope so that water would run off them.

The question of what fabric to put on the roof had been live for many months. The decision taken in the course of 1996 that the exhibition and its buildings should be temporary was made largely on the basis of cost. For a temporary building, there was little point in using a material which was designed to have a long life if a cheaper, short-life alternative were available.

Nevertheless, Millennium Central had been troubled by the legacy question for months. Faced with decisions on materials in the spring of 1997, they were in two minds. Should they commit themselves to cheaper short-term solutions, or to the more expensive alternatives, which at least kept their options open?

On the fabric there were essentially two choices: one polyester coated with PVC, the other woven glass-fibre coated with Teflon (PTFE). The first was cheap (about £6 million) but, because it degrades under ultraviolet light, would probably last satisfactorily no more than ten years. The PTFE option, it was thought, might cost as much as £15 million but would be much longer lasting. The fabric had been used in 1973 for a campus centre at LaVerne, California, in 1981 for the Haj Terminal at Jedda, Saudi Arabia, and at the same time for a sports dome in Syracuse, New York. In desert heat, in sunny California and exposed to the severe winters of New York State, PTFE could clearly function well for many years.

The choice was, as ever with this project, immensely difficult and multi-dimensional. Greenpeace were conducting a worldwide campaign against PVC, claiming that both its manufacture and its careless disposal released poisons into the environment which no millennial project should or could contemplate doing. A PVC Dome was 'a toxic, plastic, throwaway monster'.

Ian Liddell, the Buro Happold engineer, had a clear preference for PVC. The bluish light it transmitted would give a more natural feeling of daylight within the Dome than the slightly brownish light which PTFE lets through. It also admitted more daylight, perhaps about 11 per cent compared with 8 per cent for the Teflon-glass. PVC did sometimes get a little grubby and fungus might penetrate its fibres but Liddell felt sure that the PVC Dome would never have felt murky. As a material PVC was more flexible than PTFE, and so was easier to work on site. As there was a great deal of PVC being used in the coatings to the electrics in the Dome anyway, and it would never be a PVC-free site, there was no reason why they shouldn't go for the cheaper option.

Going down the OJEC route, the Dome company asked all bidders to quote for both fabrics. Five companies expressed an interest in supplying this vast order for 300,000 square metres. The initial five soon shrank to three: Koch Hightex GmbH of Germany (which later went into administration and changed its name to Chiemgauer Membran und Zeltbau), Birdair of Buffalo in New York and Cannobio of Italy. Koch and Cannobio both came in with a low price on PVC. Birdair was more expensive on PVC but offered a very sharp price on PTFE. Koch and Cannobio were both expensive on PTFE.

Only in April was a choice made: PVC from Koch Hightex. Koch were not going to manufacture it themselves but were going to procure it from either a French or one of two German suppliers. They would buy the material in large rolls from which they would fabricate specifically designed, fitted segments for the Dome roof. Those would be required on site in March 1998. PVC was the decision, robustly researched and made on utterly defensible economic grounds.

The entire environment in which this decision was to be made changed in the summer of 1997. Tony Blair, responding to a feeling in the country at large, was insistent that the Dome should be part of the physical legacy. It had to last. Otherwise the building looked like an act of pure profligacy. PVC suddenly seemed to be a problem. It was incapable of lasting. On top of that, in July, the pressure from Greenpeace came back on. It is a usual practice of Greenpeace (whose membership had dropped from 312,000 at the beginning of the decade to 215,000 in 1997) to conduct high-profile campaigns (oil exploration around Rockall, the disposal of redundant oil rigs, genetically modified crops) in the low-news season of mid summer. In 1997 it was the Dome's turn. Greenpeace threatened publicly to occupy the site. It was precisely not what the new government wanted.

The Prime Minister's requirement that the Dome should be permanent dovetailed precisely with Greenpeace's strictures against PVC. If the budget and timetable could take it, the two forces pointed in the same direction. Longevity for the Dome would be an aspect of its environmental credentials, would form part of its identity as a green, resource-efficient, water-conservative building, making a new step into a millennial future, and would represent the best practice then current.

Jennie Page asked Peter English if they still had time to go for a PTFE option. 'Yes,' he said, 'but we must place an order within a fortnight.' He got on the phone to Koch Hightex. 'We might be changing to PTFE,' he told them. 'If we do, can you stay within the programme? I want the answer today.' For two or three days they provided no answer. Eventually English got through to Michael Koch. Koch Hightex were in the middle of sourcing 'the Mina Valley job' for the Saudis. Nearly 2 million square metres of PTFE were required at Mecca for tents to house pilgrims to the Haj. The world supply was being mopped up. Suddenly it looked as if the Dome was in danger of having no fabric cladding that was acceptable. Koch said he couldn't be sure of meeting the programme because he didn't know if he could get all the PTFE that was needed.

The Dome was looking another disaster in the face. A week had passed since Page had signalled the change in material and no progress had been made. English spoke to Stan Kopaskie at Birdair in America. Were they still interested? Kopaskie thought it was a joke, or at least that NMEC was just comparing prices. Nevertheless, he said that Birdair could deliver. David Trench, NMEC's site and structures director, flew out to Buffalo, New York. Both the demands of the Dome's own programme and the state of world supply meant that time was short. Had Michael Koch confirmed that he could deliver the material, NMEC might easily have gone with him. But he didn't, so they didn't.

Once Jennie Page had established in her own mind the relevant facts, she brought the issue to Mandelson. She had told him repeatedly, as the Greenpeace campaign wound up in the press, that, largely because of the budget and timetable, it would be difficult to change from PVC in the current circumstances. The building had been designed for PVC, at least a provisional commitment had been made to Koch Hightex for its manufacture, and to change now could endanger the delivery of the Dome itself. As the papers reported both in Sydney and in Stockholm that year, Greenpeace had driven public bodies to renounce PVC. Privately Page was looking into the viability of PTFE as an alternative but she wasn't putting Mandelson fully in the picture until she was certain of where she stood. In August she raised the issue.

By the middle of the month the acute decision point was approaching fast. David Trench was at the headquarters of Birdair. He told Page on the phone that, given the international supply situation, the decision on the fabric had to be made that day. Page said, 'Give me an hour.' She was in a shed on site. It was a baking hot day. The pile-drivers were hammering into the remade Greenwich earth all around her. Page 'picked up the phone to Mandelson's office and I said, "I need five minutes on the phone with him." They put him on and I said, "I just want you to sit and listen. I don't want you to say anything. I want to tell you what the situation is. These are the options. This is what it looks like. This is what I think we ought to do. These are the risks if we do it."' Mandelson listened, thought for a moment and gave the go-ahead for PTFE. He didn't mind the need for an instant decision. Election campaigns are full of such moments. Page rang Trench in Buffalo and Trench placed the order.

The PVC contract was terminated on 19 August 1997 and the PTFE contract with Birdair signed ten days later. Birdair had built many of the USA's major stadium roofs with this material. It was a safe option. The new fabric cost £8 million more than the old and added three months to the design programme – a delay which over the coming winter, with the engineers putting in night after night of design work, establishing the new means of fitting the stiffer fabric to the cable net was, incredibly, accommodated. According to the construction programme originally devised by Buro Happold in the last months of 1996 and developed by construction managers McAlpine Laing in 1997, the first panel of roof cladding was to be installed on 23 March 1998. They hit that mark to the day.

By 13 October the masts had been welded together on site, with the huge ventilator fans fitted inside them, and were lying like a fall of spillikins, each weighing 90 tonnes, waiting to be picked up. The piles had been driven, the ring beam cast and the erection surface prepared. The anchor blocks were not quite all ready but they could be finished as the masts went up. Time was that tight. The biggest crane in Europe was hired. It arrived in parts – in 24 separate trucks. A slightly smaller crane arrived to lift and steer the foot of each mast on to the head of its pyramidal base. In something of a contrast to the shenanigans in the political world, the twelve steel masts went up in two weeks, with no hitches, precisely placed, temporarily guyed. Little wonder that engineers look down on other mortals.

Now for the cable net. The central cable ring was assembled, attached to its hanger cables and then hauled into position with winches in the heads of the masts. Rings two and three, with their radials and their hangers attached, were then winched up, then rings four and five, then six and seven. The aim was to create the largest possible pre-assemblies that could be lifted so as to minimise the number of connections that had to be made in the air.

Apart from a break at the end of January 1998, when the weather cleared for a couple of weeks, conditions were atrocious. All those putting up the cable net had a miserable time: they were searingly cold, particularly in December, in the biting wind coming in off the North Sea. High-level abseilers working for Watson Steel, led by Ian McNeill from Llanberis in North Wales, were hired to rig up the net, one by one connecting loose radials to the nodes on the circumferentials. It was needlepoint at 100 metres. McNeill, a mountaineer and North Sea veteran, handpicked his team – an inspirational crew, including an ex-Royal Marine, a Canary Wharf steelwork inspector, an Army Corps helicopter pilot, a tall-ship bosun's mate, a Christmas decoration specialist, a rock-face rescuer and a Himalayan mountaineer. In time, as the fabric was going on, there would be 82 climbers and abseilers crawling over the 72 kilometres of cable net.

The entire net now hung loosely from the masts, a baggy and formless thing, like the skin of a puppy whose body has yet to grow into it. The tension, which, in one of the comparisons those working on the Dome came to love, was equivalent to the full thrust of 25 jumbo jets at take-off, would pull the net into shape. Each paired radial cable was tightened at the same time as the one diametrically opposite on the far side of the

Dome. At the head of each of the short perimeter masts which give shape to the net at its outer edge, where the radials come down to the boundary cable, there is a stressing point. They are marked on the skin of the Dome itself by yellow rain caps. Under those caps, in Glyn Trippick's words, 'are some stonking great rigging screws that give you a foot adjustability either way'. An enormously powerful hydraulic tension jack pulled down on the radial cables and the screws were tightened to take up the slack. Slowly, first to 20 per cent, then 80, then 95 and finally to the full design tension, the cables were tightened and the net began to assume the fullness of its intended shape. The people from Watson Steel and the Buro Happold engineers monitored both the geometry and the stress in the cables. If all the perimeter masts were in the right position and at the right angle to the ground, the tension would be correct. They managed to bring every one of those masts to within 25 mm – an inch – of its intended position.

There were no more than one or two serious incidents. When the entire net had been erected and tautened, it was discovered that several sets of cables were the wrong length, some had been delivered too short and some too long. Desperate anxiety ran throughout the engineering team. The programme was too critical for it all to be taken down again. But the error, miraculously, turned out not to be as bad as it had looked. Short and long cancelled each other out. Two of the circumferential rings were not precisely at their intended position but that did not affect the performance of the net. The gap between circumferentials three and four was longer than designed, by about 10 centimetres or 4 inches. It would mean a redesign of the point where fabric panels joined, it slightly altered the shape of the Dome, which is about 30 centimetres higher than intended (because the hangers were also short), and changed the angles of the main masts by about 1.5 degrees. Apart from that, all was as it should be. A small mistake – the inevitable consequence, as one of the contractors says, 'of working at speed with this technological beast'.

The most alarming episode resulted from pure oversight. At the points where the radials are connected to the boundary cable there are large friction clamps. Unless the bolts of these clamps are properly tightened, both the clamp and the cables are in danger of slipping once the tension is applied. The forces involved are very large indeed. As the tension was brought to bear on the radial cables, one of the clamps slipped. A judder ran through the entire network and a shock wave travelled around the whole system. The principle on which the cable net is constructed means that any significant physical event in one part is immediately communicated to all others. One of the radial/boundary clamps had been tightened only two-thirds of the full amount. Possibly affected by the extra wind-pressure on the cable net produced by the newly installed fabric panels, the loosely fitted clamp had slipped along the boundary cable a distance of 2 metres.

Although they should have known about the huge amounts of redundancy in the system, so that if one cable or clamp failed, the Dome would certainly not fall down, the abseilers scrambled for the security of the giant central scaffold, a construction which was visibly self-supporting and did not depend on the tension and anchorage system by which the masts and cables were held up.

Perhaps, in this incident, one can glimpse the roots of a more general anxiety about the Dome. Its very lack of reliance on the sort of post-and-beam system which supports conventionally engineered structures; the absence of any form of reference to the ancient categories of basement, living space and attic; its elision of roof and wall; the mobility of the structure despite its vastness – skin, cables and masts all move in the wind: perhaps all these departures from conservative norms intuitively troubled a conservative nation at a time when many social and cultural certainties had also begun to seem more mobile and less dependently organised than they had been. The Dome looks as if it could be undone and redivided into its constituent parts. Although the specification changes in the second half of 1997 turned it into a permanent and, with maintenance, an everlasting building – in other words as permanent as any building is permanent – the country continued to think that it wasn't, and that they were paying for a temporary tent. Was the Dome's problem not that it was too big and too grandiose, but that it wasn't grandiose enough?

Mike Davies, the project architect, when he saw the cable net up and complete in March 1998, loved and wondered at it: 'The net is the real structure. It looks like a gossamer spider's web, minimalist, beautiful. If you take the skin off, the whole thing disappears, there's a just a bit of framework left.' For Davies, and for all those who can look confidently at the world, that lightness and anti-monumentality, the elasticity of

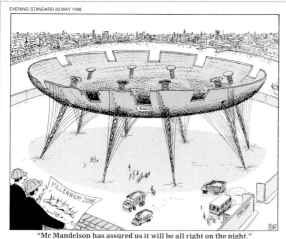

EVENING STANDARD 29 MAY 1998

"Mr Mandelson has assured us it will be all right on the night."

Even amidst the flood of vitriol, cartoons of the Dome marked the extent to which the project had entered national consciousness, a level of recognition any marketing director would envy.
Left: May 29 1998
Below: November 27 1998

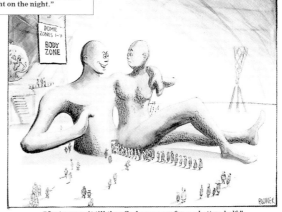

"Just you wait till they find a sponsor for my bottom half."

Below: Michael Heseltine and Peter Mandelson at the topping out ceremony on June 22 1998: an unmistakable identity of purpose beyond party allegiance.

Left: At the topping out ceremony, Blair looks up to abseilers descending from the roof of the Dome. 'A year ago,' he said, 'this was a patch of derelict land. People said it could not be built on time. Today, the masts are up, the roof is on. It is on time, on track and on budget.'

Above: By December 1998, the Dome had taken its place as a London landmark, already becoming as much a symbol of the city as the Eiffel Tower was of Paris. Anything on a smaller scale would not have had the same effect.

Left: At night, the translucent roof expressed the life inside the Dome just as much as it admitted the sunlight during the daytime. It was always part of the architect's intention that this should not be a dead monument but a responsive and living structure.

Left: In June 1998, the company had announced they would train 100 young people for the Mark Fisher/Peter Gabriel central show. 'Likely candidates,' the advertisement had said, 'will include gymnasts, trampolinists, divers, dancers, existing performers and rock climbers.' This is the stilts training class at the Circus Space in Hackney, during November that year.

Above: Politicians. Back row: Peter Mandelson; Chris Smith; Roger Freeman. Front row: Virginia Bottomley; Michael Heseltine; Charlie Falconer

Left: The Litmus Group, set up to advise NMEC on coherence, quality, entertainment and educational potential of proposed content for the Dome. Back row, left to right: John Newbigin; John Sorrell; Neil Cossons; Christopher Frayling; Simon Jenkins; Floella Benjamin; Ruth Mackenzie. Front row, left to right: Alan Yentob; Richard Rogers; Michael Grade; David Puttnam; Mike Davies.

Left: Eva Jiricna, principal designer of **Faith**.

Right: Tim Pyne, designer of **Living Island, Work, Learning** and the contents of **Shared Ground**.

Left: The central amphitheatre in June 1999. The promenade around the amphitheatre is virtually complete. The tall lighting towers around the amphitheatre are up and some of the seating is in place. On the left the bristly steel skeleton of **Body** and on the right **Talk** are both approaching their final form. The scale, which is difficult to grasp, can be measured by the two construction workers leaning against the balustrade in the foreground.

Below: Zaha Hadid, designer of **Mind**.

Left: The canting brow of the Millennium Pier – a bridge leading to the landing stage – is lifted into place on May 17 1999. 85 metres long and weighing 200 tonnes, it was designed to have no more than a 1:12 slope, even at the lowest of tides, allowing easy access for the disabled. The wall of Skyscape is in the background.

Below: Skyscape sponsored by BSkyB. NMEC hired this ready-made event building from a modular staging company, Edwin Shirley Staging. It houses two cinemas in which the Blackadder special is shown.

existence it implies, represents one of the core virtues. It makes a building not into a prison or a straitjacket, but a symbol of generosity and freedom. The new titanium-clad Guggenheim Museum in Bilbao by the American deconstructionist Frank Gehry was opened as the Dome was being created. For Davies, it represented the mirror-opposite of everything he wanted to do with his building: stiff where the Dome was 'loose-fit'; discordant where the Dome was calm; impositional where the Dome itself decided nothing about its use or content; mimicking a dynamism in its forms, but frozen into a single gesture; not allowing but dictating; a pastiche of freedom, not a vehicle for it. But the Bilbao museum immediately became the most admired new building in Europe for a decade. Did it feed precisely the appetite for monumentality from which the Dome so deliberately held back?

As the team of 80-odd abseilers and rope-access workers, using cavers' rope because it does not stretch, began to install the huge roof panels in the spring of 1998, struggling with the wind that would pick up the 1-tonne panels and flick them out of their hands, all the questions about what this great lid, this enormous act of architectural modesty, was there to contain were already well into their most critical and creative phase.

CHAPTER SEVEN

Filling It

How were they going to fill it? They could take some steers from the situation around them. Tony Blair's commitment to 'education, education, education' was at least on a safe trend. By the time Labour was elected, expenditure on education had risen by 12 per cent in real terms since the beginning of the decade. It was the one area of government spending – with health – which did not draw criticism from taxpayers. Labour was joining a train, not starting one. If the Dome could be educational as well as inspirational, it could share in that current of goodwill.

The money worries which had characterised both private and public finances in the early nineties were on their way out. Although the class and regional differences remained huge, average real income had grown steadily throughout the decade. Unemployment, which had reached a peak of 2.9 million in 1993 – a figure which Norman Lamont had described as 'a price worth paying' for the defeat of inflation – was now heading down below 2 million. Anyone going on holiday to Italy or Spain, which had seemed more expensive than Britain in the early nineties, would now find life cheaper there. The strike had faded into history. There was an optimism and a sense of opportunity in the air.

But civilisation has its discontents. There was a widespread longing for 'hope' and 'a better tomorrow'. People's busy lives seemed to harbour a kind of vacuum at their core. Stress – at least measured by the people who were said to be suffering from it – was running at 71 per cent in professionals and was higher in women than in men in all classes. This was a hunger the Dome could address: for a well-being that went beyond the pay-packet.

As both main parties had recognised during the election, 1997 Britain was far from being an Elysium. The English and Welsh in particular thought life dangerous. Their fear of being mugged was one of the highest in the world, far higher than in the United States, Northern Ireland or anywhere in Europe. The ferocious contest between the political parties to be the most socially repressive on street beggars and vagrants, a campaign which caused outrage in the liberal press, was a straightforward response to what their private polls were telling them. The contradictory complex of a fear of strangers and a sense of mutual isolation was a governing factor in many British lives. Not enough petty crimes were cleared up – 13 per cent of thefts from vehicles, 19 per cent of cases of criminal damage, 23 per cent of burglaries, all these figures were far lower than they had been ten years earlier. These were symptoms of the anonymous society. The Dome, if it was to be celebratory, could scarcely reflect that. But it could counter it and attempt to embody its opposite. The Dome's focus, as Claire Sampson, NMEC's production director, put it, was to be 'on the half-full, not the half-empty glass'. The de Tocqueville thermometer would be encouraged to rise.

This was not a culture sinking into any kind of materialist nihilism. Cinema attendance was going up, visits to museums and galleries were rising. The British Museum, the National Gallery, the Natural History Museum, the Tate Gallery and the Science Museum all showed numbers above their early nineties level. Only zoos were failing to share in the general rise. The popularity of castles and theme parks was surging upwards. Membership of all religions and churches continued to rise except among Roman Catholics (falling) and Anglicans (stable). Concern for the environment was at an all-time high. Traffic, global warming and air pollution remained the key environmental worries, particularly for people under 24. The question put by the Department of the Environment, Transport and the Regions in late 1997, 'Are you concerned about the environment?' received 'very concerned' or 'fairly concerned' from almost 90 per cent of those who answered.

People were also being kinder to their bodies. Teenage smoking was on an unexplained and inexorable rise (a third of all fifteen-year-old girls smoked) but, apart from that, the relentless government propaganda and commercial advertising about healthy living was having its effect. The British slob was a dying species. More people went for a walk, swam, cycled and did keep fit or yoga (more than twice as many women as men) in 1997 than had done at the beginning of the decade. TV watching, darts and snooker were all on the slide. The number of men playing football remained steady at 10 per cent. Nevertheless, the thing that most Britons did most of in the mid 1990s was the same as it had always been: sleep – an average of eight and three-quarter hours a day; over nine hours for women over 45. Any zone devoted to rest might well be popular.

NMEC now had two and a half years to provide something that would 'entertain, inspire and educate' this diverse nation. It was, as Claire Sampson said, 'a vast and intimidating task', not helped by PR problems, of which the Dome had its fair share that summer – the PVC roof commissioned from a German company; John Prescott telling the press that the British construction industry had a poor record; Prescott then comparing Mandelson to one of the Chinese mitten crabs which were said to be thriving in the river Thames; Tory politicians beginning to attack the Dome as a symbol of everything that was wrong about New Labour in general and Mandelson in particular: none of these made life for Jennie Page and her team, already struggling with an army of objective problems, particularly easy. When Blair returned from his summer holiday in Tuscany, he told Mandelson in the garden of 10 Downing Street that he was not happy with the way things had gone with the Dome so far, that it looked as if Mandelson was letting it slip and that he had better get a tighter hold. Mandelson did not feel that was particularly fair.

Despite those difficulties, there were many positive aspects to the new situation. The core funding from the Millennium Commission was now in place. There was certainty to a project which had never had it before. The mood of the country, still in post-election euphoria, was precisely on the upcurve of the de Tocqueville thermometer – just where the Dome needed it to be. That mood wouldn't last. As the millennium approached, the script writer Richard Curtis, the genius behind Blackadder, would suggest that 'The Millennium would have been a far more exciting time if a government had come in during 1999. A government in mid-term can never be a very exciting time.'

In June 1997, on the basis of the Alastair Burns research, sewn together with the business plan and Ken Robinson's operational requirements, a series of meetings in the offices of M. & C. Saatchi in Golden Square began to refine the ideas for the contents. There was already a scheme for a spectacular show in a vast central arena, known as the Drum. Around it, in 'the doughnut', as it was called, interspersed between the service buildings and the enclosure surrounding the vent of the Blackwall Tunnel, there was to be a series of attractions.

The 'who we are, what we do and where we live' template had given NMEC three categories. They easily broke down into nine: 'Who We Are' became 'Mind, Body and Spirit'; 'What We Do' became 'Work, Rest and Play'; 'Where We Live' became 'Local, Global and National'. These were never conceived as the whole picture. An exercise conducted early on identified for each of these zones possible industrial and commercial sectors, with a view to raising sponsorship from them. No zone fitted very intimately either with BT or with the Corporation of the City of London, both of which had already and very publicly said that they would be interested in sponsoring something in the Dome. Gift horses were always going to be provided with stables here. The terms on which those stables might be occupied would be the subject of many long and complex negotiations in the months to come. Eventually the Dome would be filled with fourteen zones (as well as Skyscape outside it) – nine from the original scheme and the others arriving later under their own banners.

To Claire Sampson and the team around her the next step was obvious: to select and brief designers. That was not how Stephen Bayley saw it. Bayley, a style guru, witty, contemptuous, candid, intemperate, epigrammatic and unkind by turn, had created and run both the Boilerhouse Project at the V & A and the Design Museum on the bank of the Thames opposite the Tower of London. He was a consultant to Ford, knew a great deal about design history and had for many years worked for Sir Terence Conran. In June Bill Muirhead at M. & C. Saatchi had suggested Bayley's name to Jennie Page as someone who would be able to oversee the look and style of the Dome's contents. It was acknowledged by design writers on both sides of the Atlantic that Bayley would add real stature to the project. He was made 'consultant creative director'.

Because he needed to keep the rest of his business going, he was only part-time on the Dome – three days a week, for which he was to be paid

£80,000 a year. He would not work in the Dome's utilitarian offices in Buckingham Palace Road, which Page's tight control on expenditure had kept spartan. Bayley thought the offices had 'the feng shui to kill a rhinoceros'.

This literal standoffishness was matched by a culture gap between him and the NMEC team, with whom he would have to work extremely closely. They saw him as disengaged, dilettante-ish and arrogant. He saw them as excluding, suspicious, uninspired and without the necessary experience and scope.

'It was absolutely mad to have taken the job,' Bayley now says. 'They simply wanted to say they had a creative director. They didn't actually want one. I'm not much given to collective activity. I have no taste for politics, committees and meetings. I made that absolutely clear. If you want strong ideas, I will give you strong ideas. But I will not do committees, I will not do meetings and I am not interested in discussing things with other people.'

Why did NMEC want him? It was well known that Bayley was congenitally incapable of staying on-message and that his team-playing skills were rudimentary. But he was a name, known for the quality of what he could do. 'It was a high-risk hiring,' Page now says. 'We all accepted it might not work and we discussed that right at the beginning. He was always on try-out. But the team needed strengthening. We needed more people. I needed to get hold of people, fast, who were high quality, available, resourceful, relevant and with enough reputation and clout to add substance to the company. There were few people around who fulfilled all of those conditions. He had achieved things too.'

There was some ambiguity to Bayley's position. It was inherent in his job title. 'Consultant creative director' is half in and half out, half advising, half controlling. There was now a core of people already at the Dome who were totally committed. Anyone coming into this atmosphere with the title 'director' attached to him was going to find life difficult.

The difficulty soon peaked. It was not, as Bayley would later describe it, about his relationship with Mandelson. He scarcely met Mandelson and, although towards the end of Bayley's time with NMEC Mandelson would become increasingly enraged by what he saw as Bayley's 'inability to offer any realistic ideas of his own', the conflict was in many ways more important than that. Bayley's favoured approach was a high-minded, principled, serious pursuit of his own vision of excellence. He was, for example, witheringly contemp-tuous of the final choice of logo, calling it 'a kitsch, pseudo-Cretan, steroid-pumped bronze female figure, a piece of design of stunning ineptitude with a complete lack of graphic intelligence'. Not much room for uncertainty there.

The clash of personality between Bayley and the Dome's content team became a vehicle for a more essential difference in view. He was adamant that they shouldn't go to the London-based community of architects, event and show designers. They should aim higher than that. The very best design minds of the world should be invited to the Dome. 'With a very few exceptions,' Bayley would write in 1998, 'the quality of the firms expressing interest [was] very low; Europe's great architects and designers almost entirely ignored the invitation. My immediate suggestion that we re-advertise and coerce entries from the best designers was also ignored.'

There was another point of difference: in the summer of 1997 Bayley suggested that NMEC should pause for six months, look at its ideas and make them deep and strong. 'Call me old fashioned, call me academic – I am basically an academic type, I'm a sort of groovy academic – but that's how you do an exhibition. You do what the *FT* always used to tell its journalists: simplify and then exaggerate. To do something about the mind you have to get people who know about the mind to write a fantastic account of what matters about the mind, and then you give it to someone like me who knows about exhibitions to write an exhibition brief and then you give it to a designer. You don't go to a designer and say: "Do me something about the mind, please."'

NMEC felt that there was a lack of realism in what Bayley said. The atmosphere in the company at the time was one of deep anxiety; they were coming under ferocious pressure from Mandelson to deliver on sponsorship and on ideas for content (no sponsors would sponsor anything until they knew what it might look like). Mandelson himself was privately going through agonies of doubt over what he had committed the government to. Blair was making it perfectly clear that Mandelson would be taking the blame if it went wrong. Blair himself was anxious about it. The press was becoming increasingly hostile. The Dome was dominating Mandelson's life. In such an environment it seemed to NMEC and the politicians that Bayley's suggestion that they should spend six months thinking hard about the content was insouciant and out of touch to the point of puerility. Bayley remained adamant that it was not. 'Six months was what any responsible professional with relevant experience would have insisted on.' Mandelson's own disdain for Bayley was not concealed.

By the late summer of 1997 Bayley was already on the sidelines, 'paring his nails', 'looking at the ceiling during meetings', 'never pulling his chair up to the table', or 'occasionally pontificating', depending on which member of NMEC you asked. Claire Sampson and Martin Newman, desperately busy, drove ahead with their scheme for briefing the designers. Having followed the usual advertising process, they chose 22 design, event and architecture practices and invited them to a meeting on 5 August. The companies would be asked to submit suggestions: two zones for each of the bigger concerns, one each for the smaller. They were to be paid £5,000 per zone for their efforts and NMEC was to retain all Intellectual Property Rights in everything submitted. They came in two groups and Sampson spoke to them. What they produced, she told them, should be educational, fun, inspirational and communal in effect. NMEC was looking for richness and variety. Schemes should attend to the needs of those who couldn't speak English, were disabled or were very young. Everything should be for everybody, 'A's to 'E's. There was to be no distinction in the audience throughout. And this, she said to the designers in the room, 'is your opportunity to do whatever you like. Anything creative, innovative or interesting, this is your chance! And we don't want a vase of cut flowers. We don't want something that will look pretty but will fade. We don't want the Chinese meal. We want plants that will take root in people's minds.'

The briefs given to each company imposed nothing and dictated nothing. They asked a set of questions. That was the NMEC position. 'Unless you suddenly became or coopted a university,' Martin Newman says, 'we were never going to have authority to give answers. We were only going to have authority to ask questions.'

The idea, according to Jennie Page, 'was to stimulate the designers, to test how they would respond, to see if they were adaptable and able to cope with change. It was not a form of intellectual self-abnegation but it was anti-didactic. It was carefully and deliberately done, precisely so that we did not impose on the exhibition a kind of stiffness and decisiveness too early, which could have prejudiced the entire show.'

This was about being open to new ways of thinking, and bringing together different sorts of designers and different sorts of ideas in what was always going to be a fluid mix. But it was also more than that. Page links the approach to a general principle in modern public life. 'We do not tell, we ask and perhaps suggest. We consult; we do not impose. The days are over when you could tell people, "This is what we are doing," and they would then do it.'

Michael Grade was adamant that this was not cynical old 'business as usual': 'In 1851 and 1951 the great and the good created wonderful tableaux, then lifted the curtain and allowed the great unwashed to have a peep at how great their leaders were. This show is different. Here it is the people themselves who are the focus. It says: "Think about your own life." The people are in charge. They can make their own mistakes. They are not being told what to be or how to act. What the Dome is saying to them is: "Here you are, folks. Here are the choices. You decide." That is a radical difference.'

A guiding force in the shaping of this philosophy was the production director, Claire Sampson. In a sometimes Jurassic NMEC environment, where big, craggy beasts slogged it out over meeting-room tables, Sampson had a different kind of presence. She had trained as a dancer, spent a great deal of time in the United States, had put on rock shows and run arts organisations. Calm; a natural and understated sense of authority; familiarity with the workings of a budget; an acute visual sense; an ability to focus on the project; balance; flexibility in a task which had little precedent; a consistently team-building and solution-seeking attitude; gentleness and subtlety, with enough toughness not to be kicked around by the bullish figures of some of the other NMEC on-site directors: these are some of the invaluable if unexpected qualities that Claire Sampson brought to her job. It occupied in many ways the most crucial node in the organisation.

The questions put to the designers were generic in the extreme: For the Body: 'Are we what we eat? Are there still seven ages of man? Can we feed the world? What about designer people?' For the Soul: 'What is the meaning of Life? Should we defend the faiths? Is God dead? Can science find Him? Or Her?' For Work: 'Does business matter if I am not a millionaire? How will technology change my life? How will I meet people?' For Play: 'What will be art? Will novels cease to exist? Can there be any new ideas?' And so on. It was little more than a blank sheet, attached to some operational requirements: a capacity for 5,000 people an hour through each zone, a completion date of November 1999 and a budget per zone. Designers were not to give a moment's thought to sponsorship possibilities but 'to concentrate on the issues as you see them'.

Sampson and Newman had been joined by Ben Evans, who had previously worked with Jennie Page at English Heritage, and was now dropped into NMEC by Peter Mandelson. He was to be a conduit on creative content between the shareholder and the company. Everybody's relationships with Bayley were worsening. In particular, people were offended by his apparent assumption that everyone was stupid. Newman felt that there was a school of narrative designers in Britain who could, more effectively than anyone else in the world, take a skeletal idea and make of it something new and exciting. There was no need for a string of 'curator-heroes' – in the Bayley mould – to preordain what the designers might do. It was an irreconcilable difference, to be resolved only in the outcome. Would the people in whom NMEC were putting their faith deliver for them? The answer to that question would be long and complex.

Mandelson felt that the need for closer control of NMEC was urgent. It had been bedevilled by too many decision-centres: the commission, NMEC itself and government. They had to be reduced to one. Almost immediately after the go-ahead had been given, Mandelson set up a coordinating group. He himself was to chair it. Michael Heseltine, Simon Jenkins (both Millennium Commissioners), Bob Ayling, officials from DCMS, and Jennie Page were to become its members. They met every Tuesday at 5 p.m. for one hour. Page could in this way see the relevant people without endlessly duplicating meetings.

The group also had a political purpose. 'It was a means of tying in Heseltine's support for the Dome,' Mandelson says, 'and so neutralising the Tory opposition. The wider intention of keeping the Dome non-partisan did not work. By February, Heseltine and Francis Maude, the Shadow Culture spokesman, were in open disagreement about the project.

The review had asked for a beefing-up of the management. Page herself had two key figures on the way: a commercial director – Kevin

Johnson, from the Swiss company ISL, where he had been in charge of developing marketing programmes for the Olympics, the World Cup and other giant events; and a finance director, Steve Brown from Center Parcs. Mandelson wanted to broaden NMEC's connections with the worlds of business, media and entertainment still further. Others were brought in. Michael Grade of First Leisure and previously of Channel Four, Ruth Mackenzie of the Scottish Opera (NMEC's idea) and Sir Alan Cockshaw, ex-chairman of AMEC, the engineering and construction giant, had joined the board in July. Sam Chisholm became deputy chairman of NMEC in August. An executive committee (Exco), to strengthen the board's decision-making capacity, was established, with Chisholm as its bruisingly abrupt chairman, and Grade and Page as its members. At Chisholm's suggestion, Matthew Freud, the young PR expert, and David Chance, his deputy at Sky, were coopted on to ExCo. Chisholm, as deputy chairman of the board and chairman of ExCo, was now in a powerful position to make the rapid decisions the company needed.

In some ways, what felt at times like such a proliferation of super-visors, with such a broad and urgent agenda, such atrocious press, and such an insistent timetable already hanging over her, was not the thing that Jennie Page needed in her life. At the weekly meeting of the coordinating group it was clear to those present that, at times, Page 'resented it like hell. She became curmudgeonly, dismissing lines of enquiry and becoming irritated by close questioning.'

There was far more to the relationship between shareholder and Chief Executive than that. 'It was not,' according to Peter Mandelson, 'a blame culture. All of us had our backs against the wall and so the feeling was "Better close ranks." Given the complexity of what we were trying to do, the atmosphere was actually fantastic and quite unbitter. Although it was sometimes difficult for her to give me the level of information I required, I completely trusted Jennie. She was in control of the project but I had to take responsibility for it in public. I could never have done that unless I trusted the person in charge 100 per cent.'

The choice of advertising agency for the Dome was announced early in September. M. & C. Saatchi was chosen as the winning agency for the £16 million campaign. Not only did they have a long, famous and close relationship with the Tory Party – which didn't particularly trouble Mandelson himself – but Bill Muirhead, one of its partners, had been working closely with NMEC on the repositioning of the Dome's content. Muirhead had been helping NMEC for free, and withdrew from the entire process by which an agency was chosen, but those details did not reach the headlines. The announcement was made just before that year's Labour Party conference. Party activists were nothing like as elastic in their attitude to the Saatchis as Mandelson was. He was irritated at the timing, as he had to fend off yet another batch of hostile headlines.

It is difficult to overestimate the tension and strain which the project was imposing on the people involved – and on none more than Peter Mandelson and Jennie Page. Both were desperate for the Dome to happen. 'I fought for it, was identified with it and walked through fire for it,' Mandelson says. Page could use precisely the same words. Mandelson goes on: 'I believed in it. Inside the Dome, it was high-octane anxiety and stress. It really felt like pushing a boulder uphill, having to probe, prod, question and cajole. I don't remember a period when it was painless. And I protected it. But if I was to take the flak, I had to know what was happening. No surprises!'

This was one of the central difficulties. If Mandelson was to give Parliament the information it needed, he, or Clare Pillman at DCMS for him, had to be given it by NMEC. But often, in a fluid, fast-moving, creative process, information is either difficult to get hold of or not available in a form to which anyone is ready to commit in public. NMEC was inclined to keep things back until they were in shape. Mandelson preferred to say what could be said as soon as possible, 'to embrace Parliament', to get them on side. It was more of a structural difficulty than one hinged to the characters of the protagonists. But Jennie Page felt that the actual process of giving information could harm the sometimes fragile organism which the information was about. 'We live and die this project thirty-six hours a day,' she says, 'and we have given more thought to it in detail than anyone else possibly could. I have to make sure there is a minimum amount of damage done, while recognising the shareholder has a legitimate interest in what's going on. You have to look at the whole picture and decide if any problem is a resigning issue.'

This was an anguished period. Certainly, on both sides of this divide, thoughts were given to drastic solutions. It seemed to many in NMEC that Mandelson's presence as the company's shareholder was doing damage to the project. According to Michael Grade, 'The problem, despite the cross-party presence of Heseltine and Blair, was to depoliticise the Dome. Mandelson, who deserves great credit for championing the thing, politicised it. The Tories could turn it into a political football because of his presence. We had to turn people away from him and engage them in content. But we failed. We failed to get Peter to take a back seat.' That is not how Mandelson sees it. For him, the Dome was political from the word go, conceived of by government, kicked around by opposition, on both sides of the election, a public project, not a private plaything. The Dome could never have been depoliticised, with or without him.

Certainly, Mandelson himself cut both ways for the Dome. He had provoked a large number of bitter rows with journalists over many years. When political correspondents covered the Dome, that history coloured their attitudes. But he also schmoozed them, patiently speaking to newspaper editors one at a time, working away at them and their senior commentators. A few left-leaning journalists, including Andrew Marr and John Lloyd and leader writers in the *Guardian*, *Observer* and *Mirror*, wrote favourably of the beleaguered project. Mandelson also provided political cover, catching most of the flak. He was the lightning conductor, both attracting the lightning and diverting it from the building to which he was attached. He was well aware of this. He discussed it, weighed up the balance and concluded that, in sum, he was an advantage, not an impediment.

Throughout this period, lurking like a toad in the centre of the Dome, and hanging over the relationship between Mandelson and NMEC, was the question of the Drum theatre. This enormous construction, 40 metres tall, as big as Trafalgar Square, was to house the great central show of the Millennium Experience. The show performed an important operational function. Every two hours or so it would draw into an amphitheatre about 10,000 of those who were in the Dome at the time. This provided NMEC's operational team with a pulsed time-structure for the movement of people within the building; when the show was on it would take a third of the crowds away from the zones. It would reduce queuing and overall would improve the experience.

It was also more than that. If the zones around the edges were the places where the big questions were to be asked, the Drum was where the heart was to beat faster, and where an inspirational and memorable show was to take place several times a day. The show and the theatre to house it were conceived, in many ways, as the crucible in which the audience would arrive as individuals and leave in some way connected, as a group. Here all the celebratory delight of a massive social event, the educational value of a deeply researched narrative exhibition and the sheer oomph of a great deal of very expensive technology would be fused into the one moment of which people in the future would say, 'Do you remember ... ?'

In the days after the election and before the outcome of the review was known, Mandelson had got in touch with Sir Cameron Mackintosh, the great impresario and producer of *Les Misérables*, *The Phantom of the Opera* and *Miss Saigon*. Mandelson first asked him if he would look at NMEC's proposals and advise him on their viability. After the review Mandelson took it a step further. Would Mackintosh consider becoming the maestro in charge of the Drum? He would.

Mackintosh brought in John Napier, the theatre designer. Although NMEC felt they were working hard with Napier to make a feasible scheme, as far as Mandelson could see it, the NMEC attitude to the Mackintosh team was 'a bit too much of "not invented here" '.

The design for the Drum theatre had its roots in the Imagination suggestion, made at the beginning of the year, for an auditorium in which different seating pods would themselves move and become part of the drama which the audience was there to watch. Withers's scheme had been founded on a ring of towers around the centre of the Dome, from which arms would stretch out to enclose an amphitheatre when it was needed and retract again when the show was over. Under the Imagination scheme, the Dome would, for most of the time, have remained a fluid and accessible space.

For the spectacular show which Mackintosh was to provide, which would inevitably be theatrical in style, there seemed to be a drawback to this structure. During the shows the only covering to the amphitheatre would be the translucent roof of the Dome itself. The show would usually take place in daylight. No light insulation, it seemed to Mackintosh and Napier, meant a loss of drama, because to them drama needed darkness, or at least a sharp delineation between light and dark which the Teflon-diffused daylight could not provide. No sound insulation meant noise penetration in both directions.

There was an answer to this: put a lid on it and turn the Drum into 'a biscuit box'. That decision was taken. The Drum was to become a large, dark, solid, roofed and very expensive building dominating the centre of the Dome. The Richard Rogers architects, who had viewed the Imagination winged-tower scheme with equanimity and enthusiasm, were very unhappy about the turn things had taken. Their loose-fit Dome, with all its eco-reliance on natural light, and the fluidity of the space it provided, was now being colonised by a cuckoo, a huge, black, central, old-fashioned, budget-consuming, energy-gobbling, space-destroying lump. But if Mackintosh was to provide the kind of show which the brief was asking him to provide, he needed it; the shareholder was supporting him, the NMEC board was enthusiastic and it was going ahead.

Increasingly, Jennie Page, Ken Robinson and Claire Sampson did not like the way the Drum was turning out. It stretched the budget and, apart from anything else, the Mackintosh show was going to be an operational nightmare. The plan was to have two casts of 1,000 children each, those casts changing on a regular basis so that children from all over the country could play a part (an idea which would eventually emerge in the Dome as part of 'Our Town Story'). Both casts would perform twice a day. The children would need chaperones. They would need training, housing and schooling. Projected costs for the child cast alone had become astronomic. As the storyline for the show developed – it was essentially a pageant of Britain's past triumphs and future hopes – both a squadron of 45 horses and a Harrier jump jet were cast in suitable roles. The health and safety requirements for the mobile seating were becoming nightmarish. What would happen if someone wanted to go to the loo in the middle of the show? Loos would have to be built into the back of each pod. But how would those loos be connected to the foul drainage system? Would they have umbilical cords snaking their way across the auditorium, carrying the waste away? Or would there be reservoirs built into the seating, with valves that would automatically open once the seating pod docked?

There was a worry about getting people out of the Drum during a fire or a bomb scare. Those mobile seats had to be loaded from the top, at first-floor level. During an evacuation the loading platforms had to be able to accommodate all 10,000 people as they escaped. A huge circular steel platform at that level would have to be built around the rim of the Drum, fattening it, taking it out to the foot of the masts, and massively inflating the budget. The Drum, the very centrepiece of the Dome, was starting to seem like a bad and expensive idea. By late September 1997 the projected cost of this great communal centrepiece, together with the show that was to be staged inside it, was well into nine figures.

The iron timetable was biting again. A decision had to be made by 28 November at the latest. A paper on alternatives to the Drum was submitted to the Executive Committee on 3 October. Grade was still keen to make it work, Chisholm was sceptical and Page now considered the show too ambitious, its cast too big and the building too expensive. It was in danger of overshadowing the rest of the Dome, leaving a shrivelled doughnut outside it. With that, the shareholder agreed. By 10 October ExCo had made its decision and, four days later, the Drum was dead. Claire Sampson immediately turned to Mark Fisher, the architect and designer of some of the greatest rock spectaculars there had ever been. Page, Sampson, Mike Davies and Ken Robinson felt the same sensation: relief. They could all breathe again.

The building of the Dome was going well. Relations on site were excellent. There was a real team spirit. The design briefs had been issued and the companies were addressing the questions. The management had begun to acquire greater width and depth. There were just over two years to go. But the Dome was in as stretched and desperate a condition as at any time in its life. Apart from the inherently difficult relationship of a private sector company with a public sector shareholder, the standing of the Dome in the press was catastrophically bad. Its defenders kept repeating the mantra that all other *grands projets* had always been greeted with the same loathing, but that was only some consolation. Present pain feels sharper than anything you might read about.

Gez Sagar, the very image of the modern press officer, quick, slight, restless, alternatingly direct and subtle, who had worked for the Labour Party for ten years in opposition, came over to NMEC immediately after the election. As the new head of Press and Parliamentary Affairs, he wrote a briefing document which was intended to convey the urgency of the situation:

We need to create the climate in which 12 million people will want in two years' time to visit the Millennium Experience – more than have been to any event in the UK ever. More than arrived in Euro-Disney in its first year (and that's after 50 years of building a brand that is universally recognised). That means effecting a dramatic change in public perceptions – and that has to start now.

Sagar had five clear weapons in his armoury: 'outshout negative coverage; create a sense of momentum; end perception of "silence"; reinforce message that Millennium Experience is on course, on time; provide supporters and spokespeople with language.' There would now be 'Line to Take' (LTT) briefings for key players. Four messages would underline anything that anyone said: 'It's the people's show. It's the most exciting experience of the millennium. It's good for Britain. It's going well.'

It looked as if the on-message culture of the modern political party was being grafted wholesale on to the Dome organisation. 'NMEC staff,' Sagar told them, 'should assume that anything they do will become public knowledge and plan accordingly. Any literature/video material for external use must be signed off by the head of P & PA before printing or final edit.'

Opinion-formers were to be approached in the media, the government, Parliament, London and the regions. But spin can only spin a reality. Sagar needed 'real things happening'. He wanted to stage a great launch in October, at which the Prime Minister would announce the first real contents and the first signed-up sponsors. But that was too soon. Jennie Page and Claire Sampson wanted to wait until the designers had got much further with their plans before going public. And sponsorship was thin on the ground. The October launch would not take place until the following February.

In the meantime, out of little more than thin air – but at least with the Dome itself becoming a physical object, masts raised, cable net appearing – Sagar could merely 'attempt to steer the speculation, to make it positive'. It wasn't easy. One after another Sagar had to field negative stories: Jennie Page's pay (£150,000 a year, plus £22,500 in lieu of pension, figures that would always be good for a headline); the contract with IMG, Mark McCormack's organisation, retained to raise sponsorship for which they would, if completely successful, receive a maximum of £9 million; the PVC/PTFE row, in which Prescott had become involved and which had Page, Sagar and Mandelson on the phone until one o'clock in the morning; increasingly hostile Tories; and Stephen Bayley. Bayley was not seeing the Sagar picture. He didn't grasp why he shouldn't say it was the 'death or glory aspects' of the project which had attracted him – he had always loved dangerous and exotic pursuits – or repeat the bon mot which David Hockney had written in a letter to the Dome – 'Most beautiful left empty' – at a time when NMEC was desperately trying to persuade sponsors to spend an unprecedented amount of money on its contents. 'At this point we are trying to give an impression of stability and a certain seriousness,' Sagar says. Instead, it was daily firefighting.

Many of these incidents would not have seemed so bad if there had not been a huge backlog of PR difficulties on the project. Sagar felt that 'not enough had been done early on at one-to-one meetings with different editors and journalists on why it was being done'. Its entire existence was still coloured, however unfairly, by the muddle of 1996, by the poor standing of the lottery. But more than that, because there was so much still to be decided, because the press was there watching and recording every birth-pang of this project, every childhood mistake, every adolescent error, the Dome never stood a chance. It was as if Ford were launching a car while arguments were still going on in the design department. There was too much that was still too provisional. There were, according to Gez Sagar, 'too many legitimate questions'.

The design companies were to return their submissions to the Buckingham Palace Road offices by 5 p.m. on Tuesday 4 September. By four o'clock nothing whatsoever had arrived. NMEC had asked Imagination to bid for a couple of zones, but they had turned down the offer. Was the rest of London's design world going to flop on them too? 'We had spent so much time with this project,' Claire Sampson says. 'We were desperate for something to be there.' They waited. At 4.30 it began. An onslaught of boxes and packages started to come through the door. Models arrived in boxes eight feet long and four feet wide. Suddenly rooms in NMEC's offices were stuffed to the gills with cartons and files. Sampson catalogued each item as it arrived, signing everything in. Suddenly, substance had come into their lives! For years they had been living with the notional. Now, here in front of them, was some tangible, visible, actual stuff. 'We were ecstatic at the level of response,' says Sampson. 'Just to get that level of commitment from the design community.' Jennie Page, Sampson, Martin Newman and Jeff Hawkins unwrapped the offerings. The brown paper came off to reveal the pretty models underneath. A version of what they had hoped for sparkled in front of them. The Dome could be filled.

Over the coming weeks the submissions were evaluated and the companies were interviewed. They were tested one by one, the suggestions examined from every angle. Would they be fun? Would they inspire and educate? Were they beautiful? Were they operable? Would the required number of visitors get through them? Had the designers thought about the blind or people in wheelchairs? What would happen in a fire? What about non English-speakers? Were they buildable? Was all the money going on the building and the contents being treated as an afterthought? Were they likeable? Were they sponsorable? What was the point of all these bobbles on the roof of the model when no one on the floor of the Dome would see them? (The beautiful roof is an old model-designer's trick. Unpractised decision-makers forget that roofs, the most visible part of a model, are rarely seen in reality.)

The companies were being tested too. Were these outfits they could work with? Were they dependable? Did they have a feel for procurement? Would they manage a budget? Did they understand what it was like working in the quasi-public sector? Were they thinking more about the elegance of their own building than about the vitality of the experience it might give? Would they be adaptable? Would they cope?

The designers that were eventually chosen were deliberately diverse in style, emphasis and history. It was important that the Dome did not box itself into a corner. Live options, breadth and variety were essential to its health. They fell into three groups: the architectural practices (all of whom happened to be led by women); the event and show designers, who had worked on a combination of party conferences and product launches; and what might be called the narrative designers, who filled the niche most difficult to define – partly explanatory, partly entertaining, partly educative and partly fun – but who had already begun to engage with precisely that middle ground which the Dome was hoping to explore. As the contents of the Dome developed over the next two years, it was the two companies in this last category which were to adapt most easily to the fluid and demanding circumstances of this project. Between them, they would end up designing a third of the zones.

Of these two narrative design companies, one is called 'WORK' and the other 'Land'. The names say something: very nineties, cool, laid-back, witty, intelligent, inventive, prepared to take on the challenge of looking at ideas from the raw material up. Land is responsible for Play. WORK, which began on Living Island, ended up doing Work, as well as Learning and the contents of Local, called 'Shared Ground'.

WORK is led by the architect and exhibition designer Tim Pyne. He had seen an ad in the *Architects' Journal* and got himself on to the NMEC shortlist. They gave him the brief for the National zone. 'What will we do when the oil runs out?' the questions had asked. 'Is Britain a green and pleasant land?'

In every detail, it was a clever pitch. Pyne sent his own CV in a fat, green, inflatable package which by design would not be happy in the middle of a pile of other CVs. It could only sit on the top.

Pyne had got his friends around a big table – 20 people with three cases of wine. Matthew Collings, the most brilliant art critic and TV star of his generation, was there along with various architects and other art and design people. It was the innest of in crowds. 'Everyone got pissed. It started us thinking.' The next week Pyne had his brainwave. 'We should do a pier. A pier represents man trying to overcome the environment. But there's also walking to the end of the pier: looking at infinity and the future, the whole "Dad's Army" thing and a perspective on the country you have left.' With Nicky Shaw, an independent theatre designer, he spent a Bank Holiday weekend in a borrowed MG touring the South Coast – the MG broke down in Bognor – drinking in the imagery of the English seaside.

The WORK designers produced a plan for a pier where at first everything looked beautiful – a lovely beach, a wonderful day, the sound of the surf – but which you slowly realised overlay something different. A whole series of environmental problems became apparent here. The seaside was both the ideal place and the dustbin. 'It was a mechanism for contradiction', irony in a concrete form, to be realised here with tongue-in-cheek authenticity, camp environmentalism, replica anxiety about the future of the earth, ersatz heart. Here, suddenly, for the first time, all the contradictoriness of the Dome, all its temporary fakeness, its yoking together of fun and education, its need for earnestness and entertainment, looked no longer like a set of hideously complicated hurdles but an opportunity for newness. The gut instinct which the NMEC team had been following had found a response in just the terms they had been hoping for.

WORK is too sophisticated an outfit to have given NMEC a model of the zone it planned to build. Instead, along with an account of walking through the zone written as if by a small girl and her grandfather, they delivered a huge mood model, a big table with 'lots of things you could poke and buttons you could press and which would play the national anthem out of plastic palm trees'. It seduced NMEC utterly. When, three weeks later, Pyne went in to talk to them about it, he knew the model had been a success. All the batteries were flat.

The second group of designers was different – these were the well-established event companies which had made their name in the 1980s for high-gloss presentations for political parties and big corporations. Park Avenue Productions, for example, had a longstanding relationship with BA and BMW. They had been approached in 1995 by the Millennium Commission to bid for the whole Millennium Exhibition but it was too much for them to contemplate. Now, though, their proposals for Work and for Rest – a rather Disneyish trip on beds which floated along a river through a dreamscape – offered a fairly traditional, child-friendly ride.

As the presentation made by Park Avenue for this beds-in-a-river Rest zone came to an end, the designers gave ice-creams to everyone in the room. This was to be a chill-out zone. It was a small joke. Bayley left his ice-cream in the box. A small pool of pink meltwater slowly thickened around it as the consultant creative director stared at the ceiling.

HP:ICM, similar to Park Avenue in their market position, pitched for Global and Body. According to Andrew Fitch, their project manager, 'The brief was sketchy and not like the kind of brief you get from a corporate client. There you usually have a product or a message or the essence of what you need to communicate. In those situations our skills and product are a tool for communicating someone else's product. Here, our skills were to be the product itself. The experience is the product.'

Fitch's description of the predicament is the flipside of Pyne's response. Fitch would have felt more comfortable with thoroughly worked-out ideas presented to him. What he had been confronted with was a set of questions. Where was the product? As initial suggestions, HP:ICM produced the idea for Body of a giant human figure with a baby in nappies at its feet; and, for Global, a big globe into which people would be invited.

The third group consisted of the architectural practices. For Local, muf came up with a many-windowed pavilion with an ice-rink attached. It was beautiful but the zone was a difficult one, which would remain a quandary for the next two years.

Eva Jiricna saw the Soul zone as 'a magnificent opportunity to create an environment in which we can all see that we have one thing in common: the soul'. Emerging from the tight and conflict-ridden world of the Dome's own struggles into Jiricna's vision for the zone is something of a shock. No one in NMEC was talking like this: 'The point of going into this space is a search for humanity, to celebrate life and to emerge into a garden of joy, to confront the choices you have to make, to learn and to change.' The zone she designed at this stage was a 16-metre-high glass pyramid, with a cracked, egg-shaped stone platform at its heart and beyond the platform a glass floor over running water. How about religion? Jennie Page asked her when she first saw it. Jiricna said, 'If you don't want war on your hands, you have to rise above religion.' A long and difficult evolution lay ahead.

Mind was in the hands of Zaha Hadid, the Baghdad-born deconstructionist. The subject had captured the imagination of everyone who worked with her: according to Graham Modlen, 'This was to be a symbol of what the mind might be, a sculpture, a building, a pavilion, an interior, none of those things but all of them.' They produced a little plexiglass model, at this stage with six elements, which provided 'a one-hit story' of what the zone was about. Each of the elements seemed to be either opening or closing, folding up or folding out, caught 'crablike', as Modlen puts it, 'in its unfolding, rolling state'. In its sense of the partial and the defended, in the strange invitation it made to explore its recesses, to come in and to find oneself on the outside, this deeply ambivalent structure appealed immediately to Jennie Page. 'Wonderful! A metaphor for the mind,' she said on first seeing it. From the beginning it was thought that modern BritArt and modern British science would play a central role in the Mind zone, where all the issues of self, identity, sexuality, appearance, perception, communication and the nature of mind itself could be explored. Mind, like every other zone, came up against budget problems and had to be pared down, the six elements reduced to three.

These, then, were the nine – Mind, Body and Soul, Work, Rest and Play, Global, National, Local. Of these, only Mind and National, although both were cut back, would emerge in the finished Dome in anything like their first form. The others would play a kind of demonic game of musical chairs. Soul would go through hell over the coming months, as Jiricna's initial vision of spirituality was pulled apart by the conflicting requirements of the different religious interest groups; Body would be subject to endless surgery, internal and external, and have two more design teams attached to it; Work would be removed from Park Avenue and given to WORK; Rest would move from Park Avenue to the Richard Rogers Partnership; Play would go through two major revolutions, which the design company Land heroically survived; Global would move from HP:ICM to Park Avenue, at the request of the sponsors; and Local, the biggest nightmare of them all, would move from muf to HP:ICM to Gumuchdjian and Spence and finally, for the contents, to WORK. The other six zones (including Skyscape), for which the ideas would arrive over the first half of 1998, were not exactly exempt from change either.

During the last two months of 1997 and on into the New Year, as the building down at Greenwich was proceeding (despite the slipping clamps on the cable net, the design work needed to accommodate the new fabric and problems with the cable length) calmly enough, one crisis after another surged up around the project. The House of Commons Select Committee on Culture, Media and Sport held its hearings into the Dome in November and December. There were disagreements between Page and Mandelson over the degree of candour they should show. Mandelson attempted to persuade Jennie Page that she should 'open up, embrace the MPs, make them love her'. She wasn't keen. The zones were at too embryonic a stage. Mandelson insisted. Page strongly advised him to say as little as he could, but he felt that the more he said, the more the project would be accepted. This difference in approach remained unresolved between them.

At the same time an enormous battle raged over the need for what was variously called 'a creative guru', 'a ringmaster' and 'a maestro' to sit alongside Jennie Page. By now she was clearly under almost intolerable strain. At least the ringmaster would take control of the creative elements of the process. He or she would have something of the same relationship to her as the controller of a TV channel to its director-general. Mandelson 'wanted a governing mind, a creative mind, the sort of person in an election campaign who could carry it all in his head'. The sort of figure needed was someone of real prominence, who could stand up for the project in the country and generate confidence among outsiders. Mandelson had lunch with Alan Yentob. He couldn't do it because it would put him out of the running for the director-generalship of the BBC. Michael Grade had his business at First Leisure to run. David Puttnam was now busy as a Labour politician. Steven Spielberg was asked. Others, less prominent, were interviewed by Jennie Page, chewed up and spat out as unsatisfactory. An architect such as Richard Rogers wouldn't have been suitable, but he appeared on Panorama saying that such a person was needed. Mandelson found himself in a curious position. Internally, no one was advocating the appointment of such a figure more forcefully than him, but such a figure could not be found. He had to stand up in public and defend the lack of the very thing he most wanted for the project.

'There is no hero for this,' Page says. 'This is about a whole load of people shoving together. This is about a team pulling together. How often do I have to say that?' Many were canvassed, none was found. Simon Jenkins gave Page a phrase to use against those pushing her to find the great genius. 'I can't see an elephant in this haystack,' she would say. 'Show me an elephant and I'll employ it.'

The Strategic Creative Review Group, or Litmus Group, as it was called, came in some ways to occupy the gap. It was set up in December and its members were an amalgam of those who were potential ringmasters and others who had held the Dome close to their hearts: Michael Grade, Ruth Mackenzie (on the NMEC board and general director of Scottish Opera), Floella Benjamin, the TV presenter, Neil Cossons of the Science Museum, Mike Davies, Richard Rogers, David Puttnam, John Newbigin, John Sorrell of the Design Council, Alan Yentob, Christopher Frayling of the Royal College of Art, Michael Jolly of Madame Tussaud's and Simon Jenkins.

This was a good list. As well as listening to presentations as a body, the members of the Litmus Group, along with some other individuals, were allocated a zone each, becoming 'godparents' to their zones, advising, suggesting, listening, providing contacts and references for the content editors and designers. It was a system that would work very well. Alan

Yentob also agreed to advise on how some of the ideas for the Dome could be expected to work on television.

Bayley had now effectively walled himself out of the process. He had attended to the logo, had his ideas rejected, and done little else. The relationship between Bayley and the content editors was one of mutual incomprehension.

The year came to an end with an episode of pure and painful farce. Peter Mandelson had been intending to visit the Disney organisation in Florida the previous September. It would have been done without fuss. The visit was cancelled at the last moment because Princess Diana died four days before he was due to go there. In December the Select Committee had criticised NMEC and Mandelson for not learning from Disney. So he rescheduled the trip for the few days after Christmas. He was in America on holiday anyway and was due in Washington to prepare for Blair's visit to the White House. The *Independent on Sunday* got hold of the story at the same time as Bayley was committing his one last act of indiscretion in the *Sunday Telegraph*. 'What relevance will the Dome have to someone from, say, Aberdeen?' the reporter asked him. Bayley said: 'I dare say there is some knuckle-dragging Neanderthal there who won't be disposed to being entertained and stimulated by aesthetically interesting ideas.' This was too much and it marked the end of Bayley's involvement with the Dome.

Bayley's interview formed the background to Mandelson's visit to Disney World. The minister was pursued around the site by photographers trying to catch him with Mickey. 'I had to grin and bear it. It was horrible. There is nothing in the world more godawful than someone trying to make you stand next to Mickey Mouse.' He could only hope that 1998 would be better.

CHAPTER EIGHT

Imagine What We Can Do Tomorrow

Outside the hothouse, it was a different world. In early 1998 The Cardinals, in south Leeds, was a grey-red brick, sterilised, shop-less, lifeless and deeply deprived housing estate. It was the landscape of poverty and social failure. No one who could avoid it wanted to live there. It was a social sink, a place stripped of self-esteem. The streets looked curiously naked; the people couldn't afford cars. The older inhabitants wouldn't go out at night for fear of being mugged. Relatives said they would 'only visit The Cardinals in armour'. British Telecom vans attended to faults only if accompanied by a Securicor tough who stood over the van, safeguarding its contents, while the engineer was inside the house. The place was scarcely policed. On all the measures of health, longevity, crime and sense of well-being, The Cardinals was a slum.

Gladys Kellett, a housewife and assiduous fund-raiser for her local primary school in Beeston, a mile or two away across Leeds, was angry and sickened by the conditions she and her family lived in. 'We are in the same state we were in ten years ago. Everything is in disrepair. The children are our future. We have got to give them what we never had. And it all starts at school. Needs must. Extra books, another computer. But parents shouldn't have to keep putting their hands in their pockets. The families here haven't got the money. At the summer fair last year we raised £600 for the school, by cadging things. We shouldn't have to do that. Buildings should be in the sort of state where the children are pleased to go there. I wanted happy days at school for my children. But I haven't got them. If the politicians were down here in the thick of it they would see how hard the struggle can be.'

The sense of obligation was highly developed in Mrs Kellett. There was nothing anyone could teach her about community or communication skills. But it was not enough. 'I am scared about my kids' future,' she said. 'I don't see a future for them. The pressures they're under. I push them and push them to do well at school. But what will they have at the end of it? There's no jobs. Welfare to work? That's a load of rubbish. There's not the jobs to go for. But you hope, don't you? If you haven't got hope, what have you got?'

Early in 1998 Stephen Byers, a member of the government close to the Prime Minister, visited south Leeds for the day. At the time he was Minister of State in the Department for Education and Employment (DfEE) and a member of the Social Exclusion Unit, the hit-squad charged with tackling the problems of poverty by encouraging, in the buzz-language of the time, 'some joined-up thinking between the relevant agencies'.

Down the street in The Cardinals a boy was mindlessly banging the railings with a metal rod. Forty-four per cent of The Cardinals' inhabitants were on some form of benefit, a third of them on income support. Until three or four years previously a quarter of the pupils weren't even turning up at the local comprehensive. The percentage achieving any grades from A to C at GCSE had sunk to 3 per cent (the national average was 45 per cent). This was zero country, a self-confirming social nowhere, the very bottom of the heap with no ladders out. If the Millennium Experience was to have any larger purpose, if the de Tocqueville thermometer was to mean anything at all outside the confines of event-company meeting-rooms, and if people like Mrs Kellett were to feel that 'Time to make a difference' was anything beyond an easy slogan, it was in places like the estates of south Leeds that the difference had to be felt.

The minister, in his dark, very faintly pinstriped suit, his white shirt, his round, steel-rimmed glasses, his hair cut neither puritanically short nor questionably long, was standing in the littered road. A tiny pale boy – he looked ten but was undernourished and was actually fourteen – came slinking out of one of the houses. The minister had arrived in the school minibus – the boy's mother had seen it parked in the street, spotted its name on the side, and sent her son out to investigate. The central strip of his hair was razored to the scalp but the sides were longer and dyed pink.

He had a silver ring through his left eyebrow and a very sweet, softly spoken voice. His headmaster, Colin Richardson, who was with Byers, recognised him. He had been a poor attender – the jargon for truant – but had improved recently and was now particularly keen on cooking. Byers attended closely, hands in pockets, feet straddling apart, head down, minimising the difference between minister and pauper.

'So what do you want to do?' he asked, his voice modulating towards the boy's own south Leeds accent.

'I want to be a chef,' the boy piped.

'Oh? And what do you like cooking?'

'Pasta with cheese.'

'Anything else?'

'All sorts really.'

'Do you know the kind of pasta,' Byers went on, elaborately making gestures with his hands as he described what he meant, 'that comes in tubes, with meat in? It's very good. Meat in the tubes and sauce on top? Do you cook that when you're at school? Do you know it? Cannelloni?'

'No, I don't know that one,' the boy said, brightly, enthusiastically. 'But I'm making spaghetti bolognese after the holidays.'

This moment of almost Dickensian poignancy seemed absurd and touching in equal measure. The other boy was still banging his metal rod on the railings at the far end of the street. Paper rubbish shifted about in the breeze around their legs. The buildings spoke only of degradation but here was one of the Prime Minister's right-hand men discussing varieties of pasta with a boy for whom the phrase 'social exclusion' might have been invented. The pasta-ladder out of social failure? The mechanics of the de Tocqueville thermometer might be stranger than anyone had guessed.

The idea of a national programme, connecting such dead-end lives with a great exhibition, had been part of the plan from the start. The Millennium Commission had always feared that the significance of the millennium as a national and regional event might be usurped by the scale and prominence of a central show, particularly if it was in London. Gary Withers's scheme submitted to them in 1995 had ingeniously united local with central. After visiting as many places as possible, his silver touring spheres would eventually have congregated on the site of 'Millennium Central'. Throughout 1996 the option of dispersing the exhibition around the cities of the United Kingdom had still been there if Greenwich failed to work. However insistent, demanding or glamorous the Dome might be, however 'iconic' its presence in national life, the wider picture was not to be forgotten. £50 million was still allocated to a national programme in the budget submitted to the commission in May 1997. The new government insisted that the Millennium Experience should 'be a truly national event'.

There were many factors in play. It was important that the Dome didn't belong to London and the south-east. Even if Greenwich was a poor borough, desperately in need of regeneration, the national perception was of London riches, a fat south-east of England and a natural drift towards London in the focus of a London-based government.

From the Dome's own point of view it was important that its catchment was national. Twelve million people would not come to the show from London alone. Those who were involved in the National Programme near their own home would be more likely to come to the show in Greenwich. And the big sponsoring corporations would not be interested in spending an enormous proportion of their marketing budget on something which did not have national reach.

NMEC, business and government were all acting to the same agenda, fuelled by their own researches into people's priorities: social inclusiveness; education in its widest sense as the potential engine for social regeneration; local and national business not as the enemy of a healthy and inclusive society but as centrally interested in those goals themselves, not only out of a sense of corporate citizenship but because a healthy business requires a healthy market.

This whole cluster of interests and concerns is essentially post-Thatcherite. Its central focus is on partnership, not conflict. Modern government works together with business. The modern corporation does not screw people into the ground. It is interested in their long-term welfare. The modern cultural elite does not set itself at a distance either from business or from the socially or culturally deprived. It aims to bridge the gap.

It would be perfectly possible to portray the tangle of interests involved in the Dome as being in constant conflict with each other.

Government (and its re-election); sponsors (and their commercial interests); designers (and their need to build something which reflects well on them, which means a higher budget); Dome idealists (and their concern for intellectual coherence and even purity); Dome managers (anxious about budgets and timetables); the public (and its demand to be entertained): all these forces, in the hostile picture, pull in different directions.

But you could turn that on its head. The very high-mindedness of the Dome's declared intentions, its role as social yeast, its lack of self-interest (or at least the identification of its interests with the interests of all) and the government blessing it enjoyed were all qualities which appealed to the modern corporation. 'What's in it for us?' was not a question with a straightforward answer. As Sarah Mitchell says, in charge of the millennium project for Tesco, 'We've got 170,000 staff. We live here too. And so we have got a big responsibility. We have given £44 million of computers to schools over the last seven years. Getting involved with NMEC was not a knee-jerk thing.'

The idea of a national programme was central to this. Many large corporations felt wary about the Dome itself, but the idea of being identified with a countrywide movement for social regeneration, with a wide range of local impacts, was more attractive. As it developed, the National Programme, although fostered and managed by NMEC through its twelve regional offices, was largely delivered through the sponsors' own programmes.

It is important to grasp the range and scale of the National Programme, which outside the local press scarcely received any coverage but could be seen as the most compelling thing NMEC did. Some of the programmes were already in existence and the millennium label was simply bolted on to them. Every one of them is coloured by its hybrid background of state blessing, commercial delivery, charitable purpose and market position-ing. Nevertheless, taken together, they add up to a remarkable collection of the new 'hand-up, not hand-out' initiatives. BT would sponsor a widescale educational initiative called FutureTalk to improve the way in which people communicated with each other; British Airports Authority would be involved with a new Millennium Youth Games; British Aerospace was behind another initiative for skills called Engineering Our Future to inspire teenagers with the excitements of technology;

BSkyB's Reach for the Sky was aimed at fourteen- to sixteen-year-olds, encouraging them not to lose heart at the prospects of adulthood but to cherish and develop the talents they had; McDonald's Our Town Story encouraged towns and villages all over Britain to bring their own dramas to the Dome, where they could perform them on a stage designed by the Richard Rogers Partnership; Manpower would sponsor a national skills festival, culminating in a grand national final in Birmingham in July 2000; Marks & Spencer fostered two parallel programmes: Voices of Promise encouraged children in 7,000 schools to compose songs for the millennium; Children's Promise was a hugely successful and innovative fund-raising effort for disadvantaged children; Tesco's Schoolnet 2000 created the biggest educational website in the world, incorporating an electronic Domesday Book, bringing together technology, education, personal histories and the idea of transgenerational communities. Citizen's Connection, sponsored by Camelot, making up for lost ground in its public reputation, was a website intended to become a forum for 'active citizenship' and mutual help for individuals who wanted to engage with the political process in its widest sense as it affected their own lives and environments. The social legacy of these programmes could turn out to be the most permanent effect of the Millennium Experience.

The urgency of the need to drum up sponsorship money, and to mobilise that sense of 'corporate citizenship', had been apparent to all in the autumn of 1997. The Dome was in danger of becoming stuck in a vicious web. It was difficult to design any content without knowing who the sponsors were and what their requirements might be. But sponsors would scarcely commit themselves unless they knew what they were committing themselves to. Hostile media coverage and the low standing of the Dome in public opinion that autumn did nothing to encourage boardrooms to come near the project. But the hostility would continue until there was something concrete, tangible and visible. Sponsorship cash and real content were required at the same time. The circle had to be broken.

Anxiety was running high. Time was slipping past and the company had to attend to fires on all fronts. The death of Princess Diana on 31

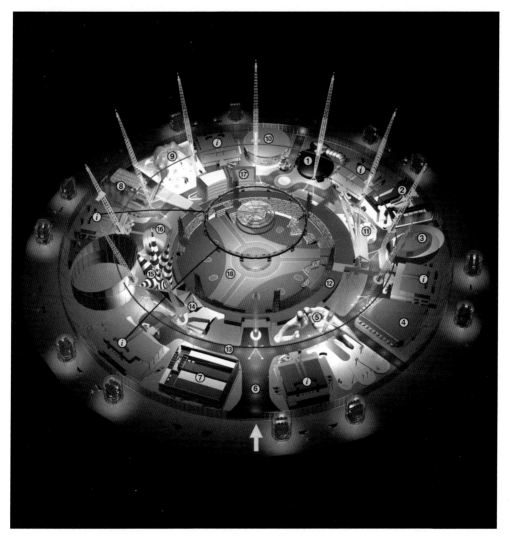

The Dome is organised in a series of concentric rings: the central arena (big enough to accommodate St Paul's Cathedral) where the spectacular Mark Fisher/Peter Gabriel show takes place; outside it the 'High Way' an elevated promenade; then a ring of smaller zones; around them runs the low level 'Mast Way', which passes under the legs of the twelve masts; in the outer ring the six core buildings, holding restaurants, loos and information points, and nine of the bigger zones. It is, quite intentionally, a multiplicity zoo, an overwhelmingly diverse environment.

1 **Home Planet**
2 **Living Island**
3 **Shared Ground**
4 **Play**
5 **Body**
6 Main Entrance
7 **Work and Learning**
8 **Mind**
9 **Faith**
10 **Self Portrait**
11 **Journey**
12 High Way
13 Mast Way
14 **Money**
15 Our Town Story Theatre
16 **Rest**
17 **Talk**
18 The Millennium Show Arena
 i Information

Left and below: Turning left immediately inside the entrance brings you to the building housing **Work** and **Learning**. A giant electric billboard flicks from library to factory to parkland and back. This pair of zones was godfathered by the Labour peer David Puttnam, housed together on the grounds that in the new world working and learning were inextricably connected. These were the zones in which the government took closest interest.

Below: **Rest**, originally a much larger and more expensive scheme, involving water rides on floating beds in a fantasy world, swopped places in early 1999 with the zone on national identity and transmogrified into a cool empty music-filled pavilion designed by the Richard Rogers Partnership. The contemplative parkland pavilion is its distant ancestor.

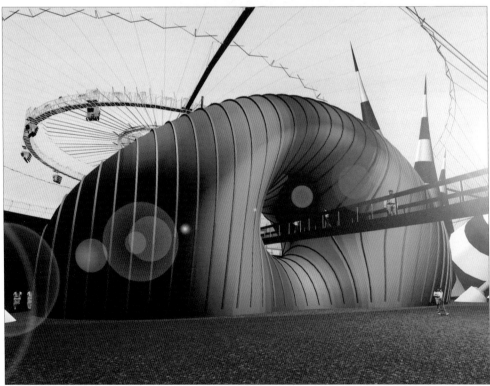

Above: **Mind** by the deconstructionist architect Zaha Hadid, coated in a shimmering skin, is filled with modern British science and modern BritArt. This zone, which in its raw state looked like a battleship in collison with iceberg, became, in its finished condition, a giant metaphor of the brain in action.

Right: The sculptor Ron Mueck with his crouching boy, a centrepiece of **Mind**.

Above: Eva Jiricna's **Faith** (ex-Soul, ex-Spirit Zone, ex-Spirit Level) was the most contentious of all during the making of the Dome. By definition, it was pulled many ways at once, needing to be accessible to more than 12 million people of all ages, all faiths and of none. Christopher Frayling, the zone's godfather, described the process as 'an extraordinary pirouette.'

Below: **Self-Portrait**, once uk@now, before that National Identity, moved halfway though its life from the site now occupied by **Rest**, was beset by budget problems, and had its designers taken off half the job three-quarters of the way through. Like the Dome itself, it portrays multiple Britain by the accumulation of layers in which diversity is the governing principle.

Right: **Home Planet** housed the only ride in the Dome, a beautifully conceived, funny and stirring journey from space back to earth. Free-flying space creatures orbited the huge floating planet beside it.

Inside the Dome with three months to go. The Mast Way runs under the pyramid base of Mast 1. The tie-down cables, which prevent the Dome roof from lifting in a high wind, are attached to the foot of the mast. **Home Planet** is on the right. In the background is the framework of **Self Portrait** on which the 'Andscape' of national imagery was to be applied. Behind that is one of the six service buildings, housing restaurants, and loos.

Left: The environmental story, which had been central to everyone's thinking about the millennium from the start, was told in many ways and in many places around the Dome, but its focus was in **Living Island**, a heightening and pastiche of a seaside resort. As Tim Pyne, the designer, described it, this was 'Monty Python and Benny Hill meet Greenpeace.' The best thought-out, most straightforward in development and earliest in delivery of all the zones, it was never able to find a sponsor.

Above: The vision complete, the Dome ready for the people, late in 1999.

Right: **Journey**, sponsored by Ford, and designed by Imagination gives some idea of the high-voltage pzazz at which Imagination excels.

Above: The Local zone, eventually called **Shared Ground**, designed by Gumuchdjian and Spence with Shigeru Ban, was made out of cardboard provided by children through the post and turned into columns in a pulp mill in Halifax. The plans for its content were radically changed in May 1999 and the whole zone remained problematic until the last.

Below: **Body**, the most prominent, the most caricatured and in many ways the most difficult of all. Three separate design teams worked on it and its contents were were among the last to be installed.

August that year ricocheted around the project. For a while Peter Mandelson seriously contemplated the idea that it should become, in shorthand, the Diana Dome. Thousands of letters arrived at the DCMS demanding that the Dome should be scrapped and a memorial built to the dead princess. What Clare Pillman, running the millennium unit at the DCMS, calls 'the heroic sponsorship total they were going for' looked, in this climate, even more remote.

NMEC knew that, in principle at least, they had BA, BT and the City Corporation on board. Although they had not publicly announced their full commitment and were not signed up, those three sponsors could be treated as givens. Apart from that, NMEC was still staring at an enormous hole. That September Bob Ayling wrote to 200 major companies to start the sponsorship ball rolling. On 14 October he and Michael Grade went to see the Prime Minister to impress on him the urgent need to enthuse sponsors. Blair grasped the point. He would do everything he could.

Over December 1997 and January 1998 the pressure to hold a powerful and convincing launch of a content/sponsorship package was becoming ever more urgent. The distractions of the Bayley affair on top of the coverage of Mandelson's visit to Disney World meant that there was no greater imperative than this: the Dome had to take control of its own public agenda. That was the purpose behind the relaunch on 24 February 1998. All the talk about the millennium being a time for people 'to take stock of their lives, their environment and their values' was wearing thin. The country needed to see what was in the Dome and to be aware of the major corporations which were supporting it.

The point of the event, the Prime Minister was told, was to convert senior business leaders, media representatives and people from the travel trade to a 'positive awareness of the project'. Cynicism was to be diffused. Enthusiasm and excitement were to be generated. Tesco, with its long history of giving computers to schools – a perfect Dome match in being high-tech, educational and community-based – was a natural Founding Partner. Dennis Stevenson, who had worked with Mandelson in the autumn on the question of the long-term future of the Dome, was instrumental in bringing in Manpower, the employment company, of which he was a director. Manpower also became a Founding Partner. Although BT, which was already engaged in developing its FutureTalk programme, with a heavy educational emphasis, was a natural candidate to take part in the event, the organisation played hard to get in the run-up towards it. With no more than a week to go an 'unofficial senior BT source' told the *Daily Mail*, 'The Dome is all but ruled out. We wanted a strong say over how our contribution would be used but we have not been given that. We wanted something for our bucks.' On the same day a still more anonymous businessman, asked about NMEC's attitude to potential sponsors, told the *Daily Telegraph*: 'There was an arrogance from the start. There seemed to be the impression that we would hand over the money and accept what they wanted to put inside the Dome.' But things were now improving. The business community was starting to feel that NMEC was getting the message. 'They have realised that to get their money we are going to have to be much more closely involved.'

Matthew Freud, the PR expert put on to NMEC's executive committee by Sam Chisholm in the previous year, was working on the media to prepare the ground for the February launch and to improve the public perception of the Dome. NMEC funds which had been allocated to a large M. & C. Saatchi-devised advertising campaign were now diverted into this less public, background preparation. Freud and Chisholm could see no point in running an expensive advertising campaign two years before any tickets could go on sale. At the same time IMG were working to raise the substantial block of sponsorship for the February launch. By the middle of January they were hoping to deliver heads of agreement and memoranda of understanding with sponsors to the value of £60–£70 million. That, it was felt, would be a credible amount, a heavy enough statement which might dispel the widespread scepticism.

In late 1997 and early 1998 Rupert Murdoch was in regular contact with Tony Blair. An earlier suggestion that Sky should put a dish in every school turned out not to be viable. The question of the Dome now came up.

Rupert Murdoch's daughter Elisabeth, with whom Freud was at that time, as he puts it, 'not yet officially going out', was then General Manager (Broadcasting) for BSkyB. Freud 'talked to Liz about it and then had a few minutes with Murdoch in LA'. He sold the Dome to them both, pitching it as something the television company should naturally be involved with. Sky was all about entertainment and leisure. The Dome was interested in those things too. It would make a good match. The sponsorship required – £12 million – was not something to frighten Murdoch.

Elisabeth Murdoch took the project on and championed it within Sky. She immediately saw the benefits it could bring the company and arranged a meeting in the Cabinet Office with Jennie Page and Peter Mandelson. Mark Booth, then managing director of BSkyB, into whose lap this scheme had been fairly abruptly dropped, and Andrea Sullivan, who would be in charge of the project, came from Sky. It was 'an easy handshake', Sullivan says. Sky were on, being steered at that point towards the zone which was being called 'Serious Play'.

The *Sun* had been consistently hostile to the Dome. Freud rang the paper. 'You may be interested to know ...' he said to Rebekah Wade, the deputy editor. 'Oh, fuck,' she said. For Freud it was 'the nicest call I ever made'. Wade concocted a leader for the paper which smoothed the path between hostility and enthusiasm. On 12 January 1998 the *Sun* had said: 'This waste of public money [should] be axed, for that's what public opinion wants ... that damned Dome has disaster written all over it.' On 17 February it thought the Dome 'has all the makings of the biggest white elephant of this or any other century ... What a terrible monument to the human ego.' On 23 February, after the Freud call, the paper, admitting it had been the 'fiercest critic', now thought: 'There is beginning to be an air of excitement about the Millennium Experience ... Griping about it will achieve nothing. Instead we should all get behind it and ensure its success.'

The pressure to get the sponsors on board and the show ready in time was desperate. Deals with sponsors were running right up to the wire. Manpower only came to an agreement the evening before, at the very moment when Blair's speech was being written in Downing Street. Concluding the design of the zones that were to be launched at the event, in the People's Palace and in the Royal Festival Hall on the South Bank were equally difficult. Eva Jiricna's beautiful pyramidal design for what had been Soul and was now being called 'Spirit Level' had been giving NMEC real worries. 'As soon as I showed it to them,' Jiricna says, 'they said, "The feedback we are getting is that this seems to be about New Age religion." They thought that was totally unacceptable.' The wrangles went on. By the time the crux came, Jiricna was away, working in Kuala Lumpur. She got a phone call in the middle of the night. The pointed tip of the pyramid had became the focus of the objections. The pyramid could not be presented to the public with a pointed tip. That, more than anything else, was said to smack of New Age religion. Certain New Ageists think that pyramids focus cosmic power. The whole Dome was in danger of being hijacked by its presence. The role of Christianity in the millennium and in the Dome was already a contentious public issue. NMEC was treading extraordinarily carefully. 'What about the spires on English churches? They're pointy, aren't they?' Jiricna asked. All the same, the Spirit Level pointiness had to go. In the middle of the night, from Malaysia, Jiricna faxed a drawing to her office of a bobbled perspex hat to sit on top of the pyramid. Her office rapidly prepared a hat for their model.

At least they now had, at the centre of the Dome, something which promised quality of a world class. When the Drum was finally killed off in November 1997, it had immediately seemed a good idea to ask Mark Fisher, the architect of spectacular rock shows, to design something here. Fisher had been in California with the Rolling Stones. Now he was driving around the American West, 'visiting old Pink Floyd covers'. He had reached Furnace Creek Ranch, opposite Zabriskie Point in Death Valley, when he got the summons by e-mail from Matthew Freud. Fisher rang Freud. Freud said, 'We're repositioning the Dome.'

For Fisher, 'It was the phone call I had been waiting for for two years. But politicians don't go to pop concerts, do they? They go to musicals. And no one ever got sacked for buying IBM.' Within a matter of days he was back in England, had seen Michael Grade, Matthew Freud, Jennie Page and Peter Mandelson and was soon being wheeled on to the Coordinating Group, of which Michael Heseltine and Simon Jenkins were members. Fisher, in suit and tie for the occasion, made his early pitch. It was a cross between Cirque de Soleil and a rock concert. It would be a collaboration with someone like Peter Gabriel or David Gilmour, a multicultural experience, in daylight, high-risk.

In this first version of his show different groups of people would, one after another, reach for the heights of the enormous space in which the show was to be performed. Politicians would promise everything and deliver nothing. Scientists, all distorted rationality, would get in a muddle and their tower would head off at an angle. Only the third group – of ordinary people, cooperating with each other – would make it to the apex of the Dome.

The man who catapulted U2 on to the stage in a 15-metre-high rotating lemon, who designed Tina Turner's 1996 *Wildest Dreams* tour and Janet

Jackson's 1998 *Velvet Rope* tour, whose *Bridges to Babylon* set for the Rolling Stones re-enacted the history and/or end of civilisation, confronted the ex-Deputy Prime Minister and the ex-editor of *The Times*. Simon Jenkins liked Fisher's suggestion for its classical three-act structure and its allusions to the manner of the Wakefield mystery plays. Michael Heseltine said, 'More people would burst into tears if a band of the Royal Marines marched across the arena than anyone ever would for your show.'

'Yes,' said Fisher, 'but not for the reasons you think.'

Despite Heseltine's doubts, Fisher was on. His scheme, in collaboration with Peter Gabriel, would over the next two years evolve into an astonishing millennial-operatic, eco-poetic, romantico-historic rock-carnival-fantasy for which there was little precedent in any of the artistic realms on which it drew.

Up until the last minute before the February launch design changes – not only to zones but to the whole layout of the site – were being made. It was all evolving very fast. Models had been commissioned, but on the basis of information that was weeks out of date. That was discovered too late to do anything about it. Gez Sagar from NMEC and Tania Watson from the event company WCT Live were coordinating the hectic, last-minute assembly of all the necessary elements. Blair's speech was being worked on overnight for the breakfast start at 8.30 on the morning of the 24th. There was no possibility of failure. Their core audience, both in the commercial world and in the media, was going to be there. Barclays, Boots, British Gas, BUPA, CBI, Canon, Carlton, Daewoo, ICI, Hambro's, Kvaerner, the Stock Exchange, M & S, Merrill Lynch, HSBC, NatWest, Nestlé, Pepsi, Philips, Rank, Swatch, Unipart, Volkswagen: senior executives from all these mingled with the editors and decision-makers from all the broadcasters and newspaper groups.

Michael Grade had been intending to run a spoof historical version of *What the Papers Say*, with the journalist Roy Greenslade presenting it. 'The Harrier jump jet, The 51 Show, *Les Misérables*: these guys always get it wrong. That would have been the message. But everyone got cold feet on the day.' It would scarcely have fitted with the fierce and evangelical tone of the Prime Minister's speech. Its intensity had deepened and sharpened as it was worked on overnight. As finally delivered, it was emotional, quasi-poetic and visionary in style, a recognition of the enormous significance of the situation. For Peter Mandelson, this was nothing short of a relaunch of the Dome. Standing in front of a huge glossy photograph of a white model of the Dome, Tony Blair delivered the words with passion and commitment.

> It's easy to say don't do something. To say it won't be done on time. That it costs too much. That no one will visit it. It takes little courage to say no to a new idea.
>
> But just suppose we gave in to the cynics and the snipers. Suppose for a second we allowed pessimism to drive out ambition. Suppose we tore down the masts, suppose we said no to the jobs and the tourists, suppose we sacked the builders, returned the land to its previous contaminated state, suppose we dismissed Britain's finest designers, musicians, directors and singers, suppose we told Richard Rogers not to build his great building in this country but to move it elsewhere, then when the eyes of the world fell on Greenwich people would see a derelict site and a signpost in the ground reading: 'Britain – year 2000. Nothing doing.' Wouldn't those same cynics feel just a bit unsettled? Wouldn't they feel that Great Britain had missed an opportunity?

This was rhetoric, but it was good rhetoric. He turned to the interests of the businessmen in front of him.

> This is a celebration that is good for British business. The Millennium Experience is a chance to demonstrate that Britain will be a breeding ground for the most successful businesses of the twenty-first century.
>
> The twenty-first-century company will be different. Many of Britain's best-known companies are already redefining traditional perceptions of the role of the corporation. They are recognising that every customer is part of a community and that social responsibility is not an optional extra.

It was a central statement of the Blair vision. All the key words were here: new, community, business, success, the future, courage, ambition, opportunity, inclusive, us and Britain. After the grandees had left, the so-called 'working press' arrived for their briefing. A tape of what the Prime Minister had just said to the businessmen was played. Peter Mandelson, Bob Ayling, Jennie Page and Michael Grade sat on the platform, watching, in Grade's words, 'the hacks' faces hanging on every word'.

BT, Manpower, Tesco and Sky were announced as founding partners, each contributing at least £12 million. Other sponsors – BAA, BA, the Corporation of London and Camelot – came in with lower figures. The total announced was £75 million. (There was another £12 million from GEC and British Aerospace just in the wings.) Models of zones (Body, Dreamscape, Living Island and Spirit Level) were launched. A draft plan of the inside of the Dome was released. BT now had their own zone, 'Time to Talk'. So did the City of London: 'Transaction'. The original idea of a Work zone, now called 'Licensed to Skill', had spawned another, about lifelong education, 'The Learning Curve', for which Tesco would be the sponsor. A zone devoted to the questions of national identity, uk@now, had also been conceived. Much of the previous autumn had been taken up with public debate on the nature of Britain, its 'rebranding', and the relative weight to be given to cultural inheritance and Cool Britannia. The Dome was now to address that explicitly too.

Much of the press after the launch was good but a steady stream of criticism persisted. Not everyone who was exposed to the Blair rhetoric was seduced by it. Like the Festival of Britain before it, the Dome summoned the anger of all kinds of cultural conservatives: those who wanted Labour to remain 'the party of belief' saw the Dome and its commercial involvement as evidence of the betrayal of principle; those who thought that the inherited institutions of the nation state, and any respect for them, were being eroded into worn, ancient stumps, saw in the Dome evidence of a sterile emptiness in modern life; those who considered the government and the state indifferent to real needs saw the Dome as the sort of place a love of presentation would value; aesthetes saw it as sham and vulgar; moralists as misguided; traditionalists as horrible; radicals as a hijacking of ideals by a diabolic combination of government and commerce.

The proposed content came in for a drubbing. According to the *Mail*, there wasn't enough emphasis on Britain's past glories, the *Express* thought the Dome should be depoliticised, the *Telegraph* asked for more profundity, the *Observer* considered it 'a vacuum held together by rhetoric'. Hugo Young in the *Guardian* called it

> 'a great megaphone for the pain-free verbiage of the new politics. It is also a test-bed for the politico-commercial complex that has become the proof of New Labour inclusiveness. What's not paid for by the lottery will be handled by the Higher Sponsorship. This will produce spectacular struggles for power, as the great corporations fight for position, treading the line between dignity and commerce, between selfless millennial patriotism and making damn sure the brand-names don't get too subliminal.'

Steve Bell, the *Guardian* cartoonist, called the contents a 'farrago of consultancy shite'.

Three days later the £100 million Millennium Festival was also launched. The money was intended for a celebration of the year 2000 in local communities, anything from historical pageants to sporting events. The projects were designed to provide a widespread balance to the glossy, centralised presence of the Dome. 'They will touch the lives of ordinary people,' said the official description from the DCMS, 'encourage activity in the community, develop an understanding of our heritage or culture, educate for the future or promote international links.' The Millennium Commission provided £25 million for the festival and the other lottery distributors £15 million each. NMEC promised £20 million but the festival was not its highest priority. No more than £10 million had come from NMEC by the autumn of 1999, even by the most generous accounting. Most of that was in kind, office work in NMEC's own National Programme offices in twelve regions around the country. The Dome itself was hungry for NMEC cash.

The February launch had been a success – Peter Mandelson considered it a watershed – but it had scarcely solved the sponsorship question. NMEC had firmed up, under heads of agreement documents, those sponsors who had been there for a long time. The first bite was the easiest and the nut was going to get harder the deeper you chewed into it. The later companies came in, the more leverage they could exert and the more demands they could make.

By the early spring Jennie Page was facing an enormous burden. It was clear that she needed someone to take the job of finding sponsorship from her shoulders. By good chance Liam Kane, who had held a string of senior management positions in newspapers and at Sky Television, was free to take the post. In April he became managing director of NMEC, and his laconic, dry, sly assurance added a new layer of ballast to the company. He was a highly experienced and prominent businessman. Other businessmen would trust him. His job, as he saw it on arrival, 'was to pick up on the commercial'. Eight sponsors had been announced at the February launch, but there was no schedule of when the deals were to be delivered and little definition of what benefits sponsorship would bring to the sponsor. Kane set about defining 'a real proposition on a rights package. It was tidying up and formalising. The focus had to be brought into that, to tell them what they were getting.' Kane's task was big but straightforward enough: to 'consider it a global beat, to service the existing guys and sell the rest of it'.

A sponsorship strategy, which would later evolve into an NMEC document known as 'A Rough Guide to Sponsorship', was devised. Sponsors could come in at a number of different levels: £12 million for a Founding Partner, £6 million for an Official Sponsor, £3 million for a Sponsor and lesser amounts for still smaller roles. Money could also be raised via licences with 'Official Suppliers', who would gain pouring rights for drinks, publishing rights for books or 'eating rights' for ice-cream and the rest of it. NMEC would accept either cash or value-in-kind. If, for example, a computer company became a sponsor, it could provide its sponsorship in the form of the information technology which NMEC needed.

NMEC's sponsorship policy was toughly framed. No one would be allowed to sponsor part of the National Programme without also being involved at the Dome. NMEC would retain full control of: the location, size and layout of everything in the Dome; all 'editorial' decisions, including the content of each zone and the overall thematic approach; the overall shape and approach of the National Programme, including its educational aspects, which they called 'The Learning Experience'; the opening hours and operation of the Dome; all access and all activities in the zones while they were being built; the design and operation of everything to do with safety; the use of their own brand and logo; the extent and use of the sponsor's brand within the Dome; and everything to do with food and catering. 'This is not logo-land,' Jennie Page would say.

NMEC would be prepared to negotiate on a subsidiary range of questions: the choice of name for the zone and of the strand of the National Programme related to it; the sponsor's proposals for storylines; the sponsor's suggestions for including specific elements in the zone; the selling of merchandised goods with the sponsor's logo on them; the design of a sponsor's corporate hospitality suite in the Dome – the scale on offer would be dependent on the scale of sponsorship but the cost would be borne by the sponsor.

Not much was being given away here. To some potential sponsors it looked like 'a cheque and go' offer – 'Thank you very much, Mr Sponsor, goodbye.' NMEC's sponsorship policy, in other words, portrayed the Dome as operating in a sellers' market. A necessary commercial front, perhaps, but not, in 1998, a strict reflection of the true state of affairs. As a footnote to the policy, there was a mention of 'tailoring to meet the needs of particular sponsors and, thereby, enhance the attractiveness of the offer while protecting the integrity of the Millennium Experience'. That, of course, was the rub. How much would the 'tailoring' be obliged to concede to sponsors if NMEC were to receive their cash?

Michael Grade maintained that over-heavy branding might have appealed to the companies but not to the public. 'There have been big rows about branding and naming. I say to all these marketing directors, "You can have your name plastered all over everything. You can have your name everywhere. It will be a propaganda festival for the company. Then the boss turns up. You will have got name recognition beyond belief, a competitive edge for your zone over every other one in the Dome. And the queues will be for everything else. And then what's the boss going to say?" They all work on the fear factor. I have spent a lifetime in commercial TV. And I tell them: "I don't know how to sell aspirin and you don't know how to put on a show."'

That may have been the tough public line, but there was some smooth talking too. The companies were to be persuaded that being part of a group of big sponsors was a good idea. The natural tendency was to wish for single prominence. Kane could only say to them: 'A bigger group will make a bigger noise. You need to be in that noise.' As the roof was being fitted, he took a string of potential sponsors on what was called the

'Works Tour'. It almost always had the desired effect: 'Deep cynics lost their cynicism when they saw the Dome.' The sell to chairmen and chief executives was relatively easy. What Kane calls the 'smoke and mirrors bit, the building the worth of your brand' always went down well with them. Marketing directors were more difficult.

Ken Robinson, the operations director who had a finger in most Dome pies, thought that 'Once you've twisted the arm of a chairman up the back that you want £12 million, that's when the real problems start because he has to explain it back at the ranch. Other people are on to it and they all try to score points off each other. That's got delay built into it.'

Another aspect of commercial psychology was at work. Once sponsors had committed verbally, the best thing they could possibly do was prevaricate. What incentive was there to say yes to anything? Just keep objecting, keep saying no, see what you can squeeze out of the project. That made life for those at the Dome who were trying to sign them up very difficult indeed. Over 150 companies were approached. Twenty-two were eventually signed up. On some zones the agreement between NMEC and the sponsor went through more than 50 different drafts before the deal was done. And the money raised was unprecedented. The £87 million in February 1998 rose to £120 million by that November, £144 million the following February and £157 million by May 1999. Some idea of the struggle can be measured by the way in which the rate of money coming in rapidly drops over time.

Kane's method was to establish with the sponsors the two outer limits of the spectrum into which any Dome deal could not stray. At one end you had the trade show: total costs for a stand borne by the company, total control of content by the company, an advertisement and manifesto for the brands and products. At the other end was what Kane calls 'the opera. You get a brass nameplate outside the opera house, you hand over your money, your brand derives cachet and standing from its association with something of such high quality and high status, but the sponsor has no control over and no say in the content. There's no rewriting of the Mozart and the divas don't wear the company logo on gold chains around their necks.'

Some in the press thought this was a trade show. Some in NMEC, at least in the early days, thought this was the opera. Neither would work here. The sponsorship team's job was to determine precisely where on the spectrum they wanted the deal to be. What they ended up with, inevitably, was a fair spread along the central band. Some of the big sponsors have approached the whole event with an understanding of what Kane calls 'the value of an unmarked place, of how a brand is better served by buying into the ethos of being a responsible citizen'. Others have not. The irrepressible Ken Robinson thinks that 'Very few sponsors understand the meaning of dignified, appropriate accreditation. They don't know that one logo in the right place is worth a thousand in the wrong places. They are all saying, "Can I make it four feet bigger? Can it flash in neon?"'

The relationship with Marks & Spencer was in many ways a model of how it might go. Their involvement had always been a possibility. Sir Richard Greenbury, the chairman, had been at Heseltine's drum-banging in the summer of 1996, but nothing had come of that. The relationship was revived by a letter to Greenbury from Bob Ayling in the autumn of 1997. The match between NMEC and the position of M & S in national life was as good as any that would evolve during the creation of the Dome.

Key to it was Ed Williams, head of the millennium project at Marks & Spencer since its inception in June 1997. The history of the company's involvement with the millennium had started earlier than that. In February that year M & S, as one of the cornerstones of national life, employing 60,000 people in the United Kingdom, was already receiving ad hoc requests from people all over the country, asking if they would 'invest in the community'. Many of the requests were already being linked to the millennium. The M & S board discussed it and decided that they couldn't respond to the ad hoc requests with ad hoc responses. Expectations of the way in which the modern corporation would behave were clearly moving in this direction. There was a need for some vision, for a strategy.

Williams, who had been head of training and management development, jumped at the opportunity. It felt like an area of real growth and he was known in the company as a safe pair of hands. Characteristically they then set up a millennium committee which included not just the bigwigs but a full cross-section of the company, from sales assistants to senior management, from all regions: 'This business doesn't work without the willingness of our employees to own and be part of everything we do.'

M & S corporate culture was already profoundly millennial in this way. The committee consulted widely and ran internal focus groups. Five hundred staff, suppliers, customers, members of the voluntary sector, Prince Charles's Business in the Community, the Prince's Trust and other charities were all spoken to. The consultation lasted for six weeks. It had to be completed quickly; M & S staff would not have been available in the Christmas peak trading period. There was no assumption that anything they might do would have any connection with NMEC or the Dome but, curiously or not, the ideas that began to emerge at M & S were deeply concordant with the Millennium Experience. 'Make an impact, leave a difference,' is how Williams puts it.

In August 1997 Williams rang Jennie Page at NMEC. 'A very spunky lady', he calls her. He went down to the Greenwich peninsula to look at the site, saw it and thought, 'How on earth …?' but then went to the top of Canary Wharf and said to himself, 'This is going to be grand!' The regenerative potential, the sense of legacy, fired the enthusiasm of this immensely energetic and enthusiastic man. 'This is important!'

Over the autumn M & S had conducted its own surveys among the public at large, asking about attitudes to the millennium. The answers were, Williams says, 'staggering in their consistency, irrespective of age, area and class'. The millennium meant the future, not the past, and was about giving, not receiving. For everyone, the recurrent terms were: partnership, community, pride and uniqueness; with a secondary cluster around inclusion, participation and involvement.

During September, over the phone, Jennie Page had mentioned quite easily, with no hard sell, that there was an opportunity to be a sponsor here. For Williams, everything – both his company's own intentions and whatever the Millennium Experience was planning to be – was at far too early a stage for any form of commitment to be made on either side. Page did not let on to him the severe pressure she was now under to deliver on sponsorship.

Late in 1997 M & S gave NMEC the results of its polling on a single piece of paper. 'Here's your brief,' Williams said to Page. 'See if you can excite us with that.' By January 1998 NMEC had come back with three ideas. M & S could become involved with a scheme to do with literacy, with a concept called 'social entrepreneurship' or with something they called 'Children's Promise', whereby millions of British citizens would be asked to commit the value of their last working hour in this millennium to the well-being of children in the next.

Williams didn't hesitate for long: the literacy suggestion looked too governmental; social entrepreneurship was a little complicated; but Children's Promise looked perfect: anyone could get the point of it in one shot; it was imaginative; it could involve a wide partnership of children's charities; the social legacy was going to be huge; and the entire country could be involved.

On a sponsorship deal of a possible £12 million, Williams was in no position to make a decision. M & S, which gives about £10.5 million every year to many different charitable ends, had never been involved in any single project of this scale before. The board members had to decide. In February he presented them with three options. They went for Children's Promise because they felt 'emotionally and intellectually that this was something that fulfilled all the criteria for all the stockholders in the company'.

For Marks & Spencer, there was no doubt that the National Programme was the draw. Children's Promise – the gift to children's charities of everybody's final hour's earnings – which started as an idea inside NMEC, did turn into an extraordinary phenomenon. Two separate pieces of market research undertaken by NMEC and M & S early in 1998 showed that 63–64 per cent of people would be prepared to give to it, potentially raising tens of millions for children. No one, anywhere, had done this before. Through 1998 and 1999 the scheme began to inspire sister projects across the world. Large numbers of British companies, 1,600 by Autumn 1999, responded by agreeing to give the money from the payroll, an American idea which makes donations for workers easy – and tax free.

Ed Williams is evangelical about the process. 'Integrity, that lies behind what we are doing. How we are doing it is terribly important. M & S has led the country in this. We set an example, nailing our colours to the mast and inviting everyone to get behind us. We haven't blasted the M & S logo all over everything. It is crucially not called the "Marks & Spencer Children's Promise". It is "Children's Promise, made possible by Marks & Spencer". That allows other organisations to take part. Where we will win, will be in the long game. It is unmeasurable. But in ten years I know I will be glad to have had a bit to do with this. We had the vision to commit to a project with the press criticising it every day. We had a board with vision and courage. I have never felt prouder of anything in my life.'

BSkyB was always going to have a slightly different agenda. Andrea Sullivan, the American powerhouse in charge of the millennium project for the company, was clear about the mutual benefits which Sky and the Dome could bring each other. 'Sky is a lead player. It's an influential company. It was always going to be good for the Millennium Experience to have a close relationship with a media partner. Sky was at the eight-year mark, entering a more mature phase, and this was the right thing to be doing, to show more public support and so become, in a way, more a part of the British Public in return. This was social marketing. We wanted to bring Sky down to earth, off the screen and get out of all that negative press.'

Social and commercial interests coalesced. There was a new government. The idea of partnership and community had taken on a new importance. According to Sullivan, 'the government alone is no longer solely responsible for growth and development. Businesses have a role to play.' Sky could also see a direct marketing advantage. 'There was a high-quality audience here for us,' Sullivan says. 'A targeted audience, a top-end audience, full of diversity and interested in the future. Any corporation would go after that.' It was not necessarily 'an opportunity to promulgate Sky products per se, but rather a chance to meet and greet consumers in a warm and personal way. This was not about selling dishes *today*. It was about associating Sky with great entertainment and positioning the company as the leader of the digital age. It was about the whole vision, including the warmer side of Sky.'

That was quite a difficult sell inside the company. Sullivan describes the priorities for marketing cash as 'the food chain: anything which will have a direct impact on sales is at the top; brand development is next; and social marketing comes behind them. It has great potential but has got to push to make itself heard.'

The development of the Play zone, of which Sky was to be the sponsor and Land the designers, became bogged down in a mismatch of visions.

Sky's involvement with it finally came to a complete end in August 1998, when their sponsorship moved over to Skyscape, the cinema and event building on the eastern side of the peninsula.

But Sky's part of the National Programme, eventually called 'Reach for the Sky', went more easily. They had done some market research in March. What did people think of Sky? The four answers were: 'Murdoch, exciting, entrepreneurial and young'. Clearly, their target audience was going to be teenagers. 'We're cool for them. We are not a company that can ask people to give their time or give to charity like M & S, but we knew we could possibly make teenagers feel there is something for them out there.' The critical point in a teenager's life is between fourteen and sixteen. The optimism which many feel at fourteen drops away in the following two years. Uncertainty enters their lives. The Sky programme aimed 'to push them over that hump, to enthuse them about their hidden talents, to imagine what they could be tomorrow. Follow your passions – see what you can be!' Sullivan says.

In June 2000 the company intended to research again, to assess the effects of Skyscape and Reach for the Sky. How much commercial value did Sky get out of it? How much of an impact did it make on teenagers? What were the social benefits? 'For Sky it is a question of "brand appreciation", the confirmation of "New Sky" and a need to show that we're working for Britain and the future.'

Throughout this period of intense growth in the project, as NMEC was fighting to bring in new sponsors, develop designs, keep its political supervisors happy, both in government and in Parliament, complete the building of the Dome itself, promote the National Programme, develop an organisational strategy for the year of operation, work out how to sell 12 million tickets, consider the marketing programme and philosophy, complete an environmental plan for Greenwich council, keep environmental pressure groups on-side, identify and gain planning permission for park-and-ride car parks around London, run a competition for the right to operate the river-boats between central London and the Dome and between historic Greenwich and the Dome, and keep tabs on the development of the Jubilee Line extension – over which anxiety was now beginning to rise – it is perhaps not surprising that some strain appeared in the way this company dealt with others.

Andrew Fitch, of the designers HP:ICM, who were initially working on both the Body and the Global zones, shared the sensation of many designers and sponsors that NMEC was a strangely cold organisation to deal with. 'NMEC was very quiet in response,' Fitch says. 'You sent stuff in and it was like sending it into a black hole, wondering whether it would emerge. Sometimes a big multinational can behave in the same way. It's often what happens in the public sector when there is a requirement to see everything done absolutely equitably. And it can happen when a company is new, with no established working relationships. NMEC was all three of those things: big, public sector and new. All three are stiffening factors.'

This is not an easy environment for any kind of creative work to feed into. 'They had no opportunity to fail in private,' Fitch says. The result was over-formality, delay and frustration. 'If only they had said to us all, all us designers, "Look, we're in this together, let's discover this together," it would have gone so much better.'

NMEC was anxious that designers should not communicate too closely with each other. Martin Newman, one of the content editors at NMEC, felt that designers getting together 'tend to make mischief'. The London design world is not big and they all knew each other. Most of them had worked together in the past. Media Projects, which was doing much of the audio-visuals across the Dome at the time, held a party for everybody at the Groucho Club. The air was thick with complaint. 'This client was learning to be a client,' Fitch says. 'And they were giving out contradictory signals. For something like this to work well, there needs to be a lot of mutual trust. There wasn't much of that here. At one minute they would be breathing over your shoulder, checking what you were doing. And then they were nowhere to be seen. It was alternately stifling and chilly.'

The content design process did not of its nature run smoothly. The work of the designers – combined with that of Claire Sampson, the content editors, the Litmus Group and the suggestions of the godparents – was essentially *iterative*. It was a word used repeatedly in NMEC, meaning that no one could jump to final solutions but had to go over and over his ideas again and again, refining and enriching them at each pass, until eventually something robust and respectable, fun and full of life, worth doing, memorable and sponsorable might emerge. Michael Grade championed and defended the Dome and its convoluted emergence, becoming in part the practised, public, non-political spokesman which the project so badly needed. It was a task he found far more difficult than running Channel Four. For Grade, asking why the process seemed to be so jerky and unsure 'was like asking someone, "Why didn't you write Draft Five first?"' Everything here was a prototype. Until opening day the Dome's whole life was a test run, a desperate stretch to fulfil contradictory ends.

By contrast, the process of actually building the Dome and its surrounding structures was exemplary. There had been delays earlier on. At Christmas 1997, because of problems with the cable net, the programme was three weeks behind. 'There was no fat in the programme,' says Cliff Smith of the McAlpine Laing joint venture. 'Any problems meant delay.' In response, they could always bring more people on. Or they could redefine the meaning of 'completion'. They realised that it was possible to begin fitting the fabric before the cable net was fully stressed. They focused on start-dates for the elements of the programme. 'People's definition of "finished" can be very wide,' Smith says. 'People's definition of "started" is either "it has" or "it hasn't". Getting things started was what mattered. If start-dates were hit, that would be a "key motivator". We've started on the day we said we would. And success breeds success.' They were aiming to complete the installation of the Dome's fabric by June 1998. Even with an accelerated programme, that was looking difficult. The section of roof around the Blackwall Tunnel vent was simply excluded from the definition of 'finished'. When, on 22 June 1998, the grand topping-out ceremony was held at Greenwich, that section of the fabric had still not been fitted. No one felt that was a problem, largely because it was said not to be a problem. 'We couldn't have told everyone, "Sorry, you can't come. There's a big hole in the roof,"' Smith says, smiling.

In fact, the great summer ceremony, held on a glorious day, was as much of a boost for everyone on site as the February event had been. In the space of a year the Dome had emerged.

The system by which the job itself was being managed was working well. All firms were contracted directly to NMEC. The McAlpine Laing joint venture was not building anything itself but was managing each of those contracts for NMEC. It was a system elegant for its simplicity: the client directs and pays bills; the construction manager manages the process; the designers design; and the builders build. The representatives from both sides of the joint venture, Bernard Ainsworth from Laing's and Cliff Smith from Sir Robert McAlpine's, felt justifiably happy in mid 1998 with the progress they were making. The standard contract they were using was 'very onerous'. If anything was delivered late, NMEC would exact a penalty without having to demonstrate that they had suffered any damages. The final payments would be made only on 'completion', not the usual terms in the building trade, which referred to 'practical completion'. 'Completion' on the Dome would mean utterly complete, with every snag snagged and the manuals to every piece of equipment handed over.

In return for this, there was a large, dangled carrot. The joint venture didn't stand back and leave people with their problems. If there was a difficulty, they would help them with it. Pragmatic views were taken. Much of this was governed by the deadline. In normal circumstances, when there is a problem, there can be a face-off. The contractor can refuse to do work until the claim is settled. The client keeps sending letters to the contractors. Such delays could not be tolerated here but people had realised for years that the Dome's deadline created perfect conditions for blackmail – 'If you don't pay us x, it won't be ready on time.' Cliff Smith of the joint venture is fairly straightforward about this: 'If someone plays silly here, we can tell them. You are now holding the McAlpine Laing joint venture to ransom. Laing's turnover is about £1 billion a year, McAlpine's about £500 million. Together we have about 20 per cent of the market in major projects.' The prospect of alienating these giant players in the contracting landscape was not particularly inviting. 'A fight is a failure,' Smith says. 'Cooperation is better in terms of quality, time and budget.'

Nevertheless, another difficult question loomed over them. The demise of the Drum had restored an integrity to the Dome. It was to be one space after all – busy, filled, multifarious but with its heart intact. The Fisher/Gabriel central show would take place in an open arena, to which all visitors would have access from the great ring promenade, the High Way, around it. This in itself was a beautiful idea, the great show of the millennium growing out of the street life of the Dome, like a pageant in the square of a small town. But there was an operational problem. The Dome had from the start set out to combat problems of queuing and overcrowding. To have 30,000-odd people cramming themselves in to watch a show for which the capacity was perhaps half that was not desirable. 'We needed another zone,' Mike Davies said, 'a lung, a pied piper to draw people away.' Another zone, outside, staging something particularly attractive, would reduce the population of the Dome itself at crucial moments. This was the birth of the Baby Dome.

Mike Davies, Andrew Morris and the RRP team set about planning the plaza between the Dome, the tube station and the river. They and Buro Happold, along with the McAlpine Laing joint venture, which was going to manage its construction, produced plan after plan in which a fabric 'dragon-tail' swirled out from the body of the Dome, enclosing a beautiful open public space, a plaza. It was just the sort of enclosed public space that Richard Rogers and Mike Davies had long wanted to create. The square next to the Centre Pompidou in Paris – where people meet, watch performances, and view the theatre of ordinary life - was precisely what they wanted here. The Baby Dome was to house 5,000 people for each performance. It was to nestle under the folds of the dragon-tail.

But there were difficulties. The Baby Dome itself swelled from 12 metres in height to 18. Fitting a cinema inside a curvy shape is not easy. It became too large to sit inside the skirts of the dragon-tail. In Davies's words, 'the lump couldn't be integrated under the cover. The Baby Dome was becoming not a robin but a cuckoo.' The architects started again. The swirling liquid forms of the early suggestions, which would have been so flattering and concordant with the Dome itself, were not working. The budget was stretched and the operability looked awkward. The requirements for retail and catering space and for service and support buildings in the plaza all proliferated. The open space started to shrink under the pressure. What Davies calls 'a more authoritarian system' seemed to be the only option. The snake or dragon-tail was abandoned. A 'wedge' building was devised as the theatre. The plaza shrank away. 'The power of a great outdoor space', as Davies put it, was now trimmed and shut in. The whole process was a source of great regret for the architects. The brief was growing and the cost of the Wedge was mounting. Finally, as the costs of this pied piper of a zone topped eight figures, in September 1998, a halt was called.

The answer, produced by Claire Sampson, was to rent. A structure designed by a combination of Edwin Shirley Staging and Urban Salon, a small London architectural practice, had been up in Battersea Power Station the year before. It was a building made from standard components which could be taken apart, enlarged, shrunk, or re-erected elsewhere. It was relatively cheap, although its PVC roof had to be replaced here with Teflon-coated fabric.

It was big, square and spiky in appearance. Mike Davies and Richard Rogers were not keen to have it positioned right next to the Dome. 'It was as big as the Sydney Opera House,' Mike Davies says, 'uncompromisingly aggressive as a structure, completely ruined the visitor approach from the pier and destroyed the glorious river-boat views of the Dome and London's skyline from the Thames Barrier.' It would look better, they felt, surrounded by its own space, on the south of the plaza next to the coach park, where it would 'contain and complete the plaza without blocking the riverside'. NMEC refused. They didn't want people having to walk too far from the Dome to reach it. A compromise was arrived at. The Edwin Shirley building was erected on the east side of the site next to the pier, not abutting the Dome but not too distant from it either. By October Sky, which had been through and finally abandoned a long and complex set of proposals for the Play zone, was married to the Edwin Shirley building, now to be called Skyscape.

Around it, the plaza changed from a fluid system to a modular one. Daisy-chains of orange steel, PTFE fabric and perspex canopies strung their way from tube station to ticket booths to Skyscape, to the pier head and the Dome itself. All were set in a sea of red tarmac – 40,000 square metres of it – both inside and outside the Dome, the orange and red as festive a combination as you could imagine, the colours of fun. Mike Davies had copied the red from the Mall. Having parked his red Jaguar there one day in early 1999, he was bending down with his red penknife and picking out a grain or two for reference when he looked up to see a policeman peering over his shoulder. What exactly was he doing? He was sourcing a colour for the floor of the Dome. The policeman sent him on his way.

The difficulties over the Baby Dome were part of a larger problem that began to affect the workings of the Greenwich offices from mid 1998 onwards. Until then the atmosphere there had been remarkably harmonious for a big, high-pressure building project. David Trench, the tough-minded, project-managing site and structures director, was the sort of figure that contractors are used to. They relished the way in which he attacked the work: no recriminatory letters, no stiffness in the hierarchy. His 'positive, galvanic approach meant it was firing on all cylinders', according to Cliff Smith. That was when the job was relatively simple: prepare the ground, put the building up, install the services. When, in the second half of 1998, NMEC started preparations for the installation of contents, the mood changed. The relationships within NMEC between site and structures on one side and operations and production on the other were not naturally harmonious. The trust between them became frayed and what had been a good team spirit grew strained. There was a culture gap. Defending the production team against criticism from the construction side, Jennie Page says, 'They didn't understand an industry where people were younger, didn't wear ties and were often female.'

There was a falling apart, accompanied by a more overt insistence from the higher management that this was one team, involved in one project. Nevertheless, the joint venture was allowed no involvement with the designers of the zones. 'Because we're builders,' one of them said wryly, 'we couldn't possibly have a relationship with the designers.'

Meanwhile, in yet another of the multiple, simultaneous threads of such a project, each of them interlocking, crossing, sometimes sharing a channel, sometimes running in their own like the braids of a river, the whole marketing strategy for the Dome was under revision through 1998. At the suggestion of Matthew Freud and after the usual hiring process had been followed, Sholto Douglas-Home, in charge of advertising and PR at BT, joined NMEC. He met the company culture in full flow. Jennie Page gave him a piercingly astringent interview. Douglas-Home mentioned 'the new century' as something to think about. Page said, 'New century? What do you mean new century? It's the new millennium we are meant to be thinking about here.'

Then he met Mandelson. 'There are four things that have got to be done,' the minister told him. 'We have got to build it and someone's doing that very well. We've got to get the sponsorship and that is coming along very nicely. We've got to define the content, which is Jennie's job. And someone has got to sell 12 million tickets, and that's your job. Your job is to make the world come to the Dome.'

Flattering, attentive, challenging, nurturing: this was a side to

Mandelson which he had failed to communicate to the public. 'Do you run or go to the gym?' he asked Douglas-Home.

'I used to be a sprinter but I can't stand long-distance running,' the Dome's new marketing director said, on slightly unfamiliar territory.

'Oh, you should. You're in your mid thirties. You have got to keep fit.'

'I do, but sometimes I creak in the mornings.'

'Creak in the mornings? That's worrying,' Mandelson said. 'You should see someone about it.'

Douglas-Home joined NMEC on 1 September 1998. He had three weeks in which to present a new marketing strategy to ExCo, chaired by the powerful and no-frills figure of Sam Chisholm. The year before, when the previous advertising campaign had been presented, Chisholm and Matthew Freud had lacerated Kevin Johnson, then the commercial and marketing director. It had been a bloodbath. Douglas-Home knew the history. This time, Chisholm began with: 'Don't give me charts. I just want it straight.' He got it straight.

Douglas-Home outlined his thinking. NMEC needed to 'own the millennium'. They needed to establish their brand, to make some sort of statement of what they were. Some of their sponsors had started to do things and NMEC wasn't doing anything. Sponsors were starting to ask, 'When are you going to get going?' There was a media expectation. And, internally, morale had been 'carved back' by the way in which the Dome had been treated over the previous eighteen months. NMEC was 'entrenched, hunkered down. It needed a lift.'

As Douglas-Home finished his presentation, there was a long pause. Chisholm turned to Freud. 'Sounds OK. Matthew, what do you think?'

Freud: 'On the button.' No one else said a word.

Chisholm said, 'Sholto, you're a fucking adornment.'

Douglas-Home said, 'Thank you,' and left the room.

The strategy was brilliant and simple. With just twelve months to go, people's expectations about the millennium itself – not about the Dome or the National Programme – needed heightening. This was deep background. The spotlight needed to be turned away from the Dome, from its tangle of argument, controversy and air of Mandelsonian manipulation, to something more inspiring, encouraging people to imagine the possibilities ahead. Simon Dicketts at M. & C. Saatchi drafted the script of an ad to be set on Easter Island. The mystery and sheer antiquity of those stone heads, their easy reach into the distant past, would bring a poetry and depth to the idea of the millennium which the press coverage had almost completely eroded in people's minds. Allied to a sense of the future, and to the idea of personal involvement in what it might be, the ad would be a way of setting the millennium firmly on track.

Easter Island belongs to Chile. Three days after the go-ahead was given for the ad, General Pinochet was arrested in London and there were anti-British riots in Santiago. It looked as if the whole scheme was up in the air. Private communications between the Foreign Office and the Chilean embassy reassured everyone that the Chilean government would do all it could to make life easy for the film crew. In this, Pinochet was a side-issue. The appearance of Easter Island on British television in connection with the millennium was important. The 60-second film was made. The imagery was beautiful, the script, read by Jeremy Irons, touching, funny, wondering whether the discovery of the sandwich and the bringing of the potato to Europe were two of the great historical moments of the last millennium. When it was first shown to NMEC staff in their offices that December, they stood there with tears in their eyes. It was difficult at times to remember what this was all for. The ad was a reminder.

Peter Mandelson, who had acutely and subtly analysed the script and approach of the film when it was first presented to him, now fell from office. As the news broke just before Christmas of his secret loan from Geoffrey Robinson, followed by his resignation from the government and from his position as shareholder of the Dome, the Easter Island ad went out on prime time TV. The sun came up over the eastern Pacific and the commercial made its invitation: 'Imagine what we can do tomorrow.'

CHAPTER NINE

Delivering the Dome

In 1999, as the Dome started to fill, each one of the giant zone buildings took up its stance. The elements of an orchestra were settling into place: the huge steel bassoon of Zaha Hadid's Mind, its vast cantilevered limbs stretching a quarter of the way across the Dome; beside it the spider legs of Eva Jiricna's Faith, teetering on the very points of its toes; the big, smooth, twinkly-skinned, round-bodied drum of Home Planet; the skeleton of the Body, bristling with armatures as complex as a clarinet, but awaiting a skin of chicken wire and concrete, to be sheened in glimmery, plastic tiles whose shot-silk colours would dance and change as you passed; the big boxes of Play and Work and Learning, scarcely articulating the secrets they would hold; the cool glass, minimalist skins of the two Talk buildings, which would in time converse with each other, flickering messages across the narrow canyon between them; the sealight-washed surreality of Living Island, where the White Cliffs of Greenwich were made of crushed cans, the lighthouse was all lightbulbs and where gulls flapping in the constant sea-breeze were recycled and reassembled parts from abandoned cars. Rudolf Steiner famously said that 'animals are the soul of a landscape'. These were the Dome's – regeneration machines: the funny, the clever and the airborne summoned from the old, the dead and the junked.

The Dome itself, the giant, loose-fit envelope, the biggest umbrella the world had ever seen, was not the purpose or the end-point of this enterprise. It was no more than an enabler, a delivery system. Even Mike Davies, the architect, hoped and intended 'for the Dome to disappear behind the experience it contained'. The substance was in the zones themselves and in the buzzing, flittering life which NMEC would provide around them. 'Content had to be king here,' said Tania Watson, one of the content editors. The Dome had to live. It was to be no cold, static, hushed museum, nor an architecture show – although some dazzling architecture was to be part of the ensemble. In the tussle, as Watson puts it, 'between architecture and story, story had to win. Each zone needs to be a building. Without a building you have no light control, no sound control, no experiential control. So you have to shut the experience inside a box. But, as we said to the designers, you mustn't lose sight of the fact that you have to spend money on the experience itself.' She jokes about the attitude of some of them: 'Oh, I see, so you want things for people to do as well?'

Here and there the Dome would have elements of architectural purity and stillness. The zone devoted to Rest and the contemplative cone at the heart of Faith were to be deep, cool, calming places, long in their rhythms, ethereal in atmosphere. The Greenwich Pavilion, outside the Dome itself on the reconstituted banks of the Thames, was to be composed and classical in its approach to the history of the site and of Greenwich. There was, by design, to be little fizz or pzazz there. Its method was clarity and elegance. By the time people reached it, as its curator Richard Burdett realised, they would, be 'exhibitioned out'.

Most of the Dome was not like that. Its contents were designed to zing. Minimalist this was not. Its means of communication aimed to be 'hot', grabbing, immediate, full of engagement with real things in real time. In the zone called Talk, sponsored by BT, you would be able to speak on a video phone to a sailor in the cockpit of a round-the-world yacht or to someone at that very moment going down the Cresta run on a bobsleigh. An entire TV studio would be in the same zone. Game shows would take place there. In Home Planet, travelling in the 'hyperlink', people would 'get the sense that they were zooming off from this spaceport, Intergalatwick, whoosh', the engine would 'spark up and fire up behind you and, this light travels over your head and then you go poww.'

Vigour was all. More than anything else, the late-twentieth-century world valued energy and vitality. If you look at the film made of visitors to the Festival of Britain in 1951 and compare them in your mind's eye with modern people, they look stiff, constrained, orderly, modest in requirements and expectations. The women wear hats. The men are in suits. Conformity colours the way they exist in the world. There is a self-containment and lack of expressiveness here which looks at us across half a century like a stilted remark from another age. Austerity has entered their souls.

The Modern is looser, freer, more fragmented and more open-necked. If, in 1951, queues were found forming for nothing, the Dome's declared policy was queuelessness. No one should have to wait for what they wanted. It was the great change of the second half of the century. And, of course, freedom from want and from many of the traditional constraints which the post-war culture enshrined – of hierarchy, respect and discretion – brought with it many of the discontents and uncertainties which the Millennium Experience aimed to address. You only had to imagine what you could do tomorrow if tradition did not ordain it for you. Liberty was now at a higher premium than order.

Peter Mandelson had always been insistent that there should be what he called both 'pow' and 'wow' in the contents of the Dome – pow being intellectual strength and coherence, wow a sense of amazement and delight. The Dome visitor was not to be a passive consumer, lying flaccid in front of his digital TV, but was there to be involved. Only those who were properly alive would be able to make a difference. The Dome aimed to vivify and to dramatise the significance of the individual and the choices before him. The individual was the prime mover here.

In Play, for example, there was a game called Kaleidoscope. The visitor stood in front of a camera. Beside it was a screen. The camera was linked to a digital music encoder. The screen showed an image of the part of the visitor's body which the camera could see. The image was not whole but broken and arranged into the sort of radially symmetrical pattern which a kaleidoscope makes. Fragments of your hand, your fingers, your blinking eye, your breathing lips would be taken by the camera and arranged in a repetitive and beautiful pattern in front of you. As you moved, the speed of your own movements would govern the tempo of the music around you. The faster you moved, the faster the image changed and the faster the music went, a mesmeric, enveloping, magical and memorable experience, so enjoyable and so alluring for the modern sensibility that two versions of it were installed in the zone.

There was, of course, a more serious and earnest side to this whole strand of the Millennium Experience. According to Chris Baines, the environmentalist and adviser on green issues at the Dome, 'The most important thing is for people to realise that the Dome is just a launch pad, a memorable experience that marks the start of the rest of their life.' Or as Tim Pyne, Living Island's designer, puts it, 'You don't have to be a tree- and bunny-hugging, whale-saving, yoghurt-eating, bearded, sandal- wearing vegan to make a difference.' The Dome was for everybody. Everybody could act in the world. Suffering the slings and arrows of outrageous fortune was not one of the modern choices. Stoicism was out. Anyone who came to Greenwich would leave with the idea that the future might not only be theirs but was malleable in their hands. The purpose was an enlargement of life.

NMEC knew that technology alone would not deliver the necessary quality of experience. The dynamism of the machine or the extraordinary reach of electronic technology had, for all its sparkle, a certain chill. There were already clear signs, in a hi-tech society, of screen fatigue. There was no point in coming to Greenwich if all you got was what the Internet could give you anyway. If the Dome was to seem genuinely communal, it needed live performers. There were to be many real people as hosts and demonstrators and explicators inside each of the zones – visitors would meet a living ET in Talk; in Journey you could hear from experts about the nature of transport in the future; Cybermen in Play would engage you in conversation; Professor Richard Gregory, the godfather of Mind, who had steered the zone away from the abstruse unintelligibilities of modern French and American identity theory, in which it had become mired, pressed for live demonstrations of prodigious feats of memory in the zone.

Outside them, a live events programme would make the Dome fizz with vitality. The shows in a string of theatres around the site, and players mingling with the people in the streets and squares of this extraordinary, condensed little millennium city, would provide what Robert Warner, head of live events, called 'the human touch. People will come to the experience, they'll enjoy their fourteen exhibitions, but they'll actually remember some wacky butler who comes up while they're eating their sandwiches and plays with them, then goes away.' Street actors, comedians, musicians, dancers, jugglers, puppeteers, figures called Clockheads, mad policemen, an Elizabeth I who would know every single detail about the life she lived in the sixteenth century – all of these would make a day at the Dome an enveloping experience from which the visitor himself would leave amazed, flattered at his own significance, restored in his self-esteem, smiling at the memory of those strange, autopiloted and wireless flying machines which orbited the giant model of the earth next to Home Planet.

Deep in the Dome's idea of its own purpose was the principle that everything here should be utterly accessible. There should be a free flow of people around the site. Everything should be easy for those in wheelchairs. Signs would be low enough for the wheelchair-bound to read them. A liquid petroleum gas land-train (very sleek, very Italian) would deliver people to wherever they wanted to be. If queues, despite the policy, happened to materialise, their members would be entertained, or persuaded to go somewhere else just as wonderful. The visitors were never to feel impotent or imposed upon. They should be able to choose. They should be confronted with experiences that would inspire or enlarge their spirits. This was to be a place without barriers. Everything should be continuous with everything else. There should be no hierarchies. In the version of the ideal future which was being revealed to us here, all forms of understanding should be open to us all. This did not need to be like the real world. Everything could be heightened and better here.

The repeated climax was the great apocalyptic spectacle of the millennium show in the central arena, devised by Mark Fisher and Peter Gabriel. The show itself was a huge-scale cross-over of street theatre, carnival, apocalyptic poetry, fantasia-engineering, dance, rock and acrobatics, lasting 20 minutes and performed five times a day. The arena and the huge spaces above it had no curtain to raise. The show could only emerge from the normality of Dome life around it. Between performances, visitors would mill about in the arena. Mark Fisher compares the space to 'a great European town square, the Campo in Siena before the Palio'. The citizens of the Dome had to be slowly shepherded to the side before the show could begin. This almost medieval sense of theatre erupting from within the crowd was one of the most exciting aspects of the show. It was a version of communal intimacy, of the absence of barriers and of a natural connection between art and life on an enormous scale.

The show started slowly, strangely, with performers moving among the audience in costumes and on stilts, disturbing and distracting them, others emerging like butterflies from a chrysalis, yet others pushing dragonfly and jellyfish mobiles into the centre of the arena. From that quiet beginning grew a spectacular, wordless (and so available to all, whatever their native language), high-energy, breakneck sky ballet, the enacting of a drama which, in three seamlessly linked acts, Fisher says, portrayed 'mankind's aspirations – to pass on wisdom from one generation to the next, to explore the idea of collaborative achievement and the ways in which less generous forms of organisation do not do as well as others'. The bad society shut you in; the good allowed you all to thrive together.

This emphasis on communality, on a public sense of togetherness, was the heart of the Millennium Experience. It provided the very thing over one brief shining day for which the atomised condition of modern life created an appetite. It was the focus of a modern pilgrimage, which Simon Jenkins had envisaged in his first proposals for a millennium exhibition five years before. This was social regeneration taking physical and concrete, if highly symbolic, form. The deep enhancement of individuality and the large-scale celebration of communality were not contradictory here, but complementary, each richer for the vitality of the other. It was in another form – and in a phrase from which NMEC itself would run a mile – the third way beyond the socialist and the Thatcherite, a deeply traditional vision of a happy world.

In the preparation for this vision, the Dome was hive-like in its busyness. An extraordinary atmosphere developed in the Greenwich offices: intense, social, removed from the rest of the world – most of which had no idea what was going on there – deeply self-absorbed, anxious, with long hours being worked and weekends usually colonised by the all-consuming demands. Speed was its governing trait. Ideas would be formed at meetings. Sketches would be roughed out imme-diately afterwards. Finished drawings would be made that afternoon. Contracts would be let. Construction would begin – on occasions within days of the first idea emerging. There were tensions between different parts of the team but also a sense of shared enterprise, a determination to make this thing happen whatever the world had said or might say. Despite, too, what Sholto Douglas-Home called 'the usual spats between creatives', and the agonising difficulties of producing work that was vital and optimistic in these often harsh and demanding circumstances, there was a growing sense of conviction and belief that the Dome would, once the exhibition was on, amaze the world. Mike Davies, the architect, sensed 'an extraordinary high, a growing feeling of triumph over doubt and vision over scepticism'.

Little of it penetrated beyond the company. The Britain for which this great fête of the nation was being prepared continued to be largely indifferent to it. A little over 30 per cent of those who were polled regularly by NMEC said they would come. It was higher among men than women and much, much higher among children, three-quarters of whom consistently said yes.

For Sam Chisholm, pure grit was at the heart of the Dome's significance. He had been brought in at the suggestion of Dennis Stevenson as deputy chairman of NMEC in 1997, was also chairman of its central and powerful Executive Committee, and the host in his Bayswater flat, each Monday morning at 7 o'clock throughout 1999, of a core gathering: Lord Falconer, Mandelson's successor as shareholder of NMEC, Michael Grade, chairman of the Litmus group, and Bob Ayling, chairman of the company. The purpose of the meeting, Chisholm said, was 'to keep an eye on how things were getting along and to make sure Jennie Page had room to do the job'.

According to Chisholm, a New Zealander, but resident in London for a decade, and with experience of big business all over the world, the Dome's success in grappling with cynicism and triumph over negative expectation were the outstanding virtues of the whole enterprise. The actual creation of the Dome and its contents was the great symbolic gesture which would make the world envious. 'It is unique,' he says. 'There is nothing like it on the face of the earth. If this can be done, on this scale, against the background that it had to put up with, then it says to the world: look what we can do.' In 1999 he was repeatedly asked by foreign businessmen and community leaders how they too could do a Dome, how they could emulate Britain. For them all, Chisholm had the same answer: 'You're too late.'

The Dome was a demonstration to the world that this country was no retrospective theme-park. Its decision-makers had the energy and conviction to do something beyond the mere restoration of faded glories or the retouching of antique perfection. 'It would have been the easiest thing in the world to have said no to it,' Chisholm says, echoing Blair. '"Too hard, let's assign it to the atomic rubbish bin and let someone else do it. Let America do it." But we didn't, we did it, and it can show us the way forward into an amazing new chapter if only we've got the courage and the vision to go out and seize it.'

This was the kernel of the regenerative process which the Dome represented. Chisholm compares the French and British railway systems. The British have pussy-footed around putting in improvements here and there. The French have built the TGV network. There is a saying current in French government circles: 'When you drain a marsh, you don't consult the frogs.' The Dome, the great white bubble that emerged on Bugsby's Marsh, with all the fizzing, dynamic energy within it, showed that the British still had the stomach for the fight. It was a curiously self-reflexive symbol: the existence of the Dome itself gave the best possible answer to the question it was intent on asking. Can Britain and Britons thrive in the new world? Yes, look, we've built the Dome. It is the modern British, communitarian equivalent of all the great building schemes of the past – the making of Versailles, the Napoleonic reshaping of Paris, the phenomenon of Manhattan: the demonstration, in the most concrete of forms, of will and capacity.

In that large sense, the Dome remained Millennium Central, the hub of an enormous, if conceptual, regenerative wheel, whose spokes spread out across the country. It had also been regenerative in a more local and measurable way. Research commissioned by NMEC showed that the Dome and other investments on the Greenwich peninsula had created or protected 13,000 jobs – 6,000 on contracts stemming from the building of the Dome, nearly 5,500 from working in the Dome in the course of 2000. Others were created all around Great Britain. Many of those jobs were transitory; others were to be long-lasting. Bob Harris, the deputy leader of Greenwich Council, who had been instrumental in bringing the Dome to Greenwich, expected 'as many as 25,000 jobs to be created in the coming seven years'. Up to 6,500 of those would be long-term jobs on the 294 acres of the old British Gas site on Greenwich peninsula itself.

In an area which had been absolutely without hope, this was a remarkable legacy. The Dome's final purpose and ownership would not be decided until April 2001. Its use as a sports centre or covered stadium was unlikely. It was, apart from anything else, the wrong shape. A stadium has to be taller at the edge than in the middle. The Dome is taller in the middle than at the edge. A more imaginative possibility was envisaged: the Dome might become the centre for a national educational network, computer-based, accessible to all, a throbbing hub, connected to everywhere. In this way, its emblematic role in the regeneration of Britain would map precisely on to its actual role in the lives of British people. The educative and interrogative impulse which lay behind the exhibition would not be cut off at midnight on 31 December 2000. The year of the exhibition would be the beginning, not the culmination, of the process.

The Dome's vision of radiant coherence which was to be presented to the public in January 2000 was not easily arrived at. It was, in its making, a theatre of conflicting interests. The ragged meeting of public sector ethos and private sector finance was never going to be easy. Inclusivity, as an ideal, was inseparable, however paradoxical this might be, from stress and argument. Nothing on this scale of sponsorship; nothing on this scale of state cultural ambition; nothing on this scale of visitor numbers; and nothing as expensive had ever been attempted in Britain. Endless wrangles stemming from these overlapping demands wound on through the year. However reluctant NMEC might have been to acknowledge the wrangling in public, it was, just as much as the ambition it embraced and the achievement it could show, inseparable from the story of the Dome. Commercial sponsors wanted their brand prominent in the sponsored zones. Sarah Henwood, for example, marketing director at Manpower, the sponsor at Work, was clear that the point of Manpower's presence in the Dome 'is to get as much commercial and brand value as possible. I am there to get commercial advantage for our brand. This is a brand which is worth millions and millions of pounds worldwide. I am a custodian of that brand. I don't trust anyone to take liberties with it. I need to make sure that our branding is there in our zone. You don't want it to stick in their gullets but you do want it to stick in their minds. So I have to ensure that the messages are a) right and b) shouted.'

Others were not quite so abrasive. Tesco, the sponsor of Learning, seemed to Ben Evans, the content editor of that zone, much easier, 'confident, friendly, patient and understanding of the slowness of progress on these things, the trials and tribulations which one has to go through'. Even so, it was of course important for Tesco to 'showcase' their Schoolnet 2000 project in the zone. They and the other big commercial players – BT in Talk, Ford in Journey, BA and the British Airports Authority in Home Planet, the City of London in Money – were all pushing and persuading NMEC to provide them with as much commercial advantage as possible from their presence here. But NMEC had been careful to hold the key elements in their hand. The company remained the central node in the process. Government, designers, members of the Litmus Group, sponsors, builders: Jennie Page, Claire Sampson and the content editors were almost always the point through which these various parties connected. Designers and sponsors, for example, except in the case of a longstanding relationship, such as BA with Park Avenue on Home Planet, had little contact unless an NMEC representative was there with them. But as Jennie Page says, 'Why should they expect to have an independent relationship with the designers? Who is controlling the budget here? Who's got editorial control? NMEC has and clearly NMEC has to control the process.'

It made, inevitably, for a highly stressful work environment. But that central ownership by NMEC of the process was a necessary part of the delivery of the exhibition. Sam Chisholm is unqualified in his praise of Jennie Page's fierce and possessive management methods. 'She's a leader and out of that energy, that feeling that the whole thing rests on her, is where you get your results,' he says. 'She has been the driving force. She understands the company. Listen, if you blindfolded your wife and said to her, "Tell me what is in the second drawer in the kitchen table," she would know, wouldn't she? You asked her where your cufflinks were this morning, didn't you? Your wife knows pretty much what's in every drawer of your house. "Mum, where's this, where's that?" That's what Jennie Page is for the Dome: she knows what's in every drawer. She was proprietorial, she did care, she got difficult, she got overtired. But you have to put up with the worst things in the best people. Her dedication, her complete mastery of the brief: there is absolutely no way that anybody could have done this. I have seen so many people in this situation and they just become overwhelmed. She hasn't.'

There was one other player in this tussle who could not be ignored. The figure Sam Chisholm calls 'Joe Sixpack, Fred Public, whatever you want to call him'. He was going to have contributed £600 million to the exhibition, either though buying lottery tickets or by paying at the door. Was he going to be happy here? During the early months of 1999 a recurrent anxiety about the Dome surfaced again. Was it balanced enough? Was there enough for the 'paddler, the swimmer and the diver'? Was there sufficient 'wow'? Matthew Freud, the PR specialist with a hotline to the tabloids, who was on NMEC's Executive Committee, felt that the core team at NMEC was too highbrow. The zones in the Dome were 'tactful' and as such seemed 'a total insult to the people who had paid for it'. For Freud, 'The important question to ask was: are you telling stories that are only available to people who have been to university? What newspaper is this? That's what you had to ask. The majority of what was in there at the time was the *Guardian* and the *Independent*. A minority dropped to the *Mail* and the *Express*. There wasn't a red top amongst them. And as I said to them all, and as Michael Grade was saying and Bob Ayling was saying and Sam Chisholm was saying, if you are going to cut off anyone, cut the top off.' Freud thought it a haven for intellectual architecture-groupies. 'Anyone who subscribed to *Blueprint*,' he said, 'all 8,500 of them, were going to have the greatest day of their lives.' At one meeting Freud 'mentioned the name of a man who had been the producer of *Noel's House Party* and the reaction was as if I'd crapped on the floor.'

This, of course, was more than just a reflection of the much larger scale debate about high and low culture and the relationship between them. It had huge political and commercial implications. It was important that the Dome got the people through the gate. 'Bums on seats', in Michael Grade's phrase, or, in the words of Lord Falconer, 'numbers who come', was always going to be the first measure of success. Critical acclaim came a good second. The business plan was based around a figure of 12 million visitors and the last four months of the Dome's operation in 2000 were dependent on having acquired the ticket income earlier in the year. If they didn't come in those first eight months, the Dome would be looking at a revenue shortfall it couldn't sustain. The figures started to go wrong financially under 9 million. For the shareholder, 'Hitting that target will be OK. Above it will be success.'

The Litmus Group was in fact equally anxious to have 'zones that kicked'. The push for a less highbrow tone to the content was coming at the designers and the NMEC team from all sides. As Michael Grade, chairman of the Litmus Group, said, they kept throwing in the darts, asking the questions: '"That's crap," we would say to them. "That's pretentious. Where's the fun?"'

At the suggestion of Michael Grade, an effort was made at the beginning of 1999 to bring in a set of producers from film, TV and the world of commercials; they were invited to examine four of the zones which seemed to be having most difficulty in delivering a bright, accessible, non-intellectualised product. Two soon dropped out, deciding that the Dome was too different from what they normally did. A third remained to work on the innards of the Body.

By April, still pushing on the same tender spot, Lord Falconer decided that the Dome needed 'a populism audit', a measure of how much the contents of the Dome would be accessible to all. He, as much as any of them, was struggling with the notions of balance, inclusiveness, fun and a longer-lasting quality which went beyond mere entertainment. 'You want some sense that people thought it was worthwhile, that people thought the contents both good and worth coming to see. But there's lots of it. There are bits to score on a culture basis and bits to score on an entertainment basis.'

How did he stand on the Reithian question? How much did the Dome have a mission to explain, to spread civilisation to the masses? 'I don't suspect that my children would have found a Reithian BBC that appealing,' he said in early May. 'But definitely you do want Reithian in the sense that you want to explain high culture in an easy way but you want as well straightforwardly populist elements. Twelve million people is not twelve million Brian Sewells.'

But what was the impetus behind the populism audit? Was the implication of the audit that the contents weren't populist enough?

'No,' he said, 'and the reason it is a "no" is that the contents are in the process of being put together. I don't want to quibble but the contents aren't anything. They are not complete.' Because the contents did not yet exist in a finished form, they could not be assigned a quality of any kind, populist or not populist. They were, technically speaking, non-existent.

If this was something of a lawyer's answer in the spring of 1999, Michael Grade had a ready explanation. 'We are at a point in the project now where there is a lot of nervousness,' he said. 'The shareholder needs reassurance. "Is there something I should be doing?" It is the question everybody asks at this stage. Everyone is insecure. Christ, we don't half need an audience.'

It was perhaps a necessary and inevitable moment. The ambitious stance which the Dome adopted – wonderful for everybody in every way – was inherently difficult and and certain to produce anxieties. The V & A didn't need 12 million visitors. Blackpool Pleasure Beach didn't need to satisfy the broadsheet press. If the Dome had not been accused of being too highbrow, it would have been accused of being too lowbrow. As it was, the set of questions was the same in zone after zone: Lowest common denominator? Or highest common multiple? The establishment view or something that embraced the marginal and the minority? Bland and easy or rich and complex? Thinking of the future or attending to sources and origins? Technological or experiential? National or global? For enthusiasts, the mildly interested or the frankly not bothered? Or more precisely, how do you find something which can accommodate all of those? Nowhere was this more intense than in the zone that dealt with spirituality.

Eva Jiricna's original suggestion of a nearly content-free, beautiful, contemplative space for the Spirit zone immediately summoned the anxieties of Jennie Page and her team. 'It was clear to me from Day One that we needed to accommodate dogma,' Page says. They did not want this to become a shrine for the New Ageists or anyone else. They were equally aware that a zone about the soul, the spirit, or, as it was eventually called, Faith, could not ignore the long history of world religion. On purely intellectual grounds, a rubbed-down, feelgood 'souliness' would be a shirking of the issue. The Dome had to engage with this most intractable of historical problems.

The outside pressures were equally definitive. The churches, the Conservative Party and the *Daily Telegraph* were proclaiming loudly the fact that the millennium was a Christian anniversary, that Christ should be at the heart of it and that any Millennium Dome which neglected the centrality of Christ would be signalling the moral collapse of the nation. 'There will be celebrations of commerce and the media,' said Charles Moore, editor of the *Daily Telegraph*. 'There will be rock stars and TV stars and fireworks and there will be Tony Blair. It's not far short of the Tower of Babel.' The Bishop of London said he wanted to advertise his own cathedral, St Paul's, with the slogan 'The Dome that knows what's inside it'. But if the overtly Christian element was to be admitted, the other faiths had to be admitted too. The task of accommodating within a single organism the deliberately distinct and contradictory tenets of the world's religions had become one of the central necessities of the Dome.

It was not as if the Dome had tumbled to this problem overnight. In the early autumn of 1996 a Millennium Coordinating Group had been set up by the government. Clare Pillman, the official in charge of the millennium unit at the DNH, remembers 'Jennie Page once saying that my job was to worry about the four "imponderables" – religion; devolution; the economy and the rest of the world – while she got on and built the Dome. I don't think I can claim much credit for keeping any of them under control, but in good civil service fashion we set up committees to deal with three of them and left the Treasury to get on with the fourth.'

The Lambeth Group was the first of the sub-groups of the Millennium Coordinating Group to get off the ground. It met roughly every three months, bringing together government, the Royal Household, the major Christian denominations and representatives of some of the other faith communities in Britain: Hindus, Jews, Muslims and Sikhs in particular. Baha'is, Buddhists, Jains and Zoroastrians were also represented through an existing organisation called the Inter-Faith Network. It was never an easy business for any of the parties involved, but it was constantly pushed and persuaded forward by Jennie Page's personal interest in the work of the group and her sensitivity to the issues involved.

There was another point. From the perspective of the government, the Millennium Commission and NMEC itself, the setting up of such a group reassured an important and vocal constituency by showing that the Christian nature of the anniversary was being taken seriously and that the inclusivity question was being properly addressed. As these two objectives might easily have become contradictory, that was good management.

Not surprisingly, it did not run smoothly. Throughout 1997 the Lambeth Group strived to produce a pamphlet which was intended as a guidebook to sensitivities. (It was eventually published by DCMS and the Inter-Faith Network in 1998 as 'Marking the Millennium in a Multi-Faith Context'.) 'Consult widely before planning,' it said. Go carefully.

'Do not unwittingly compromise the integrity of belief of any participants … No one is being asked to assent to beliefs they do not hold.' Some who had no truck with the millennium would, of necessity, exclude themselves. Others who had no religious belief of any kind might wish to participate. Denigration of others could in no way be millennial. Trivialisation or ridicule was anathema. On the other hand, there were many identifiable strands common to all religions on the subjects of 'shared social action, service and social justice'.

In July 1997 the Lambeth Group produced a further document called 'Values at Greenwich', designed to give NMEC a steer on what the faith communities in Britain might hope for from the Dome. It repeats much of the vocabulary with which the Dome had been familiar for years, from all sources: togetherness, openness, dialogue, learning, reflection, hope, future, available to all, principles, diversity. But it also began to express a series of fairly hard-edged expectations, veering towards concrete demands. 'A "Tomorrow's World" approach which is spellbound by the technological possibilities may hide the real issues.' The Dome was not to be thrilled at the prospect of globalisation without making its drawbacks explicit. The failings of Britain's imperial episode should not be glossed over. The Industrial Revolution should be described in terms of its 'costs as well as its benefits'. There was to be no blurring of difficulties: 'Being bland should not be an option.' The Dome should not become a slave to its sponsors. 'It is important that space does not go to the highest bidder.'

The group's document, not surprisingly, did nothing to distinguish between the positions of the many bodies of which it was made up. Its essential message was straightforward enough: we are the religious, we are here and we need to be in the Dome.

Canon Colin Fletcher, the co-chairman with Clare Pillman of the group, and chaplain to George Carey, the Archbishop of Canterbury, saw the task of integrating the different agendas which were orbiting this subject 'as a cliff to climb. The Dome was part of it but not all of it. This was a question for the country as a whole: this was a Christian celebration but it was also part of the life of the nation. That double focus had to be sustained.'

There was a crudely reductivist option available. All faiths are the same. All religions lead to God. Why differentiate? Over the 1980s and

1990s a great deal of work had already been done along those lines between different churches and different faiths in Britain. But by the late 1990s the current of thinking in the religious communities had swung against that. As Colin Fletcher says, 'We weren't interested in stirring in all the colours in here and hoping they turned out white.'

This was not, in other words, to be a syncretistic shrine. Multiplicity, but distinction between the elements, was important. The arrival of the initial Eva Jiricna scheme was just the reverse of what the group wanted. She and they were approaching from precisely opposite ends of the spirituality street. For her, spirituality did not need religion. For them, it could be properly embodied in no other way. 'To me,' Jiricna said, 'religion is dogma, the religious are possessive of their dogma, and it is sad that people who are part of religion don't have the courage and guts to realise that they are losing people by this possessiveness. Religion often cuts people's wings. And people, or at least their spirits, want to fly.' For the Lambeth Group, that 'New Age stuff would have dished the whole thing'.

The first Jiricna design for the zone was revealed to the press at the February 1998 launch before the Lambeth Group had seen it. 'Howls of anger from the constituency' came pouring into the offices of the archbishop. Page, a regular churchgoer herself, was well aware that she had to address the question of many faiths in one zone at length and in detail. And the zone's content editors, Tim Gardom and Alison Grey, had already begun to consult faith groups around the country. 'We were struck by the sincerity of everyone we talked to,' Alison Grey says. 'The passion to explain what their faith meant to them. At some meetings we all ended up in tears.'

The handling of religious content in the zone; the balancing of parts; the relative priorities to be given to Christianity and the other faiths; the concern for accessibility; the need for integrity and for an overall vision that went beyond doom and gloom: all these factors meant that the content and the overall design of the zone went through draft after draft. The design company Jasper Jacob Associates was closely involved. For Eva Jiricna, it was 'an infernal battle. You have to keep your sense of humour as an architect. "We can't afford it. We don't like it." That's all usual. But here we asked ourselves every day, "Should we give up? Or in the circumstances should we just make it as good as possible?" You will never get a sense of freedom from being an architect. It will always be a defeat. One has to learn to lose and to lose gracefully.'

Sponsorship was nowhere in sight. Liam Kane had let his thoughts slip to the press: 'I say a prayer every night that the next day I will find a sponsor for the Spirit zone.' Sponsorship for the zone was always going to come from many different sources, but no one in IMG was able to get the ball rolling. Peter Mandelson brought together Sir Tim Sainsbury, the ex-Tory MP who was close to Lambeth Palace, and Stuart Bell, the Labour MP who was a church commissioner, to begin to drum up some sponsorship. Eva Jiricna's original pyramid proposal had envisaged enormous amounts of glass. Glass manufacturers had been approached to sponsor the zone but that route had become redundant when the design changed to a lightweight tent.

Ever since the launch in February 1998, however, there was another large potential sponsor on the scene: Srichand P. Hinduja, known as 'SP', the reclusive Indian billionaire, patriarch of 800 businesses, and one of four Hinduja brothers who describe themselves not as Hindu but as adherents to the Vedic tradition, based on the Vedas, the Sanskrit scriptures written down in about 3000 BC. He had known and worked with Michael Heseltine for many years. Peter Mandelson, as Minister without Portfolio, had visited the Hinduja offices in Haymarket. The Hinduja Foundation had applied to the Millennium Commission for a £50 million grant towards a £100 million multi-cultural theme-park outside Peterborough called Concordia. 'The human race is about to enter the most important phase of its development,' Hinduja had written, 'a phase in which it can either destroy itself or sow the seeds for a new future of peace, co-operation and progress.' The application had been turned down, but Hinduja felt that perhaps some of Concordia's principles of universal brotherhood might be applied to the Spirit zone.

The brothers had long been interested in what SP called 'the commonalities and shared values of each faith'. There was a clear commercial motive too. 'The emphasis on multicultural understanding will promote economic growth and social welfare for further generations. As businessmen we firmly believe this will be the best gift for the new millennium.' And on top of that, sponsoring a central element of a government-owned exhibition would clearly do the Hindujas no harm. They had always been aware of the benefits of remaining close to government. The press would suggest, when Mandelson became Secretary of State for Trade and Industry, that it was a question of 'cash for favours'. But according to Darin Jewell, the Hindujas' spokesman on millennium affairs, 'That was simply not the case.' SP Hinduja offered to underwrite the zone to the tune of £3 million.

The balancing act was difficult in the extreme but slowly a solution emerged. Draft Brief Six of the zone, which appeared in mid 1998, was a milestone. Although it was still far from conclusive, it combined, as Colin Fletcher says, 'a balanced emphasis on the significance of Christianity and on the importance of other faiths, on which everyone felt happy to build'. From now on, at every point in the story, faith was to be entwined with life. The focus of the zone came to settle on the question: 'How shall I live?' A narrative and an atmosphere was slowly teased out of it. The cycle of a person's life provides moments at which religion has its greatest impact: at birth, on emergence into adulthood, at marriage and at death. Those are the moments when all people are most aware of the spiritual dimension to their lives. They are also the moments which religion most carefully formalises; they are the focus of the great rituals. Four of the world's leading photographers – Tim Page, Abbas, Jenny Matthews and Gideon Mendel – were commissioned to photograph religious practices all over the country, 'in people's homes, their temples, their most private and sacred rituals,' as Tim Gardom remembers. Jenny Matthews almost drowned at a total immersion baptism at Brighton Beach.

Some deals were struck. As Christopher Frayling, the godfather of the zone says, 'There was one really fascinating moment on the Lambeth Group. We looked at all the great sayings of Jesus to find out how many axioms could be signed up to by all the faith groups. We found eight. They tended to be the social everyday things like "Blessed are the meek". The moment you get on to the Trinity and the afterlife, you're in trouble. So these are the axioms that are shown around the zone because they won't offend anyone.'

The question of the funding was still to be worked out in the early months of 1999. The Hinduja offer had been for £3 million worth of underwriting. There was an assumption, in other words, that other money would be forthcoming. In addition, there was a clear political and presentational advantage in not having all the sponsorship for the zone coming from a single source. A meeting with the Hindujas, Jennie Page and the leading Jewish peer Lord Levy was held at the House of Lords. The Hinduja offer of £3 million had been magnificent but NMEC and the government were now hot on the trail of money from both Christian and Jewish sources. Only £1 million of the offer need be taken up. Making use of the good offices of the Archbishop of Canterbury, Sir Tim Sainsbury and Stuart Bell, £2 million was given by the trusts of the Laing family, and £300,000 from the Jerusalem Trust, controlled by the Sainsbury family. The remaining £700,000 for the £4 million target was made up from other committed Christian sources.

The Faith zone that emerged from this process was in many ways the richest and most beautiful thing in the Dome. It was astonishingly complex in the integration of its elements, and substantially enriched by the complexity of the process which had given birth to it. Christians from all walks of life explained how people or events from Christian history inspired or shaped the inherited ideas of justice, freedom and education. Masterpieces of Christian art and writing were reproduced here, from the Tyndale Bible to Holman Hunt's *The Light of the World*. The shaping of the British landscape by its religious inheritance formed an entire subsection. On the way out of the zone, 3 million visitors were expected to leave their own 'Message for the Millennium' – a unique account of the thoughts, hopes and fears of Britons at the end of the twentieth century.

'Nothing here is going to be in your face,' Armand Terruli of the designers Jasper Jacobs Associates said. Although there was a great deal of content to the zone, none of it was pushed at you in the way of a formal exhibition. Suggestivity and evanescence coloured the experience. The conflict between faiths was not dodged and the core of contemplation not erased. At the heart of the zone was a tall conical space drenched in light, a work by the American Quaker and light-installationist James Turrell. Here the modern, minimalist understanding of spirituality, stripped of the towering complexities which all religions have constructed over it, found its expression.

'I remain very grateful to Jennie Page,' Eva Jiricna says. 'She always accepted what was very important to me, that we should have a contemplation space in the centre of the zone. Its height, 16 metres, the same height as the original pyramid, draws you up, into the realm of freedom and the imagination.' Turrell was Jiricna's idea. She introduced him to Page, and although including his installation in the zone stretched the budget and meant other elements had to be cut, Page was always supportive of the idea. For the architect, the sequence of Mind, Body and Faith nevertheless remained an anomaly. The natural trios were either Philosophy, Medicine and Faith or Mind, Body and Soul. All the same, the central space continues to retain the contemplative qualities she was seeking. For her, as for Turrell, 'Light is abstract, the most spiritual thing on earth.'

Outside the zone, two rather more traditional spaces balanced it. There was a prayer room for Muslims, who have an obligation to make daily prayers, on the site but not in the Dome, because lotteries are not acceptable to strict Muslims. And there is a prayer space in the Harrison building inside the Dome to be used by Christians for services twice a day and to be freely available to everyone at all other times. Each of the nine major religions in Britain, with the addition of the Chinese community who would come for their New Year, would be invited to celebrate one of its festivals in the Dome.

The story of the zone devoted to Faith can be seen as something of a triumph for the Dome. It stands for a great deal of what was done by NMEC and its allies in government. The vastly ambitious target was to create an exploration of a subject that was central to human life. It was not going to make a museum of religious art. Nor was it going to be a place simply for worship. It wanted to make something that was new in form, a narrative exhibition which through words, images, sounds and a sense of space and light was both emotionally and aesthetically gripping. The Great Exhibition had no religious element beyond Pugin's Ecclesiastical Court, which was essentially an exercise in style. And the Festival of Britain had no religious element whatsoever. This was new territory for a national exhibition, but an old battleground for the religions and their advocates. This was a combination which had danger written all over it. The side issue, with which much of the press was concerned, of whether the Archbishop of Canterbury should or should not say a prayer in the Dome near midnight on 31 December 1999, obscured a more central reality: the bridging of chasms which few imagined could ever be bridged.

*　　*　　*

238

For those who expected the Dome to be a shrine to any one of the modern demons with which it was associated in the public mind from the start – stupidity, commercialism, materialism, control freakery, vacuity – the Mind zone, designed by the office of Zaha Hadid, godfathered by Professor Richard Gregory and with Martin Newman as its content editor, could be rolled out as the big slapping denial. That is not to say that its design evolution was without wrinkle. It makes an interesting contrast to its neighbour, Faith. There, the form of the zone underwent radical adaptation to accommodate the insistent challenges of its content. For Mind, where the equivalent of the religious – schools of philosophers – have no equivalent power, the form as originally conceived by Hadid, if trimmed by budget pressures, has remained essentially the same. The building was to be a building of the kind Hadid envisaged before any thoughts were given to what it might contain.

Hadid does not like right angles, particularly when modern art is in question, as it was to be in this zone from the beginning: 'Recent [art] practices have invented various shifts in perception, identity, and social behaviour. Given a programme for an institution that exhibits contemporary art, we can and should get away from the box, from 90-degree angles.' The idea of a square white box, conceived of by intellectual conservatives as neutral, a blank space on which the object could be seen cleanly and for itself, was a form of self-delusion and ignorance. '"Neutral space" is a wishful oxymoron,' Hadid said. 'All space is coloured by individual memory and experience.' The white box was a kind of sanctifying distortion. Only a structure with 'multiple perceptions and distant views' would 'create a richer, more perplexing experience, taking your body through a journey of compression, release and reflection.' Hadid used these words to describe her Contemporary Arts Center in Cincinnati but they apply to her Mind zone too.

The folded lasagna forms of the zone, almost like loops of film fallen from the camera, which was originally bigger, was intended to have its own exit through the skin of the Dome and to connect to its neighbours, shrank under money pressure, had elements withdrawn, simplified and turned through 180 degrees. Nevertheless the essence of 'an exteriorless form, made of decks and screens, full of references to the involutions of the brain', as Graham Modlen of the Hadid office describes it, is pretty much what emerged. Its cladding of translucent, glass-reinforced plastic

(GRP) backed on to honeycombed aluminium boarding, would glow greyish green from within like a muted turquoise brain thinking.

From the start, the building was seen as the context within which visitors could be made to think. BritArt, chosen with the assistance of Doris Saatchi and Mark Cousins from the Architectural Association, much of it deriving from the Saatchi collection and the Sensation show at the Royal Academy which drew on it, would provide the stimulus for the thought. They would have, for example, the late Helen Chadwick's famous Piss Flowers – a series of moulds taken from the cavities created when she pissed in the snow. The sponsors of the zone, GEC-Marconi and British Aerospace, thought not. The debate came and went. Even if the work was called *Untitled*, it was not considered acceptable.

If the attempt to have GEC accept the beauty of a piss flower was among the Dome's finest moments, and a measure of the chasm-bridging on which it had bravely embarked, the Mind zone had a more essential problem. The difficult and confusing world of deconstructionist aesthetics of which Hadid is a leading proponent, and the complex of French Derridaist and Foucaultist theoreticians to which it is attached, do not naturally lend themselves to the kind of exhibition by which Joe Sixpack might be 'involved, engaged, entertained, educated and transformed', as NMEC's mission statement put it. The theorising had to be cleaned up.

Professor Richard Gregory, with long experience of science shows and interactive exhibitions at the Exploratory in Bristol and the London ICA, was brought in by Jennie Page and Simon Jenkins. The approach was to become 'more empirical'. There was to be a new and clarified structure. The three structural elements to which the zone had now been reduced were to attend to: the input which the world transmits to the mind through the senses; the process of mind in action, either in isolation or communally; and the output, the shaping influence of mind on one's own sense of identity and on the future, the action of will on circumstance.

The simplicity of this conventional understanding of the mind and its relationship to the world allowed Gregory and Newman to shape a kind of suggestive narrative out of the zone. The spaces which the Hadid structure gave them were not the most convenient for an exhibition – there was nowhere very suitable, for example, for them to set their robots to play. And only one space was acoustically separated from the rest of

Dome. The need to integrate the Gregory narrative, the approval of the sponsors, the artists' preferences, the architects' requirements, the engineers' strictures and the operational estimate for 'the churn through', as Graham Modlen puts it, of 3,000-plus visitors an hour sometimes left the architects 'beside ourselves with frustration'.

Nevertheless, this exercise in coordination, accommodation and harmonisation, yet another microcosm of the process by which the Dome as a whole came into existence, has achieved an exhibition of a kind not seen before. Science and technology of the most modern sort – imaging systems, remote detection systems – are integrated with leading edge art and leading edge architecture. Visual jokes and puzzles disrupt the sense of the ordinary. Robots seem to flock together, come to be fed by visitors, seem to look after little ones if they are frightened or lonely. Even the giant mirror, which coats the enormous 'ski-slope' or banner at the front of the zone, takes on extra significance in this hyper-suggestive context: here is mind as a reflection of the world. The piss flower did not make it but Chadwick's so-called *Self-Portrait* – the artist's hands holding a brain – is here, almost at the beginning. South American leaf-cutter ants demonstrate – but this is never expressed so straightforwardly in the zone – communal, instinctive minds, working together, carrying bright flecks of leaf along paths designed to resemble the tracks on a silicon chip. The zone remains consistently suggestive and interrogative. Ron Mueck's 4.6-metre-high 'flesh-realistic' resin sculpture of a crouching boy gazes enigmatically at the Lilliputian humans around him. Newman sees the figure 'as the thinker for the millennium', in the great tradition of pensive sculptural figures'. He says nothing. No message is attached to him. But his deep, slow eyes ask the questions: Who are you? And what are you doing with your life?

The zone as a whole, Richard Gregory says, 'is an appraisal of where we have got to, allied to the idea that destiny is in your own hands. You write your own novel. Don't drift on the stream. You are author of your own life. The zone is a mind-switch, it is a place in which you can switch your mind on.'

Sarah Straight had become transport manager for the Dome in September 1996. Looking for 'a gentle, calm, unstressful task after four years at Department of Transport privatising railways', her job was to get people to the Dome. Greenwich was never going to be suitable for a car-based show. From the very beginning it was always going to be reliant on public transport. 'Don't let's overstate this,' Straight says. 'It's only the same number of people as visit Harrods on a normal day: 35,000 people. They get 300,000 during the sales and pre-Christmas.'

Nevertheless, she was faced with knitting together a small battalion of conflicting interests. 'The phone rings 30 times an hour,' she said in mid-1999. The bodies she had to deal with, every one of which had different priorities and objectives, were: the Association of Train Operating Companies, London Transport, all the other wings of NMEC, English Partnerships, the London Borough of Greenwich, the Highways Authority, the Traffic Director for London, London Transport Buses, for whom Straight had unqualified admiration, the Government Office for London, the Association of London Government, DCMS and Glenda Jackson. With her, as Minister for Transport in London, there were long discussions over whether people should be allowed to drop off their friends at the Dome by car (so-called 'kiss-and-ride') and if so what provision should be made. Or whether the provision of a place to do that, as Jackson maintained, would encourage too many people to try, clogging up the access roads and running contrary to the Dome's no-car policy. Jackson won the dispute in the end: no kiss-and-ride at the Dome, producing headlines in October 1999: 'DOME BANS SNOGGING'.

The river-boats and piers (once Prescott had removed them from the slow and undynamic management of the Port of London Authority), the dedicated guided bus route from Charlton, the arrangements for park-and-ride car parks around London and special ticket deals with coach and train operators: all this went smoothly enough. It was the tube which gradually became the problem. The delivery date for the Jubilee Line extension had originally been March 1998. NMEC needed it in operation then to get workers to the site. But the construction was hit by a number of problems: the failure of a tunnel at Heathrow which was being built by the same method as some of the Jubilee Line; poor industrial relations, stemming in part from a management team which had worked previously on the new railway in Hong Kong and had attempted to bring Far Eastern work methods to an English site; and the sheer ambitiousness of the scheme, both in the grandeur of its architecture, the difficulty of the conditions at Westminster and Canary Wharf, and the sophistication of its technology, in particular the new 'moving block' signal system, whereby each train carried its own exclusion zone along with it. The conventional signalling system identifies blocks of track in which no more than one train is allowed at time. This limits capacity to 24 trains an hour. The moving block system can bring that up to 32 trains an hour. But it wasn't going to work in time for the Dome's opening and had to be abandoned. In addition, the health and safety requirements of the Railways Inspectorate were proving difficult to meet.

Anxieties at NMEC started to rise in mid 1998. The Dome needed 24 trains an hour to deliver 14,000 people in the morning peak for the 10 a.m. opening in comfort. Because of the signalling difficulties, the Underground was saying it might be able to deliver no more than sixteen or eighteen trains. Conditions on such few trains would have been very crushed.

On top of that, NMEC considered the Underground 'an utterly unreconstructed nationalised industry', with profoundly dysfunctional relationships within its own organisation. On the tube's part, they clearly resented the existence of the Dome. The design of the tube and bus interchange at Greenwich had to be looked at again to take account of the winds coming off the Dome. More generally, the Jubilee Line would not have come under the intense political pressure it did, from Prescott in particular, and would not have had the ass-kicking management of Bechtel, a tough Midwestern outfit recommended by Lord Levene, imposed upon them, if it hadn't been for this deadline. Without the Dome, 1 January 2000 would have been just another day. The Jubilee Line could have gone on slipping for years.

From the autumn of 1998 tremors of alarm ran through NMEC. If the tube failed to be delivered, there was no fall-back. Without the tube, the Dome would not work. In September Page was asked by the NMEC board to write to John Prescott to say that the responsibility for delivering the line lay with the government. All NMEC board members had to impress on members of the government, whenever they came across them in the course of their business, the urgency and importance of this situation. There needed to be extra links between NMEC and the tube, including NMEC representation on the Jubilee Line Project Management board. By 13 October Jennie Page was attending JLE

Project Executive Committee meetings 'to monitor progress'. NMEC had already had the London Underground management up before their own board to explain the situation. In November Page requested from the DETR copies of the regular independent reports on the line from Ove Arup. London Underground had to be pushed and goaded into delivery. The key link of the Jubilee Line, from Waterloo to North Greenwich, was finally opened to paying passengers at the very end of September 1999, without fanfare and without Southwark station. This shame-faced creeping into operation of a system that had cost £3.2 billion and included some of the most magnificent public buildings in London – each tube station by a different architect, the whole ensemble conceived on the scale of a French *grand projet* – did not go down well with ministers.

In NMEC's Buckingham Palace Road offices an electronic display in the lobby ticked off the days, hours, minutes and seconds to the millennium. On the office wall of Sholto Douglas-Home, the marketing director, the clock-face was numbered in reverse. What looked like quarter to three was actually quarter past nine. The marker days began to fall like closing doors: 300 to go, 200, 100. Gradually, the form of the finished exhibition site began to emerge. The Dome's earlier, strange, blank hugeness, in which the scale was unintelligible because there was nothing to measure it by – although NMEC put a red London bus in it, simply so that visitors could understand that this building enclosed a space the size of a town centre – was starting to become a world of its own, not a site but a place.

The energised, shifting images of the kaleidoscope started to play across the peninsula. The largest commission of new art ever seen in the United Kingdom was given to seven of Britain's leading sculptors. Antony Gormley's *Quantum Cloud* would become one of the lasting symbols of the experience: 29 metres high by 10 wide and 8 deep. Gormley's work addressed the question repeatedly posed by the Dome: what was the nature of the modern self? With the help of a computer, Gormley arranged 'a metallic cloud of 3,500 steel tubes' so that from some angles the human form inside them would be fleetingly apparent. From others it would disappear, leaving no more than a cloud of randomness made visible. It was the sculptor's own turning aside from the hugely substantial metal bodies on which he had been engaged for years. Here, now, Gormley had locked on to one of the identifying marks of the age and of the whole Greenwich phenomenon. The 1851 Exhibition had been about objects and the ways in which they might be improved; the 1951 Festival had been about society, and the ways in which the post-war years might offer a better future for the British people; the 2001 Experience was about that evanescent thing, the modern self, and the ways in which it could be made whole.

Anish Kapoor came up with a proposal for the Rest zone – a huge internally silvered double egg. But the site was over the Blackwall Tunnel, the egg was too heavy and the cost of its foundations would have eaten the lion's share of £4 million. A lightweight, cool and smooth-contoured pavilion, 'the colours of a box of Caran d'Ache crayons' on the outside, was designed for the place by the Richard Rogers Partnership. Any work by Damien Hirst, the most famous British artist of his generation, was notable by its absence from the site. His proposal for a giant DNA molecule was thought too expensive and failed to excite the decision-makers at NMEC.

Hugh Hudson, the director of *Chariots of Fire*, was taken on to make a film about people on the planet which would form the climax of Home Planet. Arguments raged between Hudson and British Airways over exactly how upbeat his film was to be, or how inclusive of sorrow or failure or ugliness. Simon Jenkins issued a reminder to all those involved on the Dome not to use anything but the most straightforward English. In Money, £1 million in £50 notes was secured from the Bank of England. They would – behind plastic – form a tunnel for those entering the zone. Only unseen, on the back, would the bank overprint them with the careful word 'SPECIMEN'. Real diamonds from de Beers were to glitter there, as they had done in the Crystal Palace. Every decision, every way in which each zone might impact on the others, passed through the central node of NMEC, the Glue Group, or its inner core, Superglue, where Jennie Page, Mike Davies, Claire Sampson and Ken Robinson wrestled to make one coherent whole from the multitudinous elements they had drawn into their project: lighting, the prominence of vending machines, the view which the Queen might have, security, terrorism, a big interactive map showing all the other projects funded by the Millennium Commission across Britain and Northern Ireland, the subtle and not-so-subtle ways in which sponsors might want to introduce their brand colours into the zones (not allowed), the overall question of colour. Superglue was busy: on the evening of Friday 22 October 1999 Mike Davies had 186 items on his list of things to do.

The outside world had little inkling of the scale of some of the challenges here. The Dome had to be prepared for up to 80,000 meals a day, moving from zero to full capacity in the space of 24 hours. That could not be maintained by artisan cheesemakers. NMEC had to engage with the large-scale commercial catering organisations, and perhaps expect to get some stick over it in the food columns of the broadsheet press.

Ever since the Heseltine phase in 1996 McDonald's had been on the target list of sponsors. By mid August 1998 NMEC was confidently awaiting their commitment. All that was needed was the approval of the McDonald's US board. They finally went public that autumn as a £12 million official sponsor, engaged with solidly communitarian projects: producing learning materials for schools, building an education centre at the Dome and hosting the Our Town Story project – an invitation to towns and villages all over the country to come and put on at the Dome a performance which could tell the world who they were.

They also had a huge catering presence at the Dome. In the main square they had a 1,300-square-metre restaurant, capable of seating 400, which after the Millennium Experience closed would be removed and erected as a drive-thru in Leeds. Inside the Dome, in core 9, there was another 400-seater McDonald's on one and a half floors. The other half floor was take up by an Aroma café, a brand which after April 1999 – and after the Dome deal was finalised – would also belong to McDonald's. Here, as in all the branded catering outlets across the Dome, the food on offer was to be the standard high street fare at standard high street prices.

Negotiations with potential suppliers were long and hard. Caterers wanted vetos on who their neighbours might be. In each category, competitors were to be excluded entirely. A burger supplier would need a commitment from NMEC that not only other burger suppliers but also outlets offering fried chicken, pizzas and ice-cream should be absent. NMEC conceded on the fried chicken but stuck their heels in over pizzas and ice-cream. Take-away was an issue. The big brands wanted it; the Dome didn't, horrified at the tidying up it would present. Large-scale eruptions occurred over that but NMEC won. No take-away, all food served on trays. None of this could ever have been called millennial in tone: it was straight, hard bargaining.

The branded operators had to pay for the fit-out of their own premises in the Dome and NMEC received a percentage of their takings. These terms alone meant that small operators could scarcely participate. All the same, the final team ended up as quite a variety of companies, including YO! Sushi, OpaJohn's, a young Dutch company wanting to break into the British market with their spicy filled Indonesian pancakes, Harry Ramsden's fish and chips, hot roast sandwiches at Hot Bites, the New Covent Garden Soup Company, the Simply Internet café, Costa, Aroma, AMT Expresso, Bakers Oven Café and the Great American Bagel Factory. Separate bars sold Coca-Cola, Wall's ice-cream and Typhoo tea.

Granada, the giant entertainment, hotel and food conglomerate, won the contract for wide sections of Dome food. There were more negotiations with them over signage, specification of fit-out – for which NMEC in this case was paying – and aesthetic conflicts with architects. Finally resolved, Granada became NMEC's 'full tapestry of food units to cover every eventuality'. World food, self-service islands, showcase counters, healthy food: all came under the Granada umbrella.

The food was symptomatic of a great deal at the Dome. The mere fact of having to accommodate such huge numbers for so long without a break meant that the idea of a farmhouse kitchen feel to the catering was never going to work. The Dome involved mass handling of people. At least it wasn't reheated aeroplane food shovelled into hungry mouths. There was going to be high-class food from a variety of chefs in the Acclaim! restaurant and the Seabar, managed jointly by Compass and Granada. The Granada operation, divided into some 20 different outlets, was not going to look monolithic. There was going to be more of an illusion of locale and variety than might have been the case. A show was going to be put on. As Ken Robinson says, 'The best management is when you don't know you are being managed.'

More and more pours into this container. The multiplicity, the very scale of the thing that was being attempted, makes it almost indescribable. Imagination recreated the history and future of transport in Journey, sponsored by Ford, one of the most ambitious and expensive of all the zones. The Tesco-sponsored Learning zone, designed by Tim Pyne and WORK, hinged around three equally extraordinary environments – a recreation of all that was worst about the old sort of school, including its nauseating smells and oppressive bells; a central part in which elements of film and theatre were sewn subtly together in another wordless performance, written by Bruce Robinson, about the beauty of learning; and a final emergence into a mirrored Orchard of Learning, the classroom without walls. The Self-Portrait zone – concentric rings in search of a national identity – was in danger of spiralling over its budget and its designers were withdrawn. Much of the contents of the local zone, still called Shared Ground, were abandoned in the middle of 1999, having failed to satisfy the Litmus Group or the populism audit. WORK took over here as well. At last, late in the day, the contents of the Body looked as if they were moving towards resolution. The government's insistence that a million schoolchildren – the subject of some titanic rows – should be admitted free to the exhibition played havoc with the budget, disrupted Ken Robinson's carefully devised operations and required the creation of an entirely new entrance building.

An elaborate and innovative water system was installed by which rainwater from the Dome roof and sinks would be recycled through reed-beds to flush the 670 loos. The margins of the Thames were reshaped by the Environment Agency to give fish a resting place when the tide turned against them. On the banks of the Thames, in the area known as Meridian Quarter, the Greenwich meridian itself was marked on the ground with a bright, millennium-yellow strip light. An enormous mirror stood next to it, 5.5 metres high, so that people could stand there and see themselves straddling the line. Gardens were designed by a team led by Dan Pearson: a long living wall of coppiced willow, concealing the NMEC offices from visitors to the exhibition; and, on the other side of the Dome, a small hill of hanging beds stacked around the ventilation shafts of the tube station. A pub was designed and built. A Blackadder film to play in Skyscape was commissioned. Vic Reeves was hired for an inspirational short film to precede it. All over the country, towns and villages signed up for the Our Town Story stage. They would have three 20-minute slots with up to 100 performers. The 20 minutes would focus it. 'We don't want a three-hour opera about Grimsby,' Robert Warner, the head of live events, said.

Through the Foreign Office, communities from all five continents would come to do the same in school holidays. Under the guidance of Micha Bergese, who had choreographed for Tina Turner, the gymnasts and acrobats learned stiltwalking and sky-diving in preparation for the millennium show. One thousand millennium products, the best of British ingenuity and design, were chosen to be featured in a spiral structure on the banks of the Thames. The Dome was a catalogue of marvels, a cabinet of rarities, a circus of miracles, a multiplicity zoo. For all the grief in its making, for all the roaring of beasts in the jungle which it involved, it was a kaleidoscope of the very best that we could do.

CHAPTER TEN

For a Nation's Confidence

What, in the end, would be the significance of this strange enterprise? The Dome struggled with that question throughout its life. It talked and talked, it issued press release after press release, it sent out its roadshows, it wooed and schmoozed, it produced mission statements and brand-identity documents, and yet still a certain perplexity hung about it. This was its method; here was its face; this was its mind; this was its body; these were its limbs; here even was its heart: but what was its point?

The purpose and governing ideology of great state shows until the twentieth century (and, for those associated with the monarchy, well into it) had been self-evident. Any state performance or exhibition or architectural display was never troubled with what it meant: glory was there to glorify the institution. A gilded throne enshrined a golden king. No agony need be expended on identifying what the true nature of the institution might be. All thought could be turned to the expression of the glory: how bright the gilding, how deep the velvet, how radiant the crimson, how rich the silk. Manner was all; motivation was a given.

The purpose of the Great Exhibition, imitating its French forebears, was equally obvious. It was commercial. The global market, and the British empire's place within it, was the point of the show. Other world powers would be invited to attend, compete and, with luck, be defeated. Although there was no gap between the aims of the state and the aims of the manufacturers – they were the backbone and lifeblood of the great imperial enterprise – it is possible to see in the Great Exhibition the first crack in the culture. The aesthetes, and the cultural elite of which they were the voice, felt divorced from much of the exhibition. 'Industry without art is brutality,' Ruskin would say, and nothing seemed more brutal than the ten miles of arranged objects in the Crystal Palace. Ruskin certainly thought the Philistines were on the inside in 1851.

The 1951 Festival of Britain was precisely what it said it was: a festival to celebrate all things British – people, place, history and products. A country which had just emerged from a war that was already seen, in John Keegan's phrase, as 'the great epic of the British nation' could justifiably celebrate what they were.

By the turn of the millennium that sense of conviction had dissolved. The state and the people were now deeply uncertain about glorifying anything at all. The glossy self-presentation of great businesses could not be sanctioned here – at least not unadorned. Pure fun was no longer acceptable. Some more serious purpose had to be engaged. But pure seriousness was equally unacceptable. This was not to be the Central Office of Information. People would not visit or pay for sobriety. The great political issues of the day – devolution and the future of the United Kingdom as a single entity; Europe and Britain's part in it, particularly over the question of the euro; the constitution of Parliament, its electoral basis and the role of the monarchy – none of these fundamental aspects of the future of the state and the relationship of government to people could be addressed in the Dome.

The only flags around which the country, and the Dome, could gather – unerringly identified, again and again, in the market research conducted by political parties, large corporations and the Dome itself – were the universal aspirations of hope, a better future, a kinder world. This became the Dome's soft heart. These were the phrases used; older terms – compassion, justice, peace – had largely dropped out of currency. NMEC's vision was 'to begin the next millennium with a brighter, happier, healthier, more fulfilling future ahead of us'.

The Dome, and everything around it, the spreading skirts of its National Programme, was to be, in other words, a lamp held up for the future, a beacon of hope. 'What's it for?' Jacques Chirac asked, when he saw a model of the Dome displayed at the Asian-European summit in the spring of 1998. The Japanese Prime Minister and the Sultan of Brunei had already had a look. One of NMEC's content editors, Ben Evans, was standing by the model, ready to explain its details. But how to answer that most universal of questions? 'It's for a nation's confidence,' Evans said from nowhere. Chirac harrumphed and turned on his heel.

Of course, in its making, the Dome was revealed not as a lamp but as a mirror, a reflection of the tensions and web of demands in a pre-millennial society, the overlapping, conflicting and often fierce requirements of government, commerce, the cultural elite, the idea of 'entertainment', the demand for inclusiveness, and its mirror-twin, the fear of dumbing down. The aim was to achieve a post-millennial effect with the methods and in the circumstances of a relentlessly pre-millennial world. The people at NMEC struggled with the agonies of creating a communal fantasy out of the viscous and intractable materials of public finance and public accountability. They suffered for months on end the loathing and contempt of the press and battened down against it. They reassured themselves that all other great enterprises of this kind had been despised in gestation and admired on delivery. Even in mid November 1999 the questions being asked continued to be the deeply uncharitable ones: were the electricians holding the Dome to ransom? Was the Jubilee Line going to be properly operative? Were all the zones going to be ready? Would anybody come?

The staff of NMEC looked for something that had never been done before, not as a writer or painter might in the privacy of his own imagination, but in the world of budgets and schedules, private polling, marketing policies, political requirements and commercial limitations, ticketing strategies, remediation programmes, projected visitor numbers, the state of the economy (by which, after some flutters about an approaching recession in late 1998, they were immensely helped, as the Labour government managed the dream combination of a soft landing to a boom and a continuation of non-inflationary growth).

Nevertheless, outside a war, it would be difficult to think of anything harder than getting the Dome right. It needed to make itself marvellous but was shut in on all sides. The nearest model was indeed warfare: build a huge team, equip it, invade with it, establish the bridgehead, react to circumstances, excise failure, reinforce success, keep the enemies at bay, keep them guessing and, within the free-fire zone which you have created, make life as inspirationally memorable as it could ever be. They were throwing a dance on Omaha Beach, arranging the candles while dodging the tracer.

Could it have been done better? In some ways, perhaps it could. Its position on the margins of public and private was at the heart of its difficulties. If it had been entirely in the private sector, as it would have been in America, or entirely a government affair, as it would have been in France, its life would have been easier, its messages more straightforward, its delivery quicker and its value for money probably greater.

But that efficiency and simplicity would have involved a loss of complexity. The Dome never wanted to impose any messages. The company banned the word 'message' from any description of what the public were expected to take away from it. Instead, the meaning of the experience, in all its diversity, was to be found embedded in the rich variety of *possibilities* which the zones presented to visitors. There were to be choices rather than predictions. Each visitor was invited to consider, embrace, applaud, question or reject the suggestions that were being made to him. There was no equivalent here, for example, of the famous Futurama pavilion sponsored by General Motors in the 1939 New York World's Fair, where the giant car manufacturer presented a vision of the future which was entirely reliant on cars, and on the vastly expensive, government-funded infrastructure of highways and interstates which they would need. The Journey zone in the Dome, sponsored by Ford, was a test case of this. Although it is true to say that where a car appeared in the zone, it was a Ford – or at least owned by Ford, which could by 1999 include Jaguars, Volvos and Mazdas – the giant American car corporation did not in the Dome present a polemic in favour of the car, but a much wider exploration of the nature of transport.

'Of course the Ford zone is a brand leadership statement,' says Adrian Caddy, who led its design at Imagination. 'On a huge level. But there is also the corporate responsibility to be seen as a good citizen. They need to be liked. They need to say, "We are giving something back." This is to put across a point of view rather than merely to sell more cars.'

A 'brand leadership statement' can probably serve the brand better by serving more than the brand. It is not, in other words, what strategists call a 'zero sum game'. There is both an entertainment and a social service here; both an intensely glamorous, interesting and exciting exhibition about the history and future of transport, including the problems of too many cars in too small a place, but describing the ways in which new vehicles might be good for the disabled or run on methanol or make a minimum impact on the land over which they run. There is a faith, here as everywhere in the Dome, that elements in society can be made to bind and do not necessarily have to wrench or to wring, to twist, disrupt or divide.

But tension, paradoxically enough, is an essential part of the binding process. Without it, and without the sparks that come from bringing together risk-takers from government and industry, commerce and the world of the arts, the Dome would not have been a child of the Britain that bore it, still struggling as it was to define a new settlement between public and private domains.

The figure that is left standing in this landscape, on whom the Dome focuses its huge attention, is the modern individual, faced with choices, hungry for information, ready to learn and to act. That vision of the potent individual, embedded in the community of which he is a part, which is familiar enough in the liberal American understanding of the relationship between self and society, has not until now been much of a presence in Britain. If the Dome manages, in some way, to liberate us into that new, ardent but humane vision of ourselves, then that will be a great legacy and the whole venture will have been more than worthwhile.